I Used to Be Cool..

Lexy Ellis

Published by Lexy Ellis, 2015.

I USED TO BE COOL..

First edition. June 13, 2015.

ISBN: 978-1514365526

Written by Lexy Ellis.

Addison Jake.

Have Courage, Kick Ass, Be Kind.

Forward Thinking...

All characters in this story are completely and utterly fictional.

Any resemblance to anybody you know or have known, or would like to know, is a complete coincidence, but well done you for knowing people who are potentially mentally ill, because *potentially* mentally ill people are the best kind of people and are definitely worth knowing.

Ok so, my fella ***is*** Irish and my name ***is*** Lexy but everything else *is potentially* fiction. Except where it is true.

I hope you enjoy this tall tale of love, misplacement of marbles, and little to no weight loss.

My diary was like my therapy during these times, so please be kind with your reviews and please remember, if somebody brings you their indescribable pain - choose courage.

Put your Pollen tubes to work....

We weren't *officially* trying.

No.

Under no circumstances were we *officially* trying.

Officially trying would have meant some sort of commitment on my part to think about the future. Which is not something I am fond of. You only have to look at the numerous red letters that plummet with a thud on to my doormat every other morning to fathom that.

Officially trying would have been stupid and irresponsible. (Something I *actually* seem to do with immense ease, without even *officially* noticing.) We had only been together seven months. *Officially* trying would have meant we were *officially* stupid.

We **were** *officially* stupid.

Waking up far too early on the morning of the 14th of June, heart hammering, head glistening with last night's makeup and a half eaten pizza stuck to my face, was not something I had noted down in my planner. (I don't own a planner.) It was Sunday morning. Sleeping was officially noted down in my planner. (See last comment.) Reaching for my phone and finding the battery had gone was not a surprise. Jumping out of bed and landing feet first on an upturned plug, *was* a surprise.

Somebody's mother was most definitely a Fecker. (To set the scene you must shout this at top volume, while hopping around on one foot, clinging on to the other with closed eyes and repeating at high speed that very rude phrase. That very, very rude phrase.)

So you've gathered by now we weren't *officially* trying right?

So imagine my shock then, if you will, when I eventually stopped cursing the plug gods, turned my phone to 'calendar' and realized with a shaking hand, I had been incredibly mistaken during the throws of passion, about the dates, the evening previous.

The Irish One had spent the weekend climbing mount Snowdon and had come home happy and horny and ready for some loving! I had spent the weekend paranoid he was going to fall off a cliff, down a manhole or off the top of a mountain so was also happy he had returned in one piece! I wasn't particularly horny, as I had spent the weekend cramming chocolate down my throat like it was going off the market. (Mmm chocolate!) But at seven months in, with the '*I love you's*' still to be uttered, he still got what he wanted, when he wanted. (All women know that once the 'I love you's are out of the way, it's your decision. Until then, it's in his hands. So to speak.)

So as we weren't *officially* trying, (In case you missed that.) The Irish One, well, he was meant to, erm?!?! Reverse. (I cannot make it clearer than that really, without being crude. And his mother may read this!) We were only having sex at the beginning and at the end of the month. I know, I know, I can hear you now - tut, tut, roll eyes, by the age of twenty-nine I should know better. Good job I'm not a sex education teacher, or any kind of teacher really.

Climbing quietly back in to bed, somehow The Irish One had slept through the commotion (Yet he can still tell me how many times a night I've scratched/snored/trumped and woken him) And flicking through the dates of my cycle, it struck me that we had fulfilled *our congenial rights as a couple who live together* (again, his mum might read this!) slap, bang, on day 14.

Big hairy sodden ovaries. (Sorry Mary.)

It sounds like a full on, hit me up the side of my head cliché, but I just knew I was impregnated. I just knew it. I sat there staring at The Irish One while my mind worked on overdrive and a mild panic started to culminate in my bowels.

I should probably point out at his point, before we go any further, that occasionally I suffer with the *odd night terror* and have been known to sit bolt upright in bed at 3am (unbeknownst to me, I am still asleep) and randomly shout things at him like;

'Darling, there is a man stood at the end of the bed.' or

'Darling, I think I just murdered the dog.'

Not the best things to be hearing in a pitch black room in the middle of the night, and so I do understand his anxiety over me waking him up. (I have to admit; sometimes I do it for comedy value. Although I would never tell him that.)

So when The Irish One came to after a gentle prod in the groin from me, and spotted me staring at him, wide eyed, looking a bit demented and in a bit of a catatonic state, he shat himself.

'What?' Startled expression. 'Who is here? Who have you murdered?'

I was pretending to be calm. 'I think I am pregnant'

'Are you even awake?' Bored expression.

'I'm am awake yes, and I am pregnant! I'm bloody pregnant! And I'm having a boy! A real life boy!' (We had also watched SHRECK the night before.)

'Shut up!' Rolls eyes.

He went back to sleep without incident. But I couldn't sleep. I kept counting the days back in my head and thinking of boy's names. (I liked Micah at the time.)

Two days later...

'How was your day Lexy?'

'I'm pregnant Irish one'

'Do you want a cup of tea Lexy?'

'Can you have tea when you are pregnant Irish one?'

'Shut up Lexy!' roll eyes.

He drank his cup of tea without incident. But I couldn't concentrate. I kept counting the days back in my head and thinking of girl's names. (I liked Lola at the time.)

Two days after that...(FYI no matter how early the pregnancy test says its accurate from - 2 days post sex is still way too early! - won't stop you trying though!)

'Lexy what are you doing in the bathroom love? You have been in there an hour.'

'Having a poo darling, why?' (Code for; six pregnancy tests darling why?)

'You've been in there an hour!' (Say's he who has an hourly shit daily!)

'I'm coming out now' (After this one last test.)

The conversations went on like this for the next few weeks. Me counting back the days in my head, *constantly* while he ignored me and watched the football, *constantly*.

In the month of June 2009, pregnancy test markets across the world soared.

Ok, well maybe not across the world. But certainly across Eccles. I must have bought and weed on *that many* sticks, the woman in the chemist thought I was a bit of a not-right. She even asked me at one point if they were all for me.

'No I'm buying them for me and *all of the women* in my aerobics class! *Of course* they are all for me! Whatever happened to *discretion*? Hellllooo?'

The sympathetic smiles soon turned to worried glances, which in time turned to frowns and eventually ended in her having the tests ready and slamming them down on the counter with the force of a small wrestler the minute my unkempt head would appear around the door.

Why she was so bothered by me I don't know. I mean, surely my contribution to your profits this month is quite high? I thought, at the very least I deserved a freebie.

Unfortunately, she didn't agree. Each time I visited, I searched every shelf and read each box meticulously. (Actually, this is probably why she was getting annoyed. No shopkeeper likes *a lurker*. Especially a nutcase one.) Guaranteed early result!! 98% accuracy guaranteed!! Ultra hormone sensitive!!! Were all advertising slogans etched on my brain. 2 blue lines - positive. 1 blue line - negative. 1 pink square positive, no pink square- negative. 1 smiley face- positive, no smiley face- negative. (Although, in all honesty I find that last one a little inappropriate and insensitive. What if you don't want a smiley face? That smiley face then becomes smug doesn't it?) All results were always negative.

But as I don't like being wrong, I didn't give up. I didn't give up because, I just knew. (To be fair though, and in the interest of complete openness and honesty, I had just *known* for the past 6 months too. Hence The Irish One not being too arsed.)

I was sitting in my favorite Chicago coffee house a few days later *droning* (I see I was quite *droneful* looking back) on about how sure I was, that this time my mistake had been valid, while repeating my endless tirade of how I knew I was pregnant, when my best friend finally lost her rag. I was one whole day past the point of no return. I was having period pains, (not that I was about to admit that.) and god love her, she suggested I try a very well-known digital brand. Now, I hadn't tried this particular brand before as it was fairly new on the market and my local establishment of drugs-R-us didn't stock it. (So, looking back, grumpy pharmacist lady did have a right to be grumpy actually. She had a shop full of *not-right lurker's* and crap tests!)

I rushed to the local high street chemist like a woman possessed, NEW DIGITAL TEST!! 99% ACCURATE!! (ooo!) UP TO SIX DAYS EARLY!! (Double ooo!)

I purchased four. Well, you can never be too sure. And I may need them again next month. (Not that I will make another mistake, honest.)

During my very many conversations with The Irish One leading up to this epiphany of 'the digital age' he had made me promise that if I was going to do a pregnancy test, I had to wait for him to be at my side, that we would share the joy/terror of a positive result together. (But look, ok, technically I didn't keep this promise. But technically I didn't break it either. Each and every time I took a test I would stand next to a photo of us on the mantelpiece (I didn't pee near the mantelpiece! What are we *animals?)* To get the results. All the while telling my unborn child, that daddy was here. In spirit.)

But ok, yeah, I had *bent* this promise (satisfied?) on so many occasions and received negative results that I felt this might be why they kept coming up negative. Maybe god could see me, (BENDING) the truth and was keeping the actual truth from me. (Catholic guilt.) So, on the evening of the 2nd of July I waited. I knew in my gut this would be the positive result I felt I deserved at this point, and I didn't want god teaching me anything.

So I waited.

However, I did not set a scene. I did not wait until he had relaxed upon arriving home from work. I did not make a casserole, (chance would be a fine thing) put on some soothing music and light a candle. I did not casually mention it to him half way through a foot rub. I was like a woman possessed. I all but peed *on him* the minute he walked through the door.

'Honey I'm home!' (Ok, not really but I'm setting a scene here!)

'I bought a pregnancy test Irish one.'

'And?'

'I haven't done it yet'

'Good! You are NOT pregnant!' Quite frustrated at this juncture, he was. (Sorry I don't mean to sound like Yoda.)

'I like, totally am. You will see, I am, I know I am, I went online and....'

'Do the bloody test'

Ten minutes later. Staring us up in the face as clear as day from the digital wee stick.

'You are one to two weeks pregnant'

'Told you I was *officially* pregnant' - Me.

'Holy shit you're *officially* pregnant' - Him.

'Bollocks' – barked Doodle. (Dogs can sense these things. He knew then, I am almost sure, his reign of all things below 2 foot high, was coming to an end.)

And that's where it began.

9 months (well 10 actually, 40 weeks is 10 months god damn it!) later. My little fertilized egg started to make its entrance... And all hell *officially* broke loose.

39 weeks later...

My time as **Queen of the world** is running out.

I *really* have enjoyed being pregnant.

I have reveled in bossing people about, having an excuse to be lazy, and being the centre of everybody's universe! (What? I'm only being honest here!)

And even though, I probably shouldn't admit this, I have really enjoyed *playing the pregnancy card* at every available opportunity to get my own way. I do not care about women's lib. I am pregnant. Get me a drink.

But, alas, all good things must come to an end. (Everyone keeps telling me that after the baby is born it won't be about *me* anymore. I just smile politely and ignore them because *clearly* that *can't* be right?!?! It is ***always*** about me??)

But anyway.

I have *officially* been in labour for approximately 16 hours and so far it has been as dull as double math's on an overcast and dimly lit Monday afternoon.

Dullsville, Arizona.

My waters *officially* broke 16 hours ago.

It was not very dramatic.

I felt an elastic band ping deep inside of me and the next thing I knew, my granny knickers, my pajamas and the poodle were piss wet through.

Doodle just happened to be stood underneath me at the time, as I was eating a snickers bar and I think he was hoping for a stray peanut. Quite clearly he got more than he bargained for.

His eyes say it all. He was absolutely disgusted with me.

He didn't move though. *#Justsayin.*

I finished my snickers bar and calmly went to fetch a mop.

I have been experiencing random contractions for what feels like the *last year and a half,* and so far, I have to say, I am hugely unimpressed with labour.

I am bored.

What is wrong with this picture? Where is the *rushing around?* Where is the *urgency?* Where are the *screaming ambulance sirens* and the *running midwives?* Where are the sweaty women clambering to hold my hand and screaming *PUSH!!* Why aren't I shouting out expletives at The Irish One and threatening to cut his *gonads* off if he comes near me again? Where is the *drama?* I asked you a question! Did you miss it? I repeat, where *the hell* is the *DRAMA?*

I was promised drama!

Every book I have perused through (because who has time to read a book when there is this much eating to be done?) over the last 10 months has regaled me with tales of Drama, screaming, torn womanly bits and romantic endings.

I was positively wetting myself in anticipation for my movie moment.

I *live* for the *drama!*

Labour is supposed to be *high octave.* Labour is supposed to be all *Go! Go! Go!* Isn't it? I've waited 10 months for this moment for god sake! All previous dramas have been leading up to this monumental occurrence! This is *the main event!* This is what I have been in training for *my whole life!*

Surely, I am not supposed to be *just* sat here on a damp and fraying old towel, munching on a bacon sandwich while moaning about the weather, in my own home, watching The Irish One play Mario Kart?

He bought me a Wii and a Wii fit last week as a pre *'thank you for having my baby, this will help you get your figure back'* present.

The Wii fit was dented beyond repair when I launched it at his stupid hairy face and the only reason the Wii (fat) still works is because I deem it so.

Up until about an hour ago, I was playing too out of sheer frustration. (If you can't *beat* him (literally) then you may as well join him I say) and if *nobody* was going to pay me any attention, then I thought I might as well enjoy my last moments 'of freedom' by kicking The Irish One's arse with Bowser the Wonder Dragon!

But unfortunately even that didn't go to plan as the minute I would get in the lead and start to whoop, I would become distracted by my highly un-dramatic contractions. Eventually I had to make my excuses to the Flower cup and bow out. So technically I didn't lose. I *retired*! (I am not sure why this was an important point but it was. And don't you dare say hormones.)

Anyway. I am in labour. Get me a drink.

I need to stop thinking about food (I want a Doritos sandwich) and start counting my contractions. The thing is, these *random* contractions are a pain in the arse. (No pun intended) as I can't *even* time them. They are so *totally* random. When I feel one starting, by the time I switched on the stopwatch on my iPhone, they are finished

They don't *even* hurt that much. They are just uncomfortable. I really don't know what all the fuss is about.

A contraction feels like a very sharp period pain (the ones you get when you feel like someone is shoving a hot poker up your bum) followed by a bit of a *periody* ache and then like a leg cramp, but across the belly. Does that make sense?

Not too bad at all really.

Maybe next time instead of timing them, I will name them. That would make a nice change wouldn't it?

'How long was that one Lexy?'

The Irish One is so focused on Mario Kart, he asks me this without even taking his eyes from the screen. *So* supportive.

Meanwhile I am bent over the birthing ball behaving like a donkey might, when it is trying to shit out a watermelon.

'I don't know Irish One. But it was called Veronica. And she was a bitch.'

Yes. I think I will name them instead. That would be much more fun.

EEEEEEEE OOOOOOOOOOR.

That's my donkey breathing technique.

Time seems to have slowed right down to a complete stop.

So far the *only* excitement has been my waters breaking.

And I am pretty sure that shouldn't have even happened yet.

It was that bloody chili and that freaky bloody film. I knew I shouldn't have eaten that chili, but he put the plate in front of me, so what choice did I have?

It was as *hot as hell* and I found it nearly impossible to jump up and down to cool my mouth down afterwards. (*Everybody knows* that is the official way you cool your mouth down.)

Instead of being sat here now, I could have been out shopping for post pregnancy *wears.*

I miss shopping.

I miss shopping and I need some new skinny jeans.

Do they do skinny jeans with a kangaroo pouch? Because *apparently* I will be left with a kangaroo pouch, although to be honest I doubt it. Everyone says the weight will drop off, and in all honesty I was pretty skinny before so it shouldn't be an issue.

I want to go shopping for **post** pregnancy clothes. I wonder what size I will be at first.

I didn't *mean* to put on so much weight.

It just sort of, happened.

I just sort of, kept eating.

After every mouthful, every meal and every king-size MacDonald's meal I would promise myself tomorrow, tomorrow I will be good. I will eat healthy.

But tomorrow just never came. So five stone later (at *least* one stone will be baby right? This baby is going to be ***huge.)*** I am a bit of a heffa. A pregnant heffa, and like I say, if this baby ever gets its arse in gear and moves down my canal, I will lose like, what? 3 stone immediately? It will be fine. I am not even supposed to be in labour yet! I blame Leonardo de Caprio and those red hot chili peppers. (Too obvious a joke? Fuck it. I'm using it anyway.)

The excitement (Doodle huffs when I call it this) began at 11pm last night. We had just watched Shutter Island, which by the way is a god-awful film in my opinion.

As a rule, I am not fond of lunatics, as I see too much of myself in them. It was all a bit too close to the bone.

I think it would be very easy for me to slip in to a quiet corner and repeatedly count to one hundred over and over again, with a tissue on my head. I sometimes think it must be lovely to be a lunatic, like taking a break from your brain. Which is precisely why I don't like lunacy. It's *too* relatable. And maybe I'm a little bit jealous that they don't have to work.

Anyway back to the *exciting* bit.

I took another bite on my snickers, bent down to pull up my knickers (hey that rhymes! God I am talented) and as I stood up straight I heard and felt them go. I grabbed my bump in faux movie shock and immediately set off at a rush to the toilet. (When I say *I rushed*, I use this term lightly. Think of perhaps, what an elephant would look like rushing.) I then called out to The Irish One who was watching the football.

'Honey I've weed myself again.' (And who said romance was dead?)

'Ok babes, I'll be there is a second.' (He is well used to this by now.)

Just for the record, we have now *officially* been together a grand total of 16 months. During which time this man has seen away more of me than I had *officially* planned for him to.

Pregnancy; killing romance **dead,** fart by fart.

Anyway, It was while I was trying to remove my Basque and sexy thong, (ha ha yeah right! Have you ever seen an elephant in a thong?

No?

Well there is a reason for that!

I was *actually* wearing the oldest tattiest jogging bottoms I own. They are *comfy! Comfort is key* at this stage! And with sex well and truly out of the window anyway why bother making an effort? (Did I mention the elephant in a thong?)

When the water (slime...) continued to wane and gush out of me like a leaky tap, I realized this probably meant something more *monumental* than *another* bed wetting incident. *(Yes, I did say another.)*

'Honey?' (Starting to panic.)

'Yes babes?' (Shut up woman! I'm watching match of the day!)

'I haven't weed myself actually.'

'Oh well done yourself, do you want a cup of tea?' (That should shut her up.)

Sigh.

'No I mean, I think my waters have broken.'

'Is this another joke? Because I am not laughing. It is **not** funny.'

Have you ever read a fable called 'The boy who cried wolf?'

Let's just say he has an annoying habit of not listening to me, and I have an annoying habit of trying to shock him out of his football reverie in order to get his attention (so he can get me a drink, or give me a foot massage, or something equally as necessary! I am pregnant. Get me a bloody drink!)

It was funny at the time.

'No I'm serious. COME HERE!'

'You said that last time, piss off and get your own drink.'

Serves *me* right.

'No, I'm serious. Please *come here*!! It's everywhere and the dog is licking it up.'

'That's disgusting Lexy.'

'COME HERE YOU BLOODY MORON!'

'Coming....'

We rang the hospital not long after, and I was shouting and sobbing down the phone before they even picked up. (It heightened the drama.)

'My waters have broken and I am scared.' (Which was true, I was.)

'Pardon?' The midwife picked up, she seemed a little confused.

'My name is Lexy Ellis, my waters have broken and although my due date is tomorrow I am really scared.'

It has begun!!! Surely you were waiting for my call with baited breath?? I mean, the world will clearly **never** *be the same again, for I, Lexy Ellis am having a baby! Help me!!*

'And what do you want love?' she sounded bored.

'Er, well, I don't know. I just thought I should inform you, as I don't know what to do.'

'Well, ok.' she finally answered 'if I were you I would go to the nearest hospital'

'is this not the maternity unit at Hope hospital?' I whispered, wishing The Irish One wasn't listening.

'No love, its Picolino's Pizza on Oxford road.' (I am sure she was creasing herself laughing but I can't be sure.)

Arghhhhhh! Wrong number! Damn it!

'But ooo Pizza. Irish One do you fancy....' I look at his face, 'Ok. No Pizza. Wrong number, sorry!'

Ok. Deep breath.

I dialed again. This time checking I had the *right number*, and was connected immediately.

'Hello? Are you a midwife?'

'Yes. How can I help?'

'Are you sure you are a midwife?'

'Pretty sure, yes.'

'And is this Hope Hospital?'

'Yes'

'and you're definitely a midwife?'

'Yes, how can I help?' beginning to lose her rag now.

'My waters have broken and I am embarrassed. And a bit scared.'

'Ok, Are you having contractions?' she asked patiently.

'I'm not sure'

'that probably means you aren't.'

How rude!!!

'But come down and see us and we will check you out anyway.'

So we did. And because my contractions were too *random and pathetic,* they sent us home and told us to come back when my contractions were five minutes apart. They are now every, either 17 minutes, or every hour. Depending on how they feel.

My due date is tomorrow. So maybe, like me, *the pleb* is just hanging around, as he or she likes to be punctual. There is nothing worse than turning up early for a party is there? So I understand *the pleb's* rationale to be honest.

(*The pleb* is my *cute* name for the baby.)

Maybe I will have another game on Mario Kart. Show The Irish One how amazing I am at multi-tasking. Or maybe I will make him go get me a Big Mac.

I am in labour. Get me food.

But I tell you this.
If this is labour?
It's all a bit grim.
And it really isn't that bad.
Why do all these women *go on* like its hell on earth?
It's not even that painful.

For the love of...

Sixty-five hours ago, when this all started, I may have been a *tad* premature in my labelling of labour as *a doddle.* (Yes. Sixty FIVE hours ago.)

Perhaps I came across as a *tad* cocky. (If I had been walking I would have had a gangster limp. That's how cocky I felt. As it was, I was limping because I developed bum grapes. Lovely.)

Did I really use the words *'not even that painful?'*

(I think I may have even repeated myself to the midwife at one point too. Oh the shame! I was *pooing* all over her 6 hours later....)

I am mortified.

Twenty seven hours ago, all bravado I may have shown previously, positively ran screaming, like a rat on speed, *out* of the birthing room at a rate of knots, leaving an arrogant (and I can see now), *massively* big headed and idiotic fat *rat shaped* hole in the wall. I cannot believe I had the pure audacity to call labour *boring.*

Just who the hell did I think I was? Mother Nature was listening, of that I am sure. And the bitch made me pay.

They wheeled me up here an hour ago, baby on my knee, and promptly sent The Irish One home.

The baby was born by the way, did I not mention that? Yes *the Pleb* was born *eventually.*

(Don't you dare say congratulations yet either! I haven't got my make up on and I look like a clapped out troll. You can say congratulations later when I've got the feeling back in my flute and my eyeliner is back on my eyes and not smudged around my belly button. Don't you dare utter the words. Now is ***not the time***

to be congratulating me. I just fainted on the toilet. Congratulations? Are you on glue? I am humiliated!)

The Pleb is asleep beside me, his little fists clenched like Victor Meldrew. He looks a little peeved. If he could speak I am almost sure he would shout 'I don't believe it!'

And I would have to agree with him too.

I can hardly believe it myself. It is finally over. He is finally here. And he is asleep. He is gorgeous. And a bit weird looking. His face is all swollen and he looks a little like Mike Tyson, but he is definitely mine. I have the body to prove it.

Contractions, by the way, are definitely not *'just a bit achy.' (Oh the shame!)*

At one point I genuinely and honestly thought the only way the situation could possibly get any worse, was if the midwife had started too harshly and repeatedly *punch me in the face.*

That is how bad it was. In fact, at one point, I was *thinking* of asking her to *harshly and repeatedly punch me in the face.* I needed a distraction.

To get to where I am right now was probably the longest and most horrific journey I have ever been unlucky enough to experience. It certainly wasn't the total joy of a voyage I had meticulously planned. (On the back page of my 'natural is best, hypnosis is key' handbook.)

Ahh, my Birth Plan.

My wonderfully dramatic and yet serene birth plan. It just wasn't meant to be.

My birth plan unfortunately was lobbed straight out of the proverbial window the moment **'pig sperm'** was brought up.

Did you just gasp? Or was that me gasping involuntarily again?

My birth plan, was written and fondled with (in between snacks of course) *for hours,* in the lead up to the big day.

It was my midwife's fault.

She advised me to 'have an idea' of what I wanted to happen, as to 'aid' with a **pleasurable** *(lying bitch)* and **enjoyable** *(She is so gonna get it)* labour. She did warn me *(but not enough!!!)* not to expect *everything* to come off as planned *(ha!)* but had also kindly advised me with a big smile 'it is worth having goals and ideas of what you would like.' (See previous comment. She is *so* gonna get it. She wasn't even there!!!)

My birth plan included;

A birth pool. (Because it sounded cool and I like swimming.)

Candles (Because I thought I would look thinner by candle light.)

Music (I had visions of my child being born while Kings of Leon played *sex on fire* in the background. How cool would that have been? Turns out it was my *ring* that was on fire!)

(Manageable) Drama. (You know. Just to keep everybody interested. Maybe I could dramatically faint or something?)

People telling me I looked radiant. (People could lie. I would still accept it.)

Someone feeding me sweets. (Because I am the one doing **all the work.**)

The midwife commenting on my perfectly manicured feet. (Do you have *any* idea how hard *that* was to achieve at 40 weeks pregnant? Forget climbing Mount Everest. Try bending down and touching your toes with a watermelon stuffed up your jumper. Ok, make that 2 water melons and a small cow. (I ate a lot of meat.)

A quick labour (But not so quick that I couldn't milk it. *Obviously.)*

A nice anesthetist that called me brave and beautiful and told me he didn't think I needed pain relief. (At which point I would nod solemnly and soldier on. Just call me *Joan of arc.)*

An epidural, if I was simply *too* exhausted to carry on. (I would feign exhaustion. Poor me!)

My other half telling me he loved me (while I sighed and shot him dramatic dirty looks and midwifes whispered 'poor pet' under their breath 'he simply has no idea of what she is going through, she truly is a heroine.')

A bit of swearing off me. (Because that is what you are supposed to do isn't it?)

A bit of a giggle of the gas and air. (Re live my youth a little.)

A touching moment where when the child appeared, everybody stopped to stare and marveled at its beauty and elegance. 'Doesn't he/she just look the image of his/her mother?' At this point I would lie back with a sigh and would be presented with an award and a glass of water, while somebody mopped my brow in the background.

It did, ***under no circumstances***, include.

Being sent home from the hospital twice due to a lack of beds. (Do they know who I am? Do they know what I have to put up with at home? Keep me in and peel me grapes! I am in bloody labour!)

Being told repeatedly my labour wasn't progressing so I should just wait. (Wait? Like *heathens* wait?)

Being told to go for a long walk. (Off a short cliff by any chance? How rude!)

Lots of haggard and tired looking midwives looking up my *flute* and sighing heavily. (Honestly, I had more tourist action today than the bloody London eye.)

Being 3 cm dilated after 40 hours of proper labour. (PROPER LABOUR, did you hear me? Not every now and again mild labour, I mean proper, slap me across the head, beat me with a leather brush, call me Susan and inject me with ANYTHING you have handy, hell *on earth.)*

Having *Pig sperm* (Gasp!) shot up my lady parts in an attempt to encourage the little monster to make a move down. (Apparently poking my stomach and shouting The Pleb's full *Sunday* name in a manner reserved for a pissed off parent, a manner I have heard plenty of times over the years, is neither productive of necessary. Sor-ry! Just trying to help. Jeez.)

My other half popping home for a shower. (Yes, don't worry dear, you pop home and *refresh* yourself. I do not mind *at all.* I will stay here, sizzling, like a lump of lard on a frying pan and scream to the *bloody wall.* I will stay here and shove a watermelon out of my arse while you have a shower and read the paper. No, honestly. *You go.*)

Sandwich making.

An aneath*sadist* who was shaking like a *shitting dog* and sent my nervous system on a roller coaster ride. 'You may feel a little tingle' was the understatement of the BLOODY year! While my leg shot up and out like *gold member.)*

An epidural that didn't actually work. (I swear to god, he was either a full on numpty, or my ferocious yelling of 'Get the *fuck* over here and give me some bloody drugs before I come over there, grab the needle off you and shove it in my own neck!!' scared the living daylights out of him and he got so nervous, he did it bloody wrong! The Irish One says it was the latter. And apparently it serves me right. The Irish One has been walking with a limp ever since... and not a gangster limp either.)

For one side of my body to be paralyzed while the other felt **every single contraction.** (There are no words...I felt like one half of my body was laughing at the other, while the other half was screaming 'HELP ME, DON'T JUST SIT THERE, HELP ME! It was very conflicting, confusing and confounded. Awful.)

Gas and air to be as much fun as it was. (It really was fun! Sorry Irish one, I know your name isn't Jon. I don't know why I found it *quite so funny* to repeatedly call you by the wrong name. And yes, I know that is *my ex's name*... it really isn't funny. You are right. No I am not smirking!)

To be fully and properly induced. (Because, I am a half numb failure.)

For induction not to work. (For the love of god!)

To feel faint. (Real proper faint. Not dramatic *swoon* faint.)

To have to wear a gas mask like Goose in Top Gun. (If I am honest, this was funny for a while. To me anyway. Although thinking about it now, nobody else was laughing at my *'there's a mig on my tail there's a mig on my tail'* impressions. Ah well, as long as you can laugh at yourself.)

For My baby's heartbeat to slow right down. (REAL drama.)

Lights, sirens, bells and whistles to scare the living day lights out of me. (Turns out real drama? *Not so fun*!!)

After 65, yes 65 hours, to be told, if you don't push now your baby may be brain damaged, as there wasn't enough time for a C-section. (No words. I mean it this time.)

And finally;

> While basking in the pure *relief* of him being born healthy and well. While enjoying a *very much-deserved moment* of sheer joy, with him on my chest. While experiencing, without a doubt, the most romantic and loving moment of my entire life, for the midwife I shit on earlier (literally not metaphorically) to get her own back. Royally.

Her actual words.

Are you ready?

'Sorry to ruin the moment, but I just need to stick my finger up your bum, ok?'

(OK? Why bother asking OK? And why??? Couldn't you have just waited a moment or two??... Turns out she was checking for tearing. Sigh.)

Do some of my smiles look shocked in the photos? Well now you know why.

And also.

> For my bloody baby girl to be born with a Willy. (*What the hell?* It's a boy!)

So yes, 65 hours after my waters broke. He is finally here.

His name is Addison Jake. (Jake, in memory of my beautiful older brother.) He is 6lbs 14oz.

Which means I have a whole *15 year old* to lose in weight. The next year should be fun then.

Glass of water for me please! (I just had a baby. Get me a drink.)

A lovely doctor came up to see me a while ago and expressed very strongly that if I began to think he was Jesus, I should tell somebody.

I had only been joking for god's sake but apparently there is such a thing as post birth psychosis, and as today is Easter

Sunday, there may be a link. Is there such a thing as *pre-birth* psychosis? I asked her. Because I think I have *always* had that. She didn't laugh and not long after I fainted on the toilet. God pissed off with me? Yes I think so.

Addison has five fingers and five toes. Addison is perfect.

I have *no idea* what to do with him. Thankfully he is asleep. And I suppose I should be getting some sleep too. But I am too wired.

Are you aware that newborns can't sit up? Random right?

I have never changed a nappy. Do the sticky bits go at the back?

He is lovely but what the hell do I do with him?

Bloody hell. What a day.

I remember shouting out, right after his head appeared '*Did you cut me? Because if feels like you cut me! And if you did, make sure you stitch me back together properly! Make it nice and tight!*'

A head duly popped up from between my legs, looking a bit worse for wear, and stated ominously '*You will never be the same again love, it'll be like throwing a penny in a bucket of water.*'

Well ok *the head* didn't *actually* say *that*. But it may as well have.

The head from between my legs then went on to tell me that *this time next year this will all be a distant memory.*

Somehow *head*, I doubt that.

I *really* doubt that.

License and registration...

Why is it, when wearing down the grubby heels of my ridiculously *still* swollen feet, which are now beginning to resemble that of a sixty year old woman (is nothing sacred anymore? I have to lose my ankles too??) Shuffling aimlessly around the hallowed halls of this, century old, warmer than hell, filled with women moaning and groaning in pain, maternity unit, in an attempt to quell this screaming child, the only phrase that comes in to my mind is 'I see dead people?'

Moving anything hurts.

My body feels as if it has gone ten rounds with a meat grinder.

I feel like a mangled sausage.

Carefully placing one foot, deliberately in front of the other, in an attempt to keep moving without adding to the already excruciating needle like pain emanating from below, I find myself glancing down at my son.

He looks a bit like a cross between Yoda and Gordon Ramsey at this point, as he is swaddled so tight I am struggling to breathe just looking at him.

I didn't swaddle him, the midwife did, I don't even know what swaddle means, I am just throwing it in for dramatic effect at this point.

Meanwhile all I can think about it Bruce Willis and that bloody freaky film.

It is spooky that is why.

According to the midwife, motion can trick a newborn baby in to believing it is still in utero and it will stop crying.

In all honesty I doubt this to be true.

Maybe if I fed my child a Big Mac through his belly button he would be more inclined to believe this, and *then* maybe he would stop crying and sleep, but what choice do I have?

As it is, so far, my grunting and throbbing hobbling is having absolutely no effect on his high pitched death wail, however who am I to argue with a midwife? I don't have the energy, hence my persevered staggering.

I will do as I am told because if I don't I will have no idea what to do.

Being in a hospital and wide awake at 2am, staggering down the halls like a newborn calf is not something I have ever experienced before. And it's not something I am in a rush to experience again to be honest, it has to be said.

I am not the only one walking up and down the long, white washed, bleach perfumed hallway, but I can bet you 25 to one (whatever the hell that means) I am the only one picturing all manner of weird and horrible loony bin films.

There are five of us in total, all much bigger shadows of our former selves of course, carting our precious new additions the length and breadth of this ghostly hall of the post-natal unit.

I wonder if all these other women are wishing they could rewind the clock back to the eventful moment insemination took place and re-think the use of a condom.

I do not make eye contact with new mother number 3 as she limps past me again, muttering under her breath and cursing somebody named 'Martin,' I simply keep my eyes fixed forward and try to imagine some far away happy place.

Like Addison's 18 birthday, or the border crossing to Mexico.

'Try listening to a screeching cat for five hours while somebody torches your undercarriage and *then* try proving you are not insane.' I inadvertently blurt out to mother number 2 as I overtake her, becoming more confident now as the medication starts to sink in.

She doesn't respond.

'Are you ok Lexy?'

It's the doctor again. I really don't know why they won't leave me alone. I was only joking when I said I was going to steal an ambulance and head for the Channel Tunnel, Jesus!

You honestly would have thought I had threatened to *hurt* the pleb the way the doctors were bustling about my bed before, casting concerned and wary glances at one another and offering me medication out of a bag so large and long at first I mistakenly thought they were offering me a congratulatory selection of pick and mix.

I was a little disappointed I will admit, I could kill a foam banana right now.

Looking back though, I probably shouldn't have randomly vocalized just that.

It did not seem to calm them down.

He was born on a holy day, and all I do is mention in passing to the woman who appeared with my cup of tea and toast (sent from god this woman, sent from god!) that was it me or did he bear a slight resemblance to Jesus Christ our savior and could I please have some holy water and a mop, and the next thing I know 4 men in white coats bumble in from behind the curtain, cursing and brandishing stethoscopes.

I mean, I am not even *that* religious.

I ask him for stuff yeah, and I do good things in the hope that he is watching and therefor gives me the stuff I am asking for, but I'm not a churchgoer or anything. Maybe I would be if church were held on a Tuesday evening or something, but Sunday morning at 9am? Madness.

'Do you believe your child is Jesus?' doctor 1 had asked me kindly, his head cocked to the side after bursting through the curtain like a cabaret dancer on prom night.

'No.' I had resolutely responded impressed by his entrance and more than a little optimistic that maybe he was asking because he may agree. 'Why do you?'

I have to admit at this point I was kind of hopeful. I have always dreamed of being famous and how cool would it have been if someone thought my child was Jesus? I may have even appeared in HEAT magazine.

'No, We' he coughed, refusing to make eye contact with me but sweeping his hand around in the direction of the other three medics, as if to point out he was not alone, like I was now blind *and* unable to hear or see the other three gawping at me and breathing heavily all over the right side of my face 'WE do not think your child is Jesus. He is cute but definitely not Jesus.'

Gutted.

'Never mind then,' I replied politely and somewhat down heartedly, images of me in a Gucci gown on some runway somewhere being hailed as the new and much improved fabulous mother Teresa slipping disappointingly from my mind 'would have been nice.'

It was at this point they offered me some medication and suggested that perhaps I try and sleep.

Ridiculous.

Try and sleep? I should have offered the bag of medication back to him, is what I should have done!

4 or whatever years of medical school and his advice to a new mother, with a new born Pleb singing the baby version of the national anthem beside her, is to sleep?

How could I have possibly slept with the sheer volume of *din* coming from this child?

Why won't he stop crying?

He has been in my arms and out of my gut for approximately seven hours, and so far all he has done is screech.

And as if that wasn't exhausting enough, after the cast and crew of 'One flew over the cuckoo's nest' left and I was supposed to somehow be sleeping (but instead was busy searching for my phone from my handy hospital bag filled with useless items I spent weeks packing, so that I could text The Irish One, who had been sent home, and slag him off) some woman calling herself a Breast Feeding Advisor pushed her head from behind the flimsy curtain and insisted that I should try and feed him immediately as... I can't remember why, it's been a long night, but I'm sure she had her reasons.

Actually, I think she may have said, as the rest of her uninvited body followed her uninvited head in to my tiny bit of personal space, that it was something to do with Colostomy?

No, wait, not colostomy, colostrum.

Anyway, after ignoring my protests, that I am sure we would be just fine and I would try *after* she had left, and *after* I had text The Irish One and called him a lazy maggot and who the hell did he think he was leaving me like this to fend for myself, and after I had argued that in fairness I don't like getting my boobs out in front of strangers! And half of Salford Royal hospital had just seen my bum hole and *flute*, is nothing sacred anymore? The tussle to get my nightdress open, began.

'Seriously, I will be fine, angle nipple towards baby's mouth and he will suck! How hard can it be?' I repeated back to her willing her to leave me alone and half considering shouting for the police.

'Come on,' she insisted, forcefully reaching for the buttons of my flimsy nightgown and proceeding to undo them while I half-heartedly attempted to bat her hands away, 'Let's get it done.'

I was too shocked to respond as she plunged her hand in to the depths of my fleshy boob and pulled it out in all its glory, before angling it towards Addison's mouth.

I was horrified.

And in fairness, and I can't say I blame him, so was he.

His eyes shot open as she brushed my deep purple nipple (yes purple. I have no idea why they have changed colour, they just have) against the side of his cheek and I swear to god, all those books that say children are born blind?

Well I can tell you now, when this boy witnessed *that* being thrust towards his face, there is no doubt in my mind that this child can see.

Either that, or miraculously his blindness lifted and was instantly replaced by a terrified and appalled expression, as he immediately recoiled and the intensity of his screams (again, can't really blame him) quadrupled.

'Mummy get it off me!! Get it off me! Get it off me!!! Oh my god why is she trying to put it in my mouthhhhhhh, no mummy noooooooo!' He seemed to be screaming, wild eyed and begging me for help.

'Look' I said, trying to summon some strength from the depleting recourses I had remaining from far within, after half an hour of this rigmarole had passed and she had manhandled both of my boobs like one may a stress ball, taught me how to hold my child like a football, and bleated on endlessly about the need for him to *latch on* as Addison bit me between rock hard gums, I had bled like a tortured cow and she had muttered 'come on you little bugger, feed!' over and over again until I could stand it no more and was now beginning to wonder if in fact she even worked at the hospital or was just some sort of random masochist by association (like M*unchausen's* by association, but also fixated with kneading breasts? Are you with me? Look, by this point I honestly believed anything was possible) I eventually spat out 'this clearly isn't working is it, can we try again a little later?'

Well, the way she tilted her face to meet mine, you would have thought I had just smiled at her, poo'd in my hands and clapped.

'Fine.' She shot out, already about to disappear back behind the curtain leaving me holding my child like an American football and both boobs now flopping about on my belly angry and red, 'your child is hungry, but I suppose you want to bottle feed him?' and off she flounced before I could even respond.

No, ideally I would like to breastfeed. But the more you shove my boob in his face, the more distressed he is getting, so surely it makes sense to leave it a while until he has calmed down and then we can try again in ten minutes? Doesn't it?

I mean, I am no child expert clearly but...

Talk about dropping me in the deep end.

I can't believe that since then, since I had the *audacity* to politely put my foot down and ask her to stop stretching and squeezing my boobs as one may do an udder, they have just left me with him.

Don't I need a license or something?

After she had left I just stared after her in silent disbelief.

Well, it would have been silent if it were not for the four other children, including mine, that were now screaming in unison, like a terrifying choir, from behind each individual curtain that split this huge room in separate compartments, each housing a new mother, like me, all racing in to the first night of motherhood with a frozen look of shock on their faces.

The very same four mothers plus a straggler from another room, that are now back to creeping the halls with me.

Isn't there a nice introductory course you can book me in for? Surely there is an onsite crèche?

Can I call in sick?

There is no way I can look after a baby all day tomorrow as well. There is no way I am going to last much longer.

I have been conscious for 82 hours. I love him and all but can I get a night off? Things will seem more *manageable* after a few days of rest.

No?

But I have just had a baby for god sake; surely I deserve a night off?

Maybe I should have paid more attention in the antenatal classes I forced myself in to but I swear they didn't cover the first night.

I didn't pay much attention granted, because I was too busy rubbing my back and dramatically huffing 'oooo!' in the hope that The Irish One would whisk me immediately home and insist that as I was doing such a good job of growing his baby, I should settle in front of 'Grey's Anatomy' and eat my body weight in ice cream even though Manchester United were playing.

Needless to say it didn't work, mostly because United *were* playing but also because he was the one who wanted to go to the classes in the first place ('I need to know what to expect!' blah, he is *such a swat*) so I was forced to sit and listen to some woman twice my age go on about *breathing* and *bathing* and *swabs* and *pain relief* (I will be honest, I did tune in at that point) while I checked out the bumps on the other women and mentally scored myself against them. (My bump was *by far* the biggest, and I was proud. Of course most of my bump was probably McDonalds but *whatever.)*

But, I have the gift of the gab; I can talk anyone round, get what I want, persuade a buyer, caress a potential sale, so I thought convincing a baby to sleep, eat and shhhh! Would be a doddle. (There is that word again.) So I wasn't concerned with the grey fuzz that was the memory of what I had learned.

But there are two things I most definitely cannot do in this moment.

I cannot talk this tough cookie around. No matter what I whisper he just won't settle, or eat, or sleep. (Yes I have tried unsuccessfully a couple of times since then to *latch him on.* Just FYI? The element of surprise doesn't work either.)

He seems to have his little heart set on crying, and I can see already he is a stubborn one. He will do what *he* wants to do. God knows where he gets *that* from.

The other thing I can't do right now is wee. And I am *desperate.*

The pain my half epidural wiped out came careening back about 4 hours ago. My legs stopped wobbling 3 hours ago (on my 15th round of the ward.) However my bladder is still on sabbatical. Or at least the little men that operate the release valve are. Maybe they are stuck in traffic. Honestly, I can picture it now.

There are piercing, loud *neenor* type sirens screaming out in to my body somewhere between my empty bump and my bowel, (Think *Armageddon* crossed with *Innerspace!)* with lots of little workers in yellow suits screaming *'Release hatch 3 man! Release hatch 3! Why won't it open? We are doomed I tell you! Doomed!'*

I watched 2012 while Preggo too. Surely I am not the only one who pictures her body as a ship? The men in my head are actually hilarious!

If I could only find the time to sit on the toilet and give my lady muscles the attention they so obviously require with this task, I am sure the sirens would abate and the little men in yellow suits could go back to plugging a leak elsewhere (you *know* where!) But Addison is less than 7 hours old. I feel it a little early in his life, and especially following on from purple nipple gate to subject him to mummy/baby toilet time.

Imagine he caught sight of anything?

No. I just couldn't do it to him.

His face is currently squashed between my boobs in an attempt to dampen the screams as the midwives watch me walk past every ten minutes, I can feel their gazes piercing the back fat that has blossomed over the last 40 weeks. They must be well used to seeing this sort of thing by now. They probably have a right chortle about it over their custard creams.

'Oy Doreen, there goes Lexy Ellis from bay 1, bed 2 again.'

'Is she doing the *oh my god what have I done, is it too late to push him back in* marathon?'

'That's the one. Jammy dodger?'

'Don't mind if I do.'

(*Is it* too late to push him back in?)

I love my son very much. He is just beautiful. Even with his swollen nose and bunched up fists and open, wailing vocal cords, he is amazing. I just wish I knew what he wanted.

And my bits are really starting to *smart,* as my aunty Nancy used to say. (She used to say her finger smarted when she cut it, I mean. We never discussed her bits. She was old. Hence the term *smarting.* I don't mean she was old in any relation to her bits. Can we change the subject now please?) Apparently, according to Shakira in bay 1, bed 3, (the one next to mine, who's child is either called Sausage, or she is still having cravings – each to their own I suppose) they *do* Nurofen and you are even allowed gas and air if the pain gets *really* bad during the 3 hourly checkups.

Yes, someone will be partaking in a deep and meaningful with my bits every 3 hours.

There really aren't enough words in the English language that will allow me to to convey the deep and intense pleasure this will bring me.

So yeay! At least that is something to look forward to.

I like Gas and air, I think I may actually try and smuggle a cylinder in to the changing bag as we leave. I am sure it will come in handy at some stage. According to an old friend of mine who has a 3 year old, *she* could have really done with some in the first year.

Especially, she said, during the many times that her and her other half had endured screaming matches over how he never lifted a finger at 3am and refused to wash the knives and forks, leaving them sitting at the bottom of the sink as if invisible, for days, (and even though he had washed the plates!) before she would eventually, shove a broom up her arse (her words not mine) and get on with *that* as well as everything else she had to do.

So yeah, she said Gas and Air would have helped to lift her mood, as she wouldn't have had to try so hard not to kill her husband and hide his body in the back yard had she been lightheaded and chemically happy.

I am not *too* worried about The Irish One not pulling his weight to be honest, as I am sure we will be just fine, (he OWES me big time for tonight so it is all fair and square) and generally we get on really well, it's more for when he is watching football and I need a little pick me up.

Anyway, back to the crying baby.

Maybe if I sing to him he will stop, but my mind has gone completely blank.

I really should have researched some nursery rhymes instead of spending endless hours rewinding 'One born every minute' but it was like a drug, I couldn't help myself. I needed to see these women's pain to gain some understanding about what I was about to go through.

Damn it! Why aren't I more prepared for this bit? It's not like watching that helped anyway!

Along with 'I *see dead people*' and '*Wake up now you lazy Irish git and research me a nursery rhyme*' the only other thing rolling around my head right now is that prodigy song '*smack my bitch up.*'

Really not appropriate.

'Jingle bells, batman smells...'

That'll do.

There really should be some sort of theory test.

Galileo Galileo...

Do you know what really winds me up?

Thunder stealers.

It's like when you pass your driving test and you tell *one* person and the next thing you know all your friends are texting offering words of congratulations without you even having spoken to them. (True story.)

Or when you find out you're pregnant and your dizzy blonde mate, who you *have* to forgive, *because she is your dizzy blonde mate*, asks your mum, if she is looking forward to being a grandma? *Before* you have even told your mum. (True story. Was months before *mother* spoke to me again.)

Or when you push a 7-pound baby through a hole made for delicate maneuvering **only!**

Endure 65 hours of labour, followed by 22 hours without a wee, followed by an attack of the *heebie jeebies* and when you finally get 2 minutes to spare and log on to your Facebook page to tell the world of your amazing news, lying unceremoniously like a huge lump of left over blood and organs in your tiny hospital bed, hand poised over your status bar, trembling with excitement, you notice with fury, some **fucker** has already spread the word for you.

Name *and* weight, time of arrival; everything.

It has really wound me up. More so than the Russian doctor, the newest visitor of the *Random Squad* to appear behind my curtain and request a look up my flute.

The same Russian doctor who kept referring to me as 'mummy.'

That's weird *right?*

It's not just me is it?

He isn't the only one to do it either. Apparently having a baby also means you no longer have a name.

But to refer to me as mummy? Now that's just plain creepy.

He was at least 65 years old!

I am not your mummy! Stop calling me mummy! I know I am Addison's mummy but I have a name! You referring to me as mummy, while I lie here with my legs spread, whispering to me in your James Bond Baddy accent, while you examine me, is freaking me out. It's like a terrible porn film! My name is Lexy! For the love of god! As if this wasn't awkward enough!

It is winding me up even more than the fact The Irish One is merrily getting to go home at the end of each day I spend in here suffering, to 'watch a bit of telly, eat a bit of tea, and get a bit of rest!'

How lovely for him!

Meanwhile I am stuck here, listening to this child scream *for a bit,* having people look up my bits *for a bit*, and trying not to stamp my foot and cry in frustration *a bit.* (Ok, a lot.)

So all I was asking for was my moment you know? My moment to bloody shine!

I acknowledge, that because of the thunder stealer, my page was littered with over 100 messages of support and love and congratulations, all professing how wonderful my newborn must be and how they couldn't wait to see photos and how it couldn't have happened to a nicer couple, but do you understand my annoyance? (And erm, while I am on one, it doesn't feel much like it happened for '*us* as *a couple'* yet! So far it has only happened to me! ME!)

The messages of support were lovely to read but 'twas ME (the very same me with bum stitches, **purple nipples** and half a hippo still hanging from her hips) who wanted to update my Facebook status with the good news! I had planned this status update *meticulously* and daydreamed of the reaction for *months*. This was the biggest update of my Facebook career for god sake!

I had planned to write;

The baby has arrived! Rock on! Radiator Ellis was born after 100 years of labour, at 8.40pm, weighing in at a whopping 4 and a half stone *(so you see? I didn't put ANY weight on at all really)* ***The Baby is gorgeous!***

And then I planned to feed bits of information in dribs and drabs. Adding in sex and eye colour and *real name* a little later, after people have gasped;

'Radiator? That's different!'

And rumours had spread far and wide of my name choice and discussions were firmly in place amongst *everybody,* as to whether Radiator, was a girl or a boy.

You know, I wanted to *really milk it.*

But what good would that be now?

I'd be like a Dognapper asking for ransom *after* returning the puppy. (Just so you know I would never steal a puppy.)

So thanks *thunder stealer*.

Thanks to you my first post birth status read;

My arse hurts.

What? Surely that was news too?

And surprisingly a fair amount of people liked it.

Steal that thunder.

Bitch.

I don't mind at all...

'Oh Lexy you must be so proud, he is gorgeous isn't he?'

Although I **have** to agree, that my son ***is*** gorgeous, I am momentarily distracted by the size of my legs splayed out in front of me on the hospital bed.

Yes. I am <u>still</u> in hospital.

I know!!!

It feels like a whole year has already passed for me too but actually he is only 23 hours old, and *actually* (while we are on the subject of time passing, or not passing as the case may be) much to my eternal dismay, I still look like the Goodyear blimp. A walking road block. The marshmallow man at the end of Ghostbusters, you can pretty much take your pick.

23 hours isn't a lot of time to lose 5 stone, I *understand* that, but at what point does the weight drop off?

I had just assumed it would be immediate.

And even though I keep limping to the mirror to check, in between checkups, visits from that boob woman (the one who fittingly, behaves like a complete *tit*) and the random mental health squad, which for some reason still seem to be lurking about fairly frequently, so far I have seen absolutely no weight loss.

If anything, I just look fatter.

My thighs, plonked out in front of me now, literally look like two lifeless jellified tree trunks.

Or those yellow tubes you see on building sites.

Actually, Jesus Christ. They really do look like those yellow tubes you see on building sites. You know the ones right? The ones that hang precariously from the top of scaffolding? Ending about 10 feet above a skip?

When I was younger I used to profess to any adult who would ask me that I wanted to be a builder when I grew up. The reason being I thought they used to get to slide down from work at the end of each working day. I was jealous. I didn't even have a slide on my bunk bed. Come to think of it I didn't even have a bunk bed. Cruel is what my parents were. CRUEL. The fact I was an only-ish child, my brother being a very useless ten years my senior, is by the by.

And don't even get me started on my empty bump. It is horrifying.

I shake my bingo wing dispassionately, repulsed and try to focus back on the task in hand, vaguely aware that from over the sound of much joyful shrieking and forced cooing coming from behind the other three women's curtains squeezed in to this cubby hole, someone has asked me something.

'Pardon?' I calmly question the out of focus woman hovering in my peripheral vision while at the same time testing to see whether breathing in makes any difference.

It doesn't.

The bump doesn't even move.

'What was that?'

It is visiting hour.

The deathly warm ward is crammed full of crinkly pink and sickly blue helium balloons and over excited grandparents shrieking and clapping and slurping secretly at NHS regulation Luke warm tea, out of impossibly small blue plastic tea cups, they must have smuggled from the 'coffee room' down the hall.

The very same coffee room, that spits out the very same mulch labeled coffee that The Irish One has been informed superciliously on many occasions 'is just for the patients!' by some little old bag that should probably look for another job due to her annoyance at the 'bloody kids' scattered everywhere and plonked anywhere on every available surface.

Other than the metal bin directly adjacent to my head (If one more person slams it, they will have to transfer me from the *Hormonal fatty ward* (as I have come to know it) to the *maximum-security moose on the loose ward,* as I will undoubtedly stab them in the elbow with my plastic, soggy curry fork) all I can hear and smell is poo and TCP.

In spite of this entire *kafuffle* going on around him my freshly brewed boy however, is laying gently (very, very gently, due to the carnage taking place beneath him) in a heavenly, snuggly and beautiful bundle on my big fat lap, fast asleep.

He *is* bloody gorgeous. (His nose will shrink though right?)

His features are scrunched up in to a tight *'Don't mess with me or I will kick your arse'* face and he is bright orange.

The labour was as heavy going on him as it was for me.

He is honest to god the most orange baby you ever saw.

Like a miniature Umpa Lumpa, which reminds me I really need to pick him up some dungarees. Babies always look cute in dungarees, orange or not.

Earlier, as I was trying to coerce him on to my nipple, some woman stuck her head around, took one look at him and informed me briskly she would be around later with a sun bed.

I tried *not* to be thrilled, but I couldn't help it.

And I think you should know, I fully intend to get under it with him. I could do with a bit of colour myself, and I always look slimmer with a tan.

Although judging by the size of the thing being used by the woman opposite me, the only body part I will be able to fit under it at this venture is my third chin, but still, as Jessie J said, dreaming is believing.

'I said,' my best friend repeats huffily, 'you must be so proud. He is bloody gorgeous.'

Shit.

I look up realizing she isn't some random cubicle dweller, but is in fact here, to see *him* and me.

'Me', clearly being the afterthought.

Because apparently now the baby is here, I do not matter so much. Who knew?

APPARENTLY now the baby is here; I am just blubber, dark matter, unimportant! In fact I am pretty sure that if I painted myself blue and lay on a beach somewhere, (if only!) someone at some point would definitely try and make lipstick out of me or refer to me as Willy.

Proud though? Is she on *glue?*

Proud isn't how I would describe myself right now. AT ALL!

Knackered, half the woman I once was, Amazed, transfixed, confused, tired, in pain, shocked, terrified, and a little bit angry (hormones) probably sums *half* of what I am feeling right now.

But Proud? *Proud?* Proud of what?

It wasn't like I had a choice in the matter!

He *had* to be born, he *had* to come out, and didn't they just remind me of that over and over again each and every time I changed my mind about persevering with labour and tried to get up and go home. (The first time was just before I called The Irish One my ex-boyfriends name and just *after* I was denied a donkey ride. I love gas and air.)

No, no I am not *proud.* I am in shock. I am a wobbly, thirsty, *shocked* mess.

'I really am proud' I state loudly 'I cannot believe I made him. He is *so* perfect.'

'I can't believe it either to be honest,' she shakes her head in amazement, 'he looks absolutely *nothing* like you AT ALL, he is his dad all over don't you think?'

Call it exhaustion, call it the baby blues, call it what you want, but for the first time ever, I can't help but regard my best friend with a mixture of hatred and sheer un-harnessed envy.

I am hormonal. I am in pain. I am fatter than a beached whale at the end of seal season (and the bitch turned up in skinny jeans carrying the new Hermes clutch, and not the fake River Island one either, the real one) and clearly I am at the very start of the emotional roller-coaster of a lifetime. (I can just tell.) BUT COME ON WOMAN! NOT EVEN A BIT LIKE ME???

'Get out.'

'What?'

'Get out.'

'What?'

At which point I burst out crying.

Regarding me in shock she promptly picks her way through all manner of debris lying by my bed (wipes, cotton wool, discarded nappies, empty jugs of water and the never used car seat) and hugs me fiercely, a little too fiercely, but I don't mind I need it. I feel so upset.

She also successfully manages, the sneaky cow, with her arms still wrapped around me, to stop me from swapping my baby with her handbag. I only wanted to *touch* it!

'Sorry' I mutter, embarrassed by my uncontrollable mood. Shouldn't I be happy right now?

'For what?' she asks kindly, attempting to perch on the bed, but when unable to squeeze on due to the size of my rear, giving up and settling for the lonely stool, left behind by the doctor who visited an hour ago.

The very same doctor who insisted on whistling the Coronation Street theme tune while clamping my 'legs' open with that lovely freezing cold metal contraption and fiddling with my stitches.

Seriously, Coronation Street.

I think to work here you must have to pass some sort of creepy bar exam, but hey, at least he didn't call me mummy!

'Just you know, the tears.' I mumble attractively wiping the snot from under my fat nose.

As it turns out, in relation to her insisting the child looking nothing like me, she actually did me a favour.

She was simply preparing me for what was to come.

As following on from her, every visitor, every midwife, every stranger who saw the three of us together, every random granny, every family member, every student nurse, would share with me their over inflated and completely unnecessary opinion.

Their view being, all in various degrees, that he looked nothing like me.

Was I sure he was even mine?

For the most part I have been polite but I have to say, I do wish the male student nurse had not stated the likeness to my husband while he was getting an eyeful of my urethra.

It really did come across as rude.

And yes ok maybe my response, 'Do you mean my clitoris or my *boy* dick head?' Was a bit too much, but really, it was just literally adding insult to injury and I snapped.

At some point soon I am seriously considering handing out numbered tickets like they do at the butchers.

'Number 179?'

'Yes?'

'Your turn to come and look at this mess BUT BE GENTLE!'

Anyway. My point was made nonetheless.

'Oh he looks *just* like his dad - *Sorry Lexy.'*

'Oh he is the **IMAGE** of The Irish One - *sorry Lexy'*

'My god he is just like daddy *isn't he Lexy?'*

'Ha! If you didn't look so rough right now, I wouldn't be too sure it was even you who had birthed him! *Sorry Lexy!'*

Yes thanks for that.

It always ends the same way too.

We will make a joke about how he looks nothing like you, break your heart in to a million pieces (honestly, it isn't hormones) but none of it matters because we finish by saying Sorry.

When did this become an acceptable form of insulting communication?

I can't imagine I would get away with it.

'Your face looks like a bowl of vomit. Step away from my vagina. –Sorry doctor!'

But anyway, I have dealt with it now.

Saying my baby looks nothing like me is, like, totally last season.

And besides, it saves on a paternity test.

Not that we would need a paternity test. (Just to be clear.)

'My god, he is a mini Irish One isn't he? All he needs is a beard!'

He is a boy. My son is a boy. I am glad he looks like a man. I am sure if he looked like me he would have been *even more* stunning than he is now, but *whatever.*

He has my hands though. Just so you know.

And I am sure if I *really* tried I could look more like *him.*

All I would need to do is grimace occasionally as if trying to decide if I have left the oven on, scream blue murder anytime I want anything and stick my tongue out sporadically like I was trying to catch flies.

Oh and I would need to bunch my fists up ready for a fight.

Which if I am honest, if The Irish One keeps acting like he knows everything and outdoing me over and over again, with nothing more than a smug smile and short laugh, before disappearing off home like the part timer he is, may not be too hard to organize.

By all means look like your dad Addison, that wasn't your *choice*, but *prefer* him to me? I am not having that.

I am the one doing all the bloody work!

The mental squad came in again and checked on me before.

I told them I was fine *again.* Because I **am** fine.

I suppose I must have passed whatever test I didn't even realise I was even taking, because they wrote something on their clip boards, nodded and left.

They probably wrote;

'Poor Poor Irish Bastard.' (He told me to write that.)

To be honest I am just relieved they didn't need a look at my innards.

Smuggle me a rock hammer...

There should be a bell, or some sort of passing out parade, or some sort of leaving *doo* for when you first step out of the hospital, on your own, with your first born child in tow.

There should, at the very least be some sort of announcement!

Lexy is leaving everybody! Let's all give her a round of applause. (And while we are at it lets all shoot evil looks at The Irish One! Useless article he turned out to be! Poor Lexy, she really does have her work cut out for her with that one!)

And I would limp off, smiling my practiced martyr smile, while mentally adding up the time it would take me to race to Asda, buy a girdle, get home, unpack and become a vision of serene motherhood, just in time for the visitors everyone keeps warning me will visit, to arrive at the door bearing gifts.

Although to be honest I am not sure there will be many, we just don't have a lot of friends. (Oh well.)

The sparkly, clean car seat, I am now hoofing down the stairs, trying not to drop (The Irish One offered to carry it but like I say, he is MY child, and I want to be the one to carry him, I will feel like a bad mother if I don't) had been waiting like a ticking time bomb in the corner of the baby's freshly decorated room, while I sat rubbing my belly and munching on biscuits staring at it, wondering, imagining, picturing and hugely looking forward to (and slightly dreading) having a baby to put in it, for the last 6 months.

(Only dreading because I was scared. And because apparently, according to my single friend, having a baby means your life is over. Bitch.)

For the four days I have been stuck on the set of *Girl interrupted* meets *Saw 10, the birth episode*, I had all but given up hope of ever being able to bring him home.

Not because he is poorly.

No, I am very lucky, he is perfectly healthy, apart from the odd bit of jaundice which didn't 'fade' as 'quickly as they'd hoped' considering he had been under a sun bed for 13 hours straight, but that amazingly (cue completely astounded, confused and more than anything *innocent* face) seemed to bring out a lovely colour in *my* face, and all down one arm. (I tried. I couldn't fit completely under it, while holding the baby and simultaneously checking no one was coming.)

Nope, he is fine. I only have my easily torn anus and lady parts to blame as to why I have been held prisoner for the last week. (Four days in some countries is a week ok?)

I *think,* in between all the hospital curry's and cups of coffee, I have actually become institutionalized, no, not think.

I *have* been institutionalized.

I am like Andy Dusfresne from Shawshank redemption, I am desperate to escape, as I do not belong here, I am just an innocent mother, Mother Nature has wrongly accused me of being somebody who for some reason deserves internal tearing and blocked *nipple* ducts.

But I am also panicking about how am I meant to survive when I get out?

How will I cope without morning rounds? (I will honestly miss 15 students, one midwife; a hairy doctor with a foreign accent and 2 nurses all gaping inside my flute while sighing and tutting. Honestly.)

How will I cope without the gas and air? (They were forced to give in to my incessant pleading after I caught the evil

Russian doctor's glasses with the heal of my massively swollen clodhopper, and in shock and to steady himself, he slammed the palm of his hand down, hard, right in to middle my lady bits. The gel was cold ok? It was *an accident!)*

How will I cope without somebody poking at me with thermometers every half an hour?

How will I sleep without the sudden thud of the metal bin by my bed every six minutes?

How will Addison sleep without the constant bickering of breastfeeding vs. formula mums in the background?

Or the poor seventeen year old mummy, (I am yet to lay eyes on, due to being too much of a wimp to introduce myself) behind the curtain next door who's boyfriend hasn't *even been to see their* baby yet *'and is fookin dead I tell yao! I'll leather him. My brother'll right fuck him up.'*

It's going to be hard. It's going to be so quiet. There won't be piss weak coffee on tap. Or random people bobbing their heads around the curtain before having a good old stare and slowly losing all colour in their faces before apologising and slowly backing back out, a whiter shade of pale.

But even though I will clearly miss all of that; Today is the day.

Today I am being discharged.

However, limping towards freedom, the car seat now clunking against my shin with every step I take, the sunlight bouncing off the wall in front of me from just around the corner and The Irish One moaning relentlessly about how he feels he should be carrying the baby, it all feels a little underwhelming.

I cast my head around hoping to get a glance of the audience I had dreamed about.

I am leaving? Anybody notice that? I am taking the baby with me! Hello? Nobody care?

Where is my fanfare? Where is my police escort? Where are the paparazzi? Where is my *narrator?*

To be truly effective you must imagine it is not I, but Samuel L Jackson writing the next bit;

'Lexy Dusfresne limped to freedom in spite of five hundred stitches poking out of her vagina. Five hundred stitches, that's the length of five football fields, just shy of half a mile. He really is a huge baby...'

Ok so it's not accurate.

I wasn't stretched *that* much.

(I hope.)

But, if Andy Dusfresne can have drama, why can't I?

That would have been a lot more enjoyable than what actually then happened.

Which was me reaching the automatic doors, slipping and falling arse over tit the minute my chubby boot clad, swollen ankle made contact with the great outdoors, landing *fast and hard* on my coccyx, tearing 2 anal stitches in a bid to protect the car seat and being dragged, screaming and kicking back in to the hospital to be *repaired,* while The Irish One of course stood behind me, livid, muttering 'I told you! I told you I should have carried the car seat!'

Not what I pictured during many nights of romantically staring at the empty car seat, picturing that first venture out in to the world with my kid.

But still, at least I didn't have to crawl through a sewer.

Small mercies I suppose.

No lunch for me, thanks...

Well we made it home in one piece. Eventually.

Unfortunately, however, my milk didn't come in as punctually as I would have hoped and despite my repeated and best efforts to get him to latch on to the nipples Freddie Krueger left behind, Addison will now only take formula.

Interestingly though, he did eventually latch on, just as my dad popped his head around the curtain for his allotted visit, gasped, sat down for all of two minutes, made eye contact with every inch of the ceiling and wall, even whistled at one point, before making his hasty retreat back to the place where dads go when they have just been forced to witness their daughters nipples (Church to pray?)

I feel like a bad mother but what can I do? He needs to eat.

It was the breast-feeding woman that eventually suggested I try him on a bottle.

'Still going?' she had smiled appearing from behind the curtain 25 minutes after he had first successfully latched on and she had literally whooped with success, just about managing to avoid my dad as he all but rugby tackled her out of the way in his rush to leave.

'Yup.' I had stated proud as punch and equally as relieved 'He must be really hungry!'

In that short moment I felt like I had *potentia*l at this mothering lark.

3 and a half hours later however, my proud as punch face having slid in to my chins and been firmly replaced by my 'this

is agony how can anyone enjoy this torture' face, she crept back in somewhat trepidatiously and perched on the end of my bed, displaying what must be her 'deep in thought' face.

'I don't think your milk has come in yet.' She stated intelligently.

'You think?' I had responded glibly after suggesting this to her at least four times over the course of the evening in between trying not to clobber the Irish One for making inappropriate jokes about udders.

'Every time I take him off, he screams. He is sucking on empty boob!'

'Hmmm' she had replied ' well my shift is about to end, so I suppose you could try him on a bottle, poor mite must be starving, then both of you could get some sleep, and we can try again in the morning...'

I didn't need asking twice but I was disappointed.

Removing his head from my breast and wincing in pain, poor starving Addison revved up his lungs in angry protest, as at the same time the breast-feeding lady gasped.

'I will get you a tissue.'

I looked down to horrifically find both of us covered in blood.

I joined in with his screaming.

Is my son a vampire?!

'What the hell?' I screeched as she made her way back in, tissues held out in front of her to block the view.

'Your nipples are just a bit sore *that all'* she shushed and gushed while removing the child from my arms and passing me a wad of the scratchiest most awful blue tissue paper ever.

I mean seriously I am all for cost cutting but what is NHS tissue made of? Sandpaper? I could build a box to bury my dignity with it!

'We will give him a bottle tonight and in the morning you can pick the scabs off and we will try again.'

I must have looked like I had seen a ghost, which actually I would have preferred, as she stood there with a cocked head smiling placatingly at me.

'It isn't as bad as it sounds. By morning you will have had some rest and so will he. You can whip the scabs off your nipples and we will try again.'

'Whip. The. Scabs. Off. My. Nipples?' I asked her aghast 'Will I get gas and air?'

'No.' She responded stoutly before moving away to pop a dummy in Addison's mouth.

A dummy I had never seen before and not requested!

I didn't want to give him a dummy!

He was meant to be the perfect baby to compliment my perfection at motherhood! Where the hell did that dummy come from? What was I going to tell everyone? Only mothers who can't control their babies give them dummies! I can control my baby!

'No more gas and air for you.' She finished stoutly ignoring my look of outrage.

Fair enough I did ask for it morning, noon and night.

I never actually saw her again after that, as I was discharged and unfortunately, even though I did slowly and carefully remove the scabs blanketing my nipples (Shudder) Addison still refused to accept them. I can't say I blame him either.

So while he now sleeps (his eyes rolling around in the back of his head, finally content after three days of sucking on empty boob to have been given something to eat) I am sat here with my defunct and redundant, angry and aching full boobs, (because of course the minute I relented to teat, the little men in my body turned on the milk) dripping in to a cereal bowl while The Irish One looks on horrified, definitely not picturing a large portion of Coco Pops.

I am *literally* milking myself, like one may do a cow. He may have thought he was clever in the hospital, but now I can see my udders literally turning him green.

"Hungry darling?' I smile at him smugly sadistically getting my own back, while squeezing my aching and scabby mammary gland a little too hard for effect and watching in horror as the milk spurts directly across the living room and hits Doodle Square in the face.

'I have never fancied you more.' He deadpans a little *retchy*, before getting up and walking out of the living room, a glossy pale colour, to fetch a tea towel.

No point though really as before he can return, Doodle has happily licked it all up.

When he returns I have my head in my hands and I am crying.

He rests at my side, rubbing my back.

'What is the matter?' he asks shocked at the incredible change in tempo in such a short space of time.

I can't answer, as I am too ashamed.

Did I just inadvertently breastfeed the dog?

Basil thrush...

The doorbell is starting to grate on my very last nerve.

Why oh why, didn't we get one of those smiley happy *ring tone* like doorbells that play a funky little tune.

If we could have, I would have bought one that played the Basil Brush theme tune.

Now I know what you are thinking, you are thinking that would be hugely annoying if you were a popular person, who had plenty of visitors but you would be wrong.

You see, currently, my flat is getting more traffic that the M60 in rush hour.

I don't understand it as I was pretty sure we had little to no friends, but turns out the arrival of a baby is similar to how I perceive a lottery win must be. Everyone wants a bit.

So my thinking is, at least if we had a catchy doorbell, it would distract me from the throbbing (and not in some sleazy *Jackie Collins* type way) ache, that is positively making my life completely and utterly *unbearable* right now.

That's right.

Not only do I have wire **(A WIRE)** holding my lady bits together, not only am I bleeding like a wounded animal **(ROADKILL, I'M LIKE ROADKILL,)** not only is my arse *literally* in tatters, not only am I making bowls of breast milk soup every two hours, I now have thrush too. *(Wahoo! Celebrate good times c'mon! There's a party going on right here! A celebration to last throughout the years, let's all celebrate and have a good time!)*

Mother Nature is one sick, twisted bitch and it seems she is on a mission to make my life as comical (to her) and as uncomfortable (to me) as she possibly can.

The *catchy doorbell* would also distract the 8 million visitors an hour from my constant bum shuffling and random jumping up in the middle of conversation, to limp off for a cry (and a good, but incredibly careful, scratch.)

The *catchy doorbell* would also alert The Irish One to the fact there was, in fact somebody **at the door**, as currently, I am sure he believes that buzzing sound he is hearing over and over again between the hours of 8am and 10pm (Who does that?? Who visits at 10pm? My mum that's who!) Is actually inside his head, and nothing more than a figment of his over tired imagination!

'Was that the door dear?' I repeatedly ask him from between gritted teeth as I repeatedly attempt to prise the dummy from between Addison's lips.

'Er, maybe' is his constant reply as he washes 76 used tea cups ready for the next influx of tourists. Most of whom I have never seen before in my life.

'Ok brilliant. It isn't in your head darling' I will shrill 'please answer it!'

'Alright calm down' is his usual reply 'I can hear it in my dreams, I just wasn't sure...'

Maybe he too, due to tiredness, now *also* has voices in his head. Because I know I do. Another symptom they kept out of the books following childbirth!

The voices in my head have been talking to me for 3 days straight.

Usually they SHOUT 'you see, you see! We told you to use a condom!' and 'For the frigging love of god, who is this at the door now, at this time?' (Your mum that's who!)

As one coach load of visitor's leaves and the next one arrives, I can feel the polite me waning and the irritable, *itchy* me firmly taking hold.

'Yes, yes, *you* hold the baby, fifteenth cousin seven times removed, sorry, what was your name again? Oh Alice, hi! Ever so pleased to meet you. Please support his head or I will punch you in the face.'

'Pardon?' she would gasp looking to her mother, who I have also never met, but who has an uncanny resemblance to Ronald McDonald, for support.

'I said, *please support his head* or I will punch you *in the face.*'

'Come on Alice, we are leaving!' her mother, Jilly Bob Horse face, I think her name was, would gasp before The Irish One would walk in five minutes later a tray laden with tea, cakes and other food we didn't know we would need but he had to go out and buy, post baby.

'Where is everyone?'

'They left. I don't know why. I was perfectly polite.'

'Quick let's sleep while we can!!!'

Ahhh it's good to dream, but anyway, I better go, the next tour bus is about to pull up outside.

I'm off for a quick cry and a slow fumble before the next game of *pass the newborn parcel* starts.

I also need to practice my 'overwhelmed with love' face.

I can only hope this next lot support his head or when the music stops, they may be getting more than they bargained for.

The Miracle of birth...

Picture the scene.

It's Six forty five on a Saturday morning.

The house resembles a subsidiary of the Eccles and Hulme tip. It is **a bomb site.** It literally looks like we were up all night with six thousand of our closest friends and their newborn babies enjoying an all-night sit in feeding *rave.*

There are three milk bottles on the arm of the sofa, slowly beginning to curdle.

There are sleep suits and vests, miniature trousers and jumpers and dummies and wipes, tea towels and bibs splattered in every direction of the once tidy room. Man sized socks stuffed down the side of the fire place (I'll kill him).

Towels directly out of the drier sit forgotten in a pile on the kitchen work top and there are dog biscuit crumbs all over the once-blue but now greyish spit up stained, living room carpet.

It's like the dog feels too good to eat in the hallway and insists on carrying his tiny bone-shaped biscuits, one at a time, in to the living room and munching them on the carpet where he can watch the show. His version of a doggy TV dinner, if you will.

The show, of course being a bedraggled and smelly overweight woman, her hair tied back with a pair of old knickers, sitting like a creaky kneed elephant on a crusty old sofa.

The baby's breakfast is sitting regurgitated all over her top and she sits squinting through one contact lens (didn't't have time to put both in) while clutching a cup of coffee like her life depended on it in one hand, and a squirming baby in the other.

Mickey mouse is on the TV in the corner dancing and prancing around inviting his viewers to 'come inside, it's fun inside.'

She knows he is too young for this but doesn't care. Both feet in or not at all.

'Oh bugger off' she mutters under her breath 'fun inside, my arse.' (Ok, that sounded better in my head than it did on paper, but you know what I mean.)

Because really? What does Mickey know?

It's me, by the way, as if you hadn't figured it out.

I'm the overweight walking Honey Monster trying not to keel over on the couch.

I got up at 5.45 this morning, with the intention of getting some much needed house work done while the baby slept, but find myself, like I usually do, sat catatonic on the crusty vomit stained (once magnificent) sofa, staring avidly at nothing in particular while devising a few choice places Mickey Mouse can stick his clubhouse, and reminiscing on what I thought motherhood was supposed to be like. Back in the 'innocent and naïve' days.

I'm not in a bad mood. I'm just exhausted.

Being awake at five forty five on a Saturday morning is not what I signed up for. Leaky boobs, fat thighs and sleepless nights is not what I signed up for. 3 stone overweight, losing hair from my head like an oversized malting Alsatian with creaky, broken knees is not what I signed up for. All my beautiful clothes being stretched to within an inch of their lives and walking round with more muffin top than a Gregg's outlet is not what I signed up for.

I need to contact the Motherhood Union and explain in no uncertain terms this motherhood lark is not as easy as countless celebrities promised me it would be on the covers of glossy magazines.

And I have help. (I mean in the form of my other half, not an army of servants. And he is actually, as much as I hate to admit it, really rather good! Don't tell him I said that.)

It really makes me wonder how single mummies do it. Fair play and **utmost** respect to each and every single mother out there in this effing 'mummy club.'

You are unsung heroes. Really you are.

It also makes me wonder how teenagers manage.

There is no way at the age of twenty five I could have done this. Never mind in my teens.

In fact, every time I see a young teenage girl walking down the road I have to fight the urge to run up to her, grab her face in my hands and shout;

'DON'T HAVE SEX!! JUST DON'T! YOU WONT ENJOY IT YET ANYWAY! HE WILL NOT 'LOVE YOU MORE' AND YOU COULD END UP LIKE ME! LOOK AT ME! FOR THE LOVE OF GOD LOOK!'

(This is the point I would whip out my flappy belly and destroyed flower for all the world to see) 'ENJOY YOUR LIFE! FORGET SEX!'

So what did I sign up for? I signed up for a gorgeous basketball bump, 10 months of people treating me like the queen, a perfectly short and painless labour, a perfect little pink bundle which slept right through, any weight I had put on would obviously drop from my chubby arse immediately, leaving me waif like with gorgeous thick, full hair. I would also clearly have the perfect little girl who I could dress in pretty pink outfits and show off while the paparazzi, so amazed at the beauty of my bundle, would swarm around me, making me millions and we would live happy ever after. (I always wondered what it would be like to be famous and this was my daydream after all.)

But alas, I am not famous. At all. Unless you count that one night at the Chinese karaoke where I fell off the stage and exposed my breasts to an entire room of cheering and slightly drunken business men.

So imagine my surprise when I did not have the perfect basketball bump, but instead I piled on fat everywhere!

I piled on fat in places I didn't't know existed.

On a bad day, up until the 32 week stage and depending on what I was wearing, you were hard pressed to even see the bump I had so desperately wanted to show off. (And then came 32 weeks and I began to resemble Mr. Greedy.)

And then the labour.

Oh god, as more time passes the harder it gets to reminisce about.

A newly pregnant colleague of The Irish One asked me, while she was perched on the edge of my stained couch yesterday, eating all my 'supposedly not for guests' (but The Irish One was too tired to shop for more cheap ones) Oreo biscuits, what labour had felt like.

Now this is dodgy ground.

I remember asking this of many mums when I was pregnant. I remember thinking, if they told me I would be able to prepare myself mentally. But the stock answer always seemed to be 'you'll be fine' or 'I can't remember.'

At the time it really wound me up. I felt like there was some sort of conspiracy! I wanted to yell 'I can handle the truth just tell me!'

But I have to admit, when my friend asked me, I finally understood why I had been lied to.

Because honestly? You don't forget that pain. You may not be able to describe it, but you don't bloody forget it.

I just couldn't't do it to her.

Poor unsuspecting bitch.

So I muttered, (looking everywhere but in her eyes.)

'It's not that bad. And it's really quick in comparison to the REST OF YOUR LIFE, you'll be fine, I can't really remember. Just enjoy being pregnant.'

Which may have been a lie but in my mind was a lot kinder than;

'It's absolutely horrific and excruciating. The stuff horror films are made of, imagine your worst nightmare, double it and while you're at it try to imagine shitting an American football player, mahoosive shoulder pads and all, out of your bum hole, while trying to put on wet jeans.'

Or as my old boss summed up while she was eating my last banana yesterday 'if the pain and discomfort had got any worse I'm sure I would have died' (In this instance I feel the truth would definitely not have set her free.)

She smiled and ate another Oreo. 'I am definitely going to do it without drugs. No disrespect to you but I just don't want chance hurting my baby you know? I think I will probably just breathe through it. I am quite good with pain.'

This from the girl who won't poo at work in case anyone hears her.

I nodded and agreed with the most fake encouraging smile you ever could imagine.

'You do realise you will probably shit all over the midwife?' The Irish One unnecessarily rushes to my defense smiling a smile, it has to be said, that is just as fake.

She left not long after shooting him an evil look and professing she would 'text him about work stuff later.'

I doubt she will.

We closed the door and high fived.

No disrespect to me, cheeky cow.

Anyway I am done with all that life changing experience stuff.

I personally haven't poo'd *since* I poo'd on the midwife.

What the *hell am I going to do?*

Please don't punch me in the face...

I think maybe...

I am supposed to love him more than I do.

I can't believe I just admitted that.

Screw it.

It's true.

I am definitely supposed to love him more than I do.

I mean, don't get me wrong.

I love him.

But I am just not sure I love him *enough.*

People keep asking me about *the connection.* Visitors keep dropping it in to conversation. 'Isn't the *connection* to your newborn the most awesome, overwhelming and powerful feeling? The bond is so strong isn't it?'

Then they look at me expectantly.

I just nod mutely matching their hugely over excited eyes and teethy smiles.

I'm not sure I could look a nodding, over exaggerated smiling and cooing guest in the eye and say 'Actually, I am not sure I know him all that well yet.'

I am not sure that would go down too well.

His name is Addison.

Why did we pick that name?

I can't even remember saying I liked it.

He doesn't look like an Addison.

He looks like a Frank.

Or an alien.

Or a Derek.

His nose is all swollen.

I shouldn't be saying this should I?

But, I am on a roll.

Maybe I *am* just a terrible mother.

Maybe I am not cut out for this mothering *lark?*

Everything just seems so back to front at the moment.

I am disgusted with myself.

Disgusted.

I should love him more than I do.

I should blatantly be feeling some sort of overwhelming connection.

At this present time the only *overwhelming* connection I feel is the *overwhelming* connection to my painkillers. They are my best friends. If I could wrap them in a blanket and cuddle them to sleep, I bloody would.

God bless Ibuprofen. Oh how I miss Gas and Air.

Looking at him now though, asleep next to me in his crib. He *is* gorgeous. He still looks like a little boxer. His nose is huge. I hope he grows in to it. My heart swells a little, I guess. He is mine. I do love him.

But,

It's not *overwhelming*?

Everyone said it is supposed to be.

At this point in time I don't know whether this is the hormones or me talking.

I actually don't think I am *that* hormonal but people keep telling me I am. And I do keep crying. So I must be.

Although in honesty I am a bit sick of listening to that excuse, as it seems anytime I show any emotion at the moment it gets put down to 'hormones!'

I *really* was *gutted* there were no Oreo's left! That bloody *wasn't* hormones! I was *bloody* starving! I had no time to eat dinner and I wanted a bloody biscuit!! You try feeding a baby from your bloody rubbish breast for an hour and a half, until your nipple bleeds and you have to give in and administer another bottle anyway, to then find some 'friend' ate all your secret stash you stupidly shared! You'd be crying too! God it makes me indescribably angry!! It is not BLOODY HORMONES!

Addison is 14 days old today.

This time 2 weeks ago a Chinese lady had her finger up my bum.

That's not something I ever thought I would say you know? But it's the truth.

Ah motherhood. It's just magical.

Like, say, being mugged is magical.

This time last week I was looking at my little boy for the first time. I suppose that's the thing I should be concentrating on really. And ok yes, he was gorgeous. And I did cry. But I think that may have been because I was so relieved the labour was finally over.

I have so many feelings pushing for the surface right now, I just don't know.

I feel overwhelming guilt, which is something I *can* admit I do genuinely feel.

I should love him more. I should be happy that he was born safe, born with five fingers and five toes, born healthy, but all I feel is numb, and guilty.

I do love him.

I know that because I keep thinking about how I would feel if something happened to him, like I accidentally suffocated him, or didn't realise he'd stopped breathing, or didn't feed him enough or Doodle sat on him. I would be devastated.

I feel worry too. Overwhelming worry.

There just doesn't seem much room for love you know?

What is wrong with me?

I just don't know him yet.

I need to get to know him.

I love him because he is mine.

I love him because he amazes me every minute. (Ok no he doesn't. That's a lie. He can't even sit up. Did you know that? That newborn babies can't sit up?)

But it isn't *overwhelming.*

I need to make it overwhelming!

I am a terrible person.

It's just been a whirlwind fortnight you know? (Did I mention the woman, and where she put her finger?) It's just that this time two weeks ago it was just me, Doodle and The Irish One.

Now, my life has changed forever.

I wouldn't change it.

Ok maybe I would.

But only because this isn't how I expected to feel and I am scared.

What if he needs to go to the dentist? I don't even have a dentist.

How will I pay for university and his 1st birthday party? We are broke.

Oh god. How will we cope? What if he never stops crying? What if people look at me and just *know* I'm a fake?

Addison is here. He is really here.

My boobs are useless, I am in more pain than I have ever been in, I can barely walk and I am at least, still ten stone heavier than I was this time last year, and this week, adding to all this, my house has been busier than a bloody knocking shop.

I have barely seen my son.

Oh my god I have a son.

He has been too busy socializing.

Maybe that's what it is. Maybe when we spend more time together just the two of us the overwhelming bit will come?

Maybe I will be good enough if I try really, really hard.

Every time I see someone holding him I want to rugby tackle him away. So I must love him.

I just need some time on my own with him, to get to know him.

Maybe women shouldn't speak about these things.

I wonder what would happen if I was honest with another mother? Would she look at me in dismay, punch me in the face and call me a selfish bitch? Would social services ring my doorbell?

Or does every mother secretly feel a bit like this?

Would the *perfect* mother open up and be honest, and admit that maybe the ultimate, *overwhelming* bond took a little while for her too?

Maybe I will try and be honest with one of my closer friends.

See what happens.

Because surely I can't be that bad a person. I just don't know him yet.

I wish I could talk to The Irish One about this, but I think he must sense something is amiss so has backed right off.

I miss him too.

I miss myself.

I don't recognise my life anymore and all I keep thinking is –

Is this it?

Shut the hell up...

People can be so cruel.

People can be *so stupid!*

My uterus is still *huge.*

I get it.

I also *get* that at this point it most probably isn't my uterus that is hanging like a limp *pitta pocket* over my jeans, but we can ignore this for now ok?

Because if I accept that my uterus has ***possibly,*** retreated back already and what is actually hanging over my jeans is just, put plain and simple, 9 months of over indulgence, I will have a break down ok?

And I am already way too close to the edge, so let's just pretend for now, that it is still my uterus ok? And that at some point soon, it'll all just suck back up like a hoover extension cord, and I will instantly be once again, the size 6... Ok, size 14, I was before. Deal?

Moving on.

If I am ever in a supermarket, or a shop, or a park, or a museum or just about anywhere really, and I see a woman who is beautifully voluptuous, and by this I mean, she has a magnificent rack and fabulous curves, I would not and never have thought - Hey, could she be pregnant, I better ask her!

Being plus sized is a very different 'look' to being pregnant, I don't care how much curvier I am now.

So when I see women like this out and about, I usually think - wow great pair love! (If I was a lesbian I would definitely be a boob girl) and then carry on doing whatever I was doing that brought me to the park, museum, shop, supermarket, crematorium in the first place. (I like crematoriums. They are peaceful, and dead people can't hurt you) and think nothing more of it.

The point I am trying to make is, I would never look at a woman, skinny, small, petite, curvy, voluptuous, tall and feel a need to comment on them!

I would not stop what I was doing, gawp and then shout 'when are you due love?'

Can you see where I am going with this?

The point I am trying to make is, if you are the type of person to do this and you see a woman, and you are not sure if said woman is fertilized of not; keep your bloody mouth shut.

I am *never* leaving the house without Addison again.

Or at least, not until this empty uterus (we made a deal) and surrounding flubber has disappeared back in to where it came from. (Couple of weeks then right? ***RIGHT?)***

I have just visited Morrison's (I am not posh enough for Sainsbury's at the moment) for some more lady towels *sans* baby.

My first trip out without him.

I had left The Irish one boiling bottles while he slept and was quite excited at the prospect of nipping out, all on my own, with no baby dotted around anywhere on my person, for the first time in 10 months! Not inside me or out! I am freeeee....

While I was stood in aisle 6, minding my own business, checking around my person for poo, because I could smell it, and very sensibly choosing the no frills brand of lady nappies, over the better-known Tena brand, because really, at this point, what right does my vagina have to act like a snob? I could feel a pair of eyes burning in to my stomach.

A little old lady was stood by the shampoo, hand stopped midair, gawping at my empty bump.

I smiled and turned to walk away quickly; a terrifying inkling of what was about to happen preparing my soul for a 90-degree nosedive.

'It's cold out isn't it,' she called to my retreating back 'make sure you don't slip!'

'I won't, thanks!' I reply politely only half turning around in an attempt to halt the conversation in its tracks, before the question I knew was about to come out of her stupid mouth, arrived.

'When are you due?' she stupidly asked like a stupid, stupid, old stupid woman.

Bingo.

With one fat lady instead of two.

I very slowly turned away from her, the smile frozen on my face, and fled.

I am devastated.

Was it wrong to want to slap her?

In the end though, I didn't flee far enough. (The biscuit aisle reminded me of the scheduled 4pm visitors.)

She walked up behind me again, as I was biting back tears and looking for some Jammy dodgers and repeated herself.

'Sorry love, when are you due?'

What are you chasing me now? You little old *weirdo?*

So I told her.

He is 10 days old.

I have already *had* him.

Did my running from you not give you an inclination??

She was mortified.

I was mortified.

The whole situation was horrific.

I left without the Jammy dodgers.

Handle with Care...

'I am not going out again' I huff. 'I am too fat and ugly and none of my clothes fit. I have a belly that is hanging down to my knees and there is no way I am leaving the house looking like this.'

'Baby you are gorgeous,' he pleads, starving now 'let's just walk to the Italian down the road, the three of us, I love you, Addison loves you. You look fantastic.'

'*You*' I point with fury, '*are a liar!*'

'No' he begs quietly. 'I am not.'

'Yes *you* are' I strop further 'you will never fancy me again will you? How could you? *Just look at me!*' I grab handfuls of flesh and attempt to throw them at him. They sag back insubordinately like sticky, sloth like silly putty.

'Yes, you are bigger than you were, but I still love you.' He cajoles uncertainly.

'*Much* bigger?' Dangerous territory and he knows it.

'You just had a baby.' He whispers 'so yes, you are bigger than you were, but still beautiful. I will always love you. But you know, maybe it's time to lay off the chocolate for a while if you are feeling this low about it.'

My fat face turns puce.

His turns a whiter shade of pale, he has made a mistake and he knows it.

A Big, big, **big** mistake.

As I run sobbing in to the bedroom, my knees creaking under the four and a half stone (ok five) that I am now carrying. He knows he has made a human sized blunder. I know I held his hand and purposely walked him in to the *am I fat trap*. But I do not care! I am livid! How very dare he? I don't eat *that* much chocolate. I have barely eaten *any* since this morning!

There are piles of clothes strewn all across the floor in abandoned heaps, maternity clothes now mingle with my old *slim me* clothes and the two are in a heated debate about which body image is the most beautiful. I silence them instantly, by kicking and hurling them in every direction across the room.

My slim me clothes are smug. They know they have won.

My frustration though, turns to exhaustion pretty quickly (yes I am *that* unfit and miserable) and I give in, drop to my fat knees and sit in a big fat heap on the floor in floods of angry, fat, tears.

I am a red hot mess.

'Nothing has changed for you!' I scream at top volume while pounding my fists in true toddler tantrum style on the floor.

*'**NOTHING!** You just get to have a beautiful baby boy HANDED to you! Well meanwhile back in fat land, **EVERYTHING** HAS CHANGED FOR ME. EVERYTHING!'* I don't stop there, *'you get to go back to work and lead a normal life! I will be sat here, a fat dumpy unattractive mother who nobody loves with leaky boobs that I can't even feed my son with, and stains down my top and you will be off chatting up women! Pretty women! Women I used to look like!'* I don't stop there either, *'I am a shit mother, I have a horrifically, hideous body and it's all your fault!'* I had really got going now. *'EVERYTHING HAS CHANGED FOR ME, nothing has changed for you! I don't even see you anymore! All you care about is the baby. No! Don't touch me JUST LEAVE ME ALONE!'*

Understandably he backs out of the room with his hands in the air, as if facing a gunman on a rampage, while I sit trembling and heartbroken in a heap on the floor.

I know I am thinking the differences between me and a tantrumming toddler right now are few and far between, but I really cannot help the way I am behaving. It is like an out of body experience.

I know this sounds incredibly shallow but I really am heartbroken when I look in the mirror, I hadn't been proud of my body for long before I got pregnant. My self-esteem, I guess, has ashamedly, always been a little weighted on my waistline. I grew up in Marbella, if you weren't thin you had no worth. I am struggling now to find my worth beneath all of this extra flab.

(I was so proud I had managed to get away with no stretch marks and then that bitch Mother Nature heard my internal celebration and issued a decree for a light sprinkling once the baby had arrived, as if she hadn't already done enough!)

But even so, why I am acting like a lunatic I couldn't tell you.

I have had a house full for days, and have just given birth, I need some time to process what has happened - alone.

My boobs hurt and my arse hurts and no matter how many times I shower, I feel disgusting.

I feel disgusting inside, and I know I look disgusting on the outside.

It isn't long before I hear the front door close behind The Irish One, and I find myself alone.

I have no baby inside me anymore, and the house is completely still.

I curl up in the disturbed mountain of dusty, stained and redundant clothes, rest my head on my fat, but comfortable, upper arm and think about how excited I was a month ago.

By the time The Irish One comes back, I will be normal again.

I promise.

That's if he does come back.

He will come back *won't he???*

Sticky situation...

This morning The Irish One got out of bed, walked to the bathroom and screamed.

A proper girly scream too.

I didn't even bat an eyelid, why *wouldn't* he be screaming? We live in *an actual* horror movie and also, although I am relieved he did come back, we are at the point where I am beginning to struggle remembering his name isn't *'dickhead.'*

I know I sound like I am being a complete bitch but believe me, he is giving as good as he gets.

Unfortunately for him in this instance, he woke Addison up.

'What the hell is wrong with you, you have woken the baby!' I spit at him full of venom, I often feel that emotion where he is concerned now, but I couldn't for the life of me tell you why.

It is venom that rises quickly and yet, vanishes just as quickly.

'Look at me' he spits out through gritted teeth.

I unstuck my eyelids and peered in to the hazy mist surrounding the bed.

I can only have been asleep 4 minutes.

'What?' I muttered over the sound of Addison's *not cute at all* screeches.

He takes a step closer and I gasp.

There, stuck to the side of his leg, is my heavy-duty maternity pad which, if I am honest, I was surprised to note was no longer protecting my undercarriage.

I haven't stopped laughing yet.

Interestingly though, he has.

Nothing says romance like a sanitary towel.

Random advice I could do without thanks...

Yesterday I visited a friend in a posh little village outside of Manchester; I can do these things in peace now you see, since The Irish One has buggered off back to work.

It really isn't as bad as I thought it would be.

We make a good team baby and me.

I would even say it is a bit easier being alone.

Actually, screw that, I will be honest with you - I would say it is a *lot* easier.

I am totally trying not to, but it is so difficult not to resent my fellow child rearing colleague a little.

He is such a good daddy and I hate him for it.

How can he be such a natural and I am so unnatural?

He asks me all the time if I am ok, and if there is anything he can help me with but this actually makes me want to punch him in the penis.

I know I should be grateful he is a good daddy but sometimes I wish he would just piss off to the pub so I could moan about him and take some of the attention off myself.

At the moment all I seem to be doing is hating myself.

I really need to snap out of it, but even my nose seems to have grown. It is taking over my face. I am all nose and not much else.

Is nothing sacred?

And seriously, what is with this mullet I seem to be growing against my will?

All my hair has gone tufty at the front and lanky at the back. All I need is a motor home and a can of Mountain Dew and I would fit in perfectly in Arkansas, or somewhere American where they *dig* mullets.

Anyway, I was stood outside Marks and Spencer's yesterday, while she nipped in to get some caviar (or something equally as posh). I, on the other hand, am far too scruffy for '*Marksnsparks*' so was stood outside staring in to space trying to remember the last time I had a wash or brushed my hair.

I am sure passersby thought my tall, slim and childless friend was supporting some sort of outreach program for fat dumpy idiots. I wanted to shout at them 'I used to be glamorous you know! I used to wear acrylic nails like her!' but I couldn't be arsed. What would be the point?

It was a lovely day, as it always is in Cheadle, peaceful and posh.

I had given Addison a heads up earlier in the day. No tantrums in Cheadle little boy. Cheadle is far too posh for tantrums. But evidently he had decided to ignore me.

He woke up from a nap, just as I worked out it had probably been over a month since I had put make up on and decided that in no uncertain terms, he was making his presence known.

It was such a surprise, as I usually have him so doped up during the day I barely hear a peep out of him.

I am of course joking.

It wasn't a surprise at all, the only real shock was that it had taken him so long to wake.

I quickly and in a mild panic (it was really, very loud screaming for this time of day and also being a new mum - baby cries? Pick baby up. Gina Ford piss off.) I began the 'untangling baby' dance. *Clip one, rope 2, button 3, twist 4, jump up and down on your left foot 5, clasp undone 6 and he's out!*

I wrapped my arms around his little trembling, tantrumming body and began my pathetically vain attempt at soothing him.

Clearly something was the matter, as usually he would stop crying the second he was picked up. (I know I have made a rod for my back by doing this, but to be honest I don't care. I dare say that by the time he is 21 none of this will matter.)

I made a rod for my own back when I got pregnant, you think I am bothered about attaching another to it?

I felt around his person for the usual suspects, belly (wind), bum (wet patches) and neck (eczema) but all seemed to be you know, normal.

He however, insisted on continuing with his angry rant so flustered, I gave up trying to be a calm and in control mother on her first 'proper' trip out and began to search for his dummy, apologising to passersby who may have been disturbed, while flapping my hands and sweating profusely.

While we are on this subject, can I just say that dummies have special powers?

Honestly, I am sure of it.

A dummy can disappear and re-appear at will.

And also multiply!

If you do not believe me, then I beg you to get pregnant, give birth, and go and buy a skip load of dummies. You will see for yourself.

I spent half an hour searching for one this morning and only after I had turned the house upside down and given up, opting instead to give him the end of a bottle, which FYI for future reference is NOT a good idea as they fill themselves up with air. (**Hours.** Hours spent burping him while he screamed in pain) and then I look down and find three at my feet!

I finally located the illusive dummy and was about to shove it in, I mean gently place it in my sweethearts mouth, when out of nowhere a head thrust itself towards us like a turtle appearing out of a shell.

A little old lady in a green mac, a green scarf and a green head wrap with interestingly green teeth had broken all rules of personal space and was literally shaking her nobly little head in what seemed to be disgust, a mere inches away from my face.

Addison immediately stopped crying for a second due to shock I imagine, and I'll be honest, I found it rather intriguing.

Is she going to turn me in to a frog? Or maybe stab me with a spinning wheel needle so I sleep for a hundred years (actually... I wouldn't mind that one.)

'Hello?'- (step back slightly alarmed.)

'You know what you want to do?' Posh, clipped and pretentious.

'No?' Tired, gormlessly and confused.

'Put a muslin cloth over his face'

'what?!?'

'Put a muslin cloth over his face, that'll soon stop him crying.'

'You want me to place a muslin cloth, in the middle of a hot day, over my son's face, to stop him crying?'

'Yes.' She nods vehemently 'Muslin cloth.'

I search the contours of her face looking for the element of laughter, the slight lip quiver that tells me she is actually joking but do not find it.

I take a couple of steps back and avoid eye contact.

'Yeah, thanks for the advice but I'm not gonna do that.' I am now attempting to walk away while supporting his head and pushing the buggy at the same time. I do not have enough arms.

The buggy goes left and starts to spin in a backwards motion, I tilt my off kilter body and brain to the right trying to offset it and Addison, sensing my frustration decides to help in the only way he knows how, by screaming.

Leaving the house is so stressful!

But this has been playing over and over in my mind since the dotty old *Disney villain wannabe* uttered the words.

She wanted me to **put a muslin cloth over my sons little face, to stop him crying.**

Yeah, I'm sure it would stop my son crying missis. I am pretty sure it would also actually stop him breathing too as I'm not sure a baby can cry and gasp for breath at the same time.

Later, as we were walking away from the shops; me holding a plastic bag over Addison's face, (What? It totally stopped him crying?!) It got me thinking about how totally odd it is when you become public proper.

Who are these people who seem to think it is ok to stop and give me advice on being a mother?

It is more than a little annoying.

Especially seen as most of it seems to be outdated and utterly barmy.

On a *very rare* occasion it can be helpful (usually only off my mother in law who has had a lot of experience and is kind and patient with her words) but mostly I have found 'stranger danger advice' to be totally incorrect and utter crap. These 'pearls of wisdom' range from a little odd to full on 'get your coat Addy, we're off.'

This advice sharing started from the second I developed a bump too.

Advice giving and the 'Touchy feelers!'

It is almost as if you get pregnant and become public property.

Sure by all means! Just lay your hands on my uterus!

I have NO idea who you are, but why not have a squeeze of my right boob too, it's juicer than the left one. Why not just go the whole hog and cup them for me, see if you agree?

Sure I do not mind at all, come on over and feel my gut! I am only 3 months pregnant right now you see! So what you are actually fondling is my lunch!

Are you enjoying this as much as I am? GET.OFF. ME!

Is it just I who is subject to this intrusion?

And if it is, then what the hell am I doing wrong?

We never seem to get random advice when The Irish One is with us.

That's probably because he looks like a serial killer at the moment.

He isn't sleeping much and he is working all day! Do you have ANY IDEA HOW HARD HIS LIFE IS?

First world problems much.

Maybe I should put a muslin cloth over *his* face.

Social suicide of the Ex degree...

I don't care what anyone says.

Bumping in to an 'ex' is a certified nightmare.

They should issue you with an award.

An **'I bumped in to my ex and survived'** award.

Or a t-shirt. Remember those t-shirts? 'My family went to Skegness and all I got was this lousy shirt'?

Well I may start printing 'I bumped in to my ex and all I got was an evening of over analysing' t-shirt. Although I'm not sure I would have anything it would go with, to be honest as nothing fucking fits.

It can't just be.

Every woman (and maybe even some men) at the end of any relationship, regardless of how long this relationship lasted, must make themselves feel better with a casual 'next time I see him I'll make him regret it.' statement.

I am sure of it.

We have all done it, we have all thought it, and I bet most of us have said it.

Whether you are the dumper or *dumpee* is irrespective. Next time you see this person you will be, feel and most importantly look fabulous. (And thin! Thinner than I have ever been motherfucker!!!)

Unfortunately for most of us mere mortals the law of sod sees to it that this rarely, if ever happens.

I am yet to meet a woman who can tell me in all honesty she bumped in to her ex and was certain 'he regretted the moment he left me, let me tell you'

Although we know this rarely is the case it doesn't stop us repeating our mantra, post dump.

As I've mentioned. Bumping in to an ex is horrific. So why does the law of sod taunt us so?

Why can't we bump in to the Fucker that cheated, the Fucker that never called and the Fucker we lived with for 2 years who 'didn't't believe in marriage' but has since met someone who changed his mind and had him gallivanting up the aisle quicker than JLO, when we look our very best?

I'm not sure about you, but I have days when I wake up, get dressed, slap on my Morrison's eyeliner, look in the mirror and know the wardrobe gods have been on my side. You stop, double check it's actually you, you're in fact looking at and think, *jaysus.* I don't look half bad today. How did that happen?

Those days, albeit infrequent are the days when bumping in to an ex would be almost manageable. Almost.

But, alas, then there are the other kind. Like today.

The days you fall out of bed looking like a donkey. Tie your greasy hair up with a pair of old tights, (ok- an old bobble if tights are a step too far), rub last night's foundation back in around your nose, use your spit to quickly eradicate the panda eyes. (We've all done it; don't even bother to deny it.) Pull on last night's stained top and the 'these will do another day' jeans. Run to your car. Forget your keys. Run back to the house. Run back to the car. Forget the baby. (Yeah.) Run back to the house, run back to the car, sniff your armpit, wish you'd put deodorant on. Get in the car, realise your right boob is leaking, get out of car, pour half a bottle of water over your chest to hide one leaky boob, get in the car, drive to destination swearing at tardiness, get baby out of car just in time for baby to spit up on your right shoulder, pick up changing bag upside down but realise too late, just as nappies, wipes and trusty hemorrhoid cream roll all over the car park, put baby down, turn around to pick it all up and....

...BANG!! There's fucker 2. In all his glory, a shocked, but slightly relieved and possibly victorious expression on his face.

He looks good too and the Fucking Fucker knows it.

'Fuck'

'Hi Lexy'

'Hi Fucker 2'

'How's things? (Code for – bloody hell love, what have you been eating? Ever heard of a shower?)

'Grand. I just had a baby which is why I look fat. I'm not fat. I mean, well I am. But only because I just had another man's baby. A gorgeous man... (Silence)...With lots of money. And we are so happy. Really very happy. I also got a new job... (Silence)... and won the lottery. So yeah I'm really happy.......you?'

(Ground swallow me up now please.)

'I'm well Lexy. Clearly regretting leaving you, and marrying a goddess who dances on the west end.'

On this particular evening you come home and maybe you appreciate your gorgeous Irish Fucker a little more when he offers to do the night feed.

MAYBE you even thank him for his thoughtfulness and try a little harder to see the romance in him bringing you home some Laxatives, because he knows you have been unable to poo for 8 days and have the worst stomach ache in the world but are still point blank refusing to try and poo, because the pain in your bum hole is so unbelievably sore that you are too scared to.

Maybe laxatives **are** romantic, you may ponder. Maybe I don't need flowers anymore...

Eventually instead of focusing on the pain, you decide to ring your best mate for post-ex analysis.

Your first words?

'I know I just had a baby and I look like a complete skip dweller, but he well regretted leaving me. Let me tell you. The Irish One is lucky to have me, and you know what he did tonight the little sweetie? He brought me some laxatives. I know, he's a keeper right? Fucker 2 doesn't know what he is missing.'

It may be a lie. (There is no 'may' about it. Laxatives and Sanitary items, that is what we are reduced to.)

But it feels better.

And who needs that Fucker anyway?

I got myself a daddy fucker. (Ok, that sounded WAY better in my head.)

I mean, my fucker is the father of my child.

And I always look gorgeous and thin and fabulous for him anyway.

Mostly.

Oh fuck!!!

My fucking boob is leaking again!

Must. Act. Normal...

According to a person with absolutely no identity, who I am unable to describe for fear of retribution, but whom I can say with absolute certainty, is gorgeous, lovely caring, funny and a total babe.

'The Irish One is as sexy as hell'

After I had collected my eyebrows off the ceiling and settled my features back in to a look of agreement, instead of complete shock, this person then went on to tell me that somehow, he seems to have created for himself, in the work arena, the arena where the air conditioning is either set too 'Nippletastic' or 'Sahara desert at noon,' a place where the phones never stop ringing and the girls are all younger, prettier and more fun, the arena I am not allowed to talk about really and have no desire to go back to anytime soon.

'A bit of a fan club.'

The person is female too.

He made me put that in there. (He is delighted I am writing about this of course.)

'It isn't that I am homophobic or anything' he clarifies from behind me 'but just make it clear to all of your readers, that it is *actual* women that are after me ok? Lots and lots of real life women.'

'Yes darling' I murmur regretting the moment I opened my laptop and decided on writing all this down 'yes of course I will.'

'LOADS of women' he expands on his point flinging his arms wide 'Maybe hundreds!'

And with that, as I hide a deep sigh and surreptitiously role my eyes, he positively swaggers off in to the kitchen, wearing, just for the record, a pair of tatty boxers and a t-shirt displaying Addison's regurgitated chocolate all down the front.

A part of me is surprised he didn't't burp loud and proud on the way out.

Would I describe him as sexy as hell?

I'll claim the fifth on that at the moment.

The conversation got me to thinking though, after I had got over the initial shock of how quickly it had digressed from work gossip in to a *lust fest,* which weirdly seems to be the effect I am having on a fair few conversations at the moment (Clearly I am living vicariously through others) had giggled, stared at her disbelievingly, pinched myself to make sure I somehow hadn't found myself in a dream belonging to The Irish One himself and guffawed loudly.

Is he gorgeous?

I mean I know when I met him I must have thought so because I put in some *serious* effort you know?

A fact The Irish One never fails to remind me of.

I had been off sick at work with a terrible bout of flu (ahem... hangover) and upon my return, as I was busy stalking down the office in my spice girl heels thinking I was the business and just a little bit nervous at having been off sick and wondering what may await me from my boss, I noticed immediately that in my absence, a new boy with blonde hair and quite a nice bum has been installed in to the seat opposite my desk.

Turning the corner and sitting myself down wondering what his face may look like, but scared to look up having just been caught checking out his bum as he picked something off the floor, I heard his voice for the first time and I have to say my heart sank.

I am an absolute sucker for an accent.

I knew, you see, as soon as I heard it, without even looking at his face, that I would now have to make an effort to look half decent in work.

'Tanks for kallllinnnnnn...'

He murmured down the phone to a customer, before hanging up and looking up at me trying to make eye contact, which was a little awkward as by this point I was a pile of embarrassed, nervous, flushed, floppy mush, salivating and shuddering on the floor.

The new boy was well fit. I had to make him mine.

I had a plan.

It went like this;

Must. Act. Normal.

Must. Make. Him. Want. Me.

So of course, typically for me over the next few days as I struggled to appear busy and important, (to show him I had a brain) sophisticated (to show him I had style,) elegant (to show him I was a lady,) fun and carefree (to show him I could be an *animal* in bed,) classy (to show him he could take me home to meet his mother,) tasteful (to show him I was interested in him,) refined, (to show him the *animal,* would all be for him) chic (to prove he absolutely wanted me too) what actually happened was very different.

Instead of the above, I actually bumbled around like a flaming imbecile, my brain too full of things I wanted to be, to even focus on who I was actually being. (A complete knob, to show him, I was a complete knob.)

I was like a walking disaster any time he was within my general vicinity.

I tripped up and head butted the corner of my desk, I spilt coffee all down my front while wearing a white blouse (blouse

– who am I my dad? Shirt I meant shirt), I walked in to a wall while I was trying to see if he was looking at me (which he was-brilliant.) I trapped my finger in my desk drawer and couldn't help but shout 'poo' at top volume (very classy,) I made completely idiotic irrelevant jokes that made no sense, talked completed bollocks and spent the entire time in his presence, glowing bright, red hot, red.

I was a beacon of stupidity.

In the end though I just got sick of all the waiting, trying and failing and just dived in.

'Sexy accent hot rod, you busy Friday night?'

Ok, those weren't't the actual words I used, as I probably would have been fired, me being a manager and all, but I did ask him out surreptitiously and bravely!!

Dear Irish one.

Are you new in town? I want your babies.

Very brave and sure to get his attention, I thought.

The bastard turned me down.

Not one to give up though I asked him again.

'Sexy accent *hot rod,* you busy Friday night?'

Much to my horror he turned me down AGAIN.

I couldn't't understand it.

Doesn't every man want a woman in a short skirt that will walk in to a wall for him?

Not one to give up, and now seeing this as a challenge, I decided to befriend him instead, listen to his woe's and then pounce on him when he was vulnerable.

It worked.

He would be telling me all about his life and his problems without really noticing how my tops were becoming lower cut and my skirts more thigh hugging.

He would be explaining to me, in great detail, why the English were a nation the Irish would never trust but that he loved living here without noticing my perfume was becoming more enticing and my lips more pouty.

He would be raving about his favorite band and his hopes for the future without noticing that gradually I had begun to insert myself in to it.

It didn't't take long before *he* asked *me* out.

See? Genius.

They always like to think it is *their* idea don't they? I don't know why I didn't't think of that in the first instance.

Our first *date,* however did not go well.

'You ok in a pub like this?' he asked as I tottered, all dressed up and excited, in to a pub that can only be described as a toilet.

'Yes of course I am!' I laughed trying to mask my horror at the filth of the place and of the people dressed in boiler suits now leering at me dressed completely inappropriately in stupidly high heels and another tiny skirt. 'Of course!'

What then proceeded to happen will go down in history as the worst date ever.

He went to the toilet and a weirdo in a boiler suit tried to feel me up.

I called him a bad word and he left. (The weirdo in a boiler suit, not The Irish One. That would have been a **terrible** date... And one I suppose I have experienced many times before!)

I did not tell The Irish One. I wanted the date to be perfect. He went to the bar.

A weirdo in a boiler suit started whispering death threats at me.

I told him he looked like a turd and turned back around.

I did not tell The Irish One. I wanted the date to be perfect. He went to the cigarette machine.

Before any of the 'hills have eyes cast' could abuse me further I glanced around and hissed;

'Don't any of you dare, I have been waiting for his date forever and if you fuck it up I swear to god you will regret it! Leave me alone you bunch of not rights! Go crawl back in to your skips for the night! I am a woman with a plan, and I don't need you messing it up!'

Luckily for me they did leave me alone from then on.

Unlucky for me, however, and to this day without him really knowing why, they then started on The Irish One.

He still has no idea why he was punched in the face that night and I still deny I had anything to do with it.

He made me wait 6 weeks for sex after that though.

6 whole weeks.

Which was a lot for me as I was taught at the; *'if you have sex with a guy a.s.a.p. he will fall in love with you'* school of self-esteem.

6. WHOLE. WEEKS.

Turns out he had a plan too.

He didn't't just want to be a one-night stand. (What does that say about me eh? Eh? Let's not go there...)

It worked too, except now I suppose; he is lucky if he gets *it* across a period of 6. Whole. Months.

But seriously?

When did I forget he is actually quite desirable?

Was it when he was looking up my flute at the baby's head? Was it while I was screaming at him for help during my 68-hour labour and got the response that he was busy making a ham and mustard butty 'to keep him going'? Was it when I was trying not to lamp him with the side of the high chair for being a lazy bugger? Was it at 3am when we would throw filthy looks at one another during the long nights of colic?

Yesterday as I was looking for something warm to wear to an outdoor event and he was busy pestering me, as to where the nappies are kept (THE SAME PLACE THEY HAVE BEEN KEPT SINCE HE WAS BORN!) it began to dawn on me.

'Should I wear this?' I asked hoping I wasn't coming across like a pleb.

'A body warmer?' he exclaimed like I was an idiot, 'No you will still be cold, and I don't want to have to hear you moaning for the next 3 hours, put a coat on for the love of god!'

Of course, I thought, looking at him through the eyes of someone else.

He *is* gorgeous (if not a little grumpy.)

'Am I making a fool of myself with you here?' I asked worried all of a sudden, 'should I be acting all cool and put together to keep you interested? You have a fan club!'

'Lexy' he laughed grabbing my hand 'I have known you 2 long years. I have seen your uterus splash on to an operating table, I have witnessed you pissing yourself while lying in bed' (yeah thanks for bring that up) 'and I have shared with you the most incredible journey of my entire life.

I love you. NOW GO PUT ON A SODDING COAT!'

I didn't't.

I wore the body warmer, and he did have to listen to me moan all night, it's called a relationship. But you know what? Having bore (beared/bored?!) this all in mind, The Irish One may actually be getting *some* tonight if he can shut up about potatoes for long enough.

And now he really does have a swagger on.

'Irish One!' I shout after him realising once again he has peeped over my shoulder 'I said *may* be getting some... *may*....'

He doesn't hear me, he is too busy celebrating.

It's been a while.

Operation Skinny Bint...

'If you just lie back here and take a deep breath' bouncy Helen said pointing to the clapped out settee and dropping heavily on to one knee 'I will check your uterus and your stitches again.'

With her dropping on to one knee, I had almost expected something a little more romantic and a little less mortifying to come out of her mouth but alas, at six weeks past my delivery date, this was not the instruction I had been hoping for.

'Do you really have to?' I ask with a heavy sigh before climbing on to my sofa. '*Surely* I don't need to be checked *again*? There is just something so weird about you doing this *procedure* while I am lying on my *own* couch, in my *own* living room, with the neighborhood kids cavorting outside and The Irish One lurking in the kitchen.'

'I know' She replies with a sigh, having heard this every week at the same time for the last 5 weeks, 'but this is the last time today Lexy, so just lie back and think of England ok? I'll be done in a Jiffy.'

'Right' I sigh dramatically while lying back and dropping my *kecks*. 'Oh the magic of pregnancy and childbirth. It just keeps on giving.'

While I rest my head back and attempt to stop Doodle jumping up on to my chest and grabbing five minutes of much needed, abandoned and forgotten *'hey I'm your son too, so I will pin you down with doggy paws and lick your face whether you like it or not'* mammy and poodle time, Helen the unhelpful midwife plunges her hands in to the depths of my stomach.

She is elbow deep in flab and stretch marks when she looks up triumphantly and exclaims 'Well you will be happy to know your uterus has now retreated fully back to where it should be, and your stitches are healing nicely.'

She pulls off her plastic gloves and begins to stand up, clutching her back for dramatic affect. (Yes my sofa is too low, *I get it!* It is *not my fault* that the 'wooden block feet' were mistaken for 'random bits of wood' and thrown out during operation 'sort out nursery.' Move on! Have some physiotherapy!)

Meanwhile back on the sofa of doom, I gasp, splutter and stutter, 'what do you mean my uterus has gone back in?' I manage to spit out while pulling my knickers up and avoiding eye contact with Doodle. 'It can't have, it just can't have. If it has, then what is all this?' I cry, grabbing fistfuls of bump. 'If my uterus has retreated then why do I still have a bump??' I am horrified.

'That my dear,' says bouncy Helen, full of glee, 'is fat.'

And with that she packs up her assassin case of midwifery tools and heads towards the door. 'Nothing a bit of exercise won't solve, and now it has been six weeks you are good to go. Good luck.' She calls out slamming the door behind her while I stand cursing the day KFC, Pizza hut, MacDonald's, Milkshakes, Burgers, Ice cream, chocolate and Square crisps had been invented and consequently eaten, continuously over 10 months (not 9!) of sheer gluttony.

'But it was...' I pondered to the wall forlornly, imagining a camera zooming in for a teary close up... 'But it was meant to drop off?'

Looking 8 months pregnant six weeks post-delivery is not something I enjoy.

Looking like a beer swelling lager lout with a belly that sways when I rock the baby is not something I find even remotely attractive on myself, and as if to add injury to insult for some ungodly reason that only Mother Nature can answer (sick bitch) I have begun to grow thick curly black hairs on it too.

Er hello? Why don't you kick me while I'm down Cow bag!

It isn't like I was thin before.

But you have to understand. I was told it would *go.* So being left with an overhang similar to a bum bag (or 'fanny pack' if you are American) full of water hanging from my hips, does not leave me in a good mood.

Why oh why couldn't I have been one of those women you see swanning about the place with the perfect, and dare I say it? *Sexy* little bump, protruding from the front of their jeans? Why couldn't I have been an example of the perfect weight gain? Why couldn't I have only put 8 pounds on, had no morning sickness and been described as 'suiting pregnancy' on a day to day basis?

Because The Irish One introduced me to **Pasta sandwiches** as a cure for Nausea, that's why.

For 10 months (not 9!) I was made entirely of Carbohydrates, little arms and legs booting me in the *flute* and Dolmio tomato sauce. So much so, that I started to look like the woman from the cartoon advert. At one point I even drew a mole on my face and spoke with an Italian accent for the entire evening. 'You *wanta* some-a pasta ravioli Irish one-a? It's a nicer place-a to *stuffa* your face-a!' (He soon tired of this and introduced me to Magnums. I never spoke again. My mouth was always full of ice cream and chocolatey goodness.)

But oh! Had I been a thin and 'healthy' pregnant woman instead of a 'whoooaaaa huge bump!' and 'wow you're blooming!' heavily set baby maker, I could have been a thin new mummy! You know the ones I mean.

You see them camping out around the baby aisle in Asda and pushing Maxi-cosi's on massive combine harvester type trolleys. They are so tiny, the trolley engulfs them. They are so thin and perfect looking you expect to see a 12 year old crammed in to the tiny Maxi-cosi, all legs and hairy armpits, humphing and moaning about how he is 'not a child anymore muuuuummmm', but are shocked and physically curled in irritation to notice the baby is *only an hour and fifteen minutes* old.

'Yes...' They shout merrily while doing star jumps and breast feeding concurrently 'I exercised all the way through! Ate only a yoghurt and a donut daily and managed to push him out an hour ago while doing a sit up! Isn't he wonderful?'

You plod away towards the cakes wondering where it all went wrong, but comforted by the fact your uterus hasn't retreated yet so you have an excuse.

'My uterus hasn't gone in yet' I explain between mouthfuls of chocolate sponge 'when it does, I'll be thin again, like magic!!'

Then Helen visits. The bitch.

Exercise?

My son is only 6 weeks old for god's sake!

Is it morning? What is my name again? When was his last bottle? What? I'm feeding him now? Right ok, who are you? You are the father? Great! Can I go to bed? I can't? I have to rub ice cold salt and vinegar on my nipples and then stick nails in them? Right ok. What day is it? Was that the doorbell? Did the visitors just leave or have they not been yet? Who the *hell were they?* Why am I still so fat? Where are my feet? I can't see them! Has he had a bottle yet? Do you know what my name is? Where is the toilet paper? Go out in public? Are you on glue? I'm never leaving the house again. Where are the nappies? Do we have any wipes? Has he poo'd again? Have you burped him? Was that a burp? Please god say that was a burp, it sounded like a burp! Why has he been sick? Is it colic? Is that the doorbell? Who was that? I have no idea why these people are visiting! I have spoken to them once in my entire life! Do you want a cup of tea? Make it yourself I am sterilising bottles. What day is it?

Has he had a bottle recently? Why has he been sick again? Is that poo I can smell? Was that a burp? PLEASE tell me that was a burp. Exercise?????

You have **GOT TO** be joking.

The point I am trying to make is; there is **no way** I am ready to exercise at six weeks post-delivery. In fact, I think the whole six weeks and go, go, go! Thing is just too much pressure and not enough support on us poor women (me) that pregnancy spits out.

Obviously there are those women who are the exception, those women who do not struggle in the weeks immediately after the baby was born, and those who hardly put any weight on, and all joking aside, I hate you. No really, I do. (Not really.... not much, anyway... I am just jealous... I really am...)

I wasn't the perfect pregnant woman. I am yet to jump back on the cross trainer and I have put on a hell of a lot of weight.

Does the perfect pregnant woman exist?

I have lost a little over a stone in the last 6 weeks.

I totally expected him to be about 3 stone goddamn it!

I remember screaming at the midwife '6 pound what?????' before insisting her scales must be malfunctioning.

It was *clearly* a man who came out with the whole; 'all women will feel normal 42 days post tearing their arse out while giving birth! I, mister Man of Man street, Man land, came to this number by multiplying the number of times I think about sex on a daily basis, by the number of brain cells I still have remaining!'

Six weeks my arse!! (She says, grabbing it in proof.)

I *have* bought a stepper from Tesco though. It was £46 and so far all I have done is stare at it angrily.

I know I need to be healthy for my son and all that. Healthy body healthy mind maybe? But so soon?

I may try stepping later but I am not joining fat club or slimming world or even a Gym. Any pressure and I will run a mile (or not as the case may be.) I am literally going to do a bit of stepping here and there, and less chewing and swallowing there and here.

My goal is realistic.

Realistically by this time next year I fully intend on being the thinnest woman on the planet. Or at least a happy size 14 with *thighs that make you go oooo!* (MC Hammers lesser known track.)

When that time comes, I will then borrow a new-born baby and parade around town, pushing my Maxi Cosi while showing off my 'post preggo body' by wearing a full on leotard and imitating the dance to *all the single ladies*, by Beyoncé . (FYI – When I say *borrow a new born*, I mean off a friend. I don't mean from a hospital in a creepy way!) I will also sit *my newborn* on my rock hard abs while doing sit up's in the banana aisle.

I *just for once* want to know what it feels like to be seen as an upbeat new mother!!

Instead of the heavy footed, slow walking, limping Eeyore type mother I am!

My thunder thighs are constantly cursing those pasta sandwiches The Irish One assured me would cure the nausea.

It is his fault I am this fat.

Operation Skinny bint has commenced though, that is what I shall call it.

No food.

My flab.

One Goal.

Forms, Arse-holes knees and toes, knees and toes...

I am starting to think there will never be a day where we can go out, with the baby, and not end up at each other throats before we even get to the car.

I am trying very hard not to kill him at every opportunity.

Is this *actually* normal?

I think I probably would have injured him by now, were it not for the fact I am too bloody busy doing *everything else.*

Have I mentioned the fact that The Irish One is doing my head in at the moment?

That I am slowly beginning to resent him, but that I couldn't tell you exactly why at this point?

Today we have registered the baby.

The baby is now a real, life member of the British population. And oh my god what a hoo-haa!

Registering 'the baby' is something I have been dreading for some time.

Registering the baby is a task I have been putting to the back of my mind. It is not that I don't want him to be a proper member of society, no it isn't that at all.

It is just that registering the baby involves a fair few THINGS I really did not want to do.

Like;

Get dressed. (I cannot leave the house in my skuzzy jogging bottoms but as you are well aware, nothing else fits. Everything else also *hurts.* My lady parts are still undergoing *not routine at all* maintenance. Even having a wee is agony. Never mind pulling my granny knickers up. The thought of even attempting a pair of jeans makes me positively shudder, and before you ask me why I am not in leggings, I will tell you. I will never be seen *dead* in a pair of leggings. Pre pregnancy I would have attempted, but post pregnancy? Well, have you ever seen a hippo in tights? No? Well there is a reason for that.)

Leave the house. (Eh? How is this possible now? It takes a year and a half to organise everything and I always forget a crucial ingredient. Like wipes, or nappies, or formula, or a bottle, or the water for the bottle, or the changing bag, or the cuddly toy, or the muslin cloth, or the dummy, or the baby. Did I ever tell you about the time I got out to the car laden down with all of the above only to find the car seat I was carrying was empty and I had left him in his cot? I really am a terrible mother. He must have been in the house on his own, with only Doodle to look after him, for at least 4 minutes.)

Make a FINAL DECISION ON HIS NAME. Yeah I really wasn't ready to do this. And yes I am aware we have been calling him Addison since Dot, but I just, I just, I'm just not sure basically.

I have just been unable to decide whether I like his name enough to make it permanent. Before he was born I loved it. But then before he was born I usually referred to him as The Pleb.

When people ask, how did you choose his name, I really don't have an answer.

I heard it on Grey's anatomy but thought it was a girl's name.

Then The Irish One mentioned it to me when he was reading through a baby name book. (The worst baby name book I have ever heard of too, by the way. It had no meanings and under where it said 'Addison' it said – Like the actor out of Grey's anatomy. Good for a girl or a boy. – Seriously. That is what it said. Worst. Book ever. 'Tom' – like the cat Tom out of Tom and Jerry or Tom Cruise. Seriously?)

So even though I had my heart set on another name at the time, a name which The Irish One said was too popular and therefore didn't like it (idiot; it is popular because it is great!) we plumped for Addison because he really liked it, it would be fine whatever the gender, and I was too tired (and probably had a mouth too full of burger) to argue.

I was all right about it though, because I wanted a name that was funky.

And even though Addison, in my opinion is still a girl's name it does suit my boy.

I had 3 girls names picked out in the early days.

Girl's names are easier to choose in my opinion.

I had buckets of them, but never mind.

I think I will grow to like it the more time that passes, I hope.

But you see this is why I never got a tattoo, and why I took so long naming the dog, because, as my school report always detailed 'Lexy is flighty, easily distracted and a bit of a butterfly' and nothing much changed as the years flew past.

What I love today, I may not necessarily even like tomorrow, do you see the problem?

Like, I used to love Brad Pitt, but now I am very secretly more about One Direction.

Things get old too quickly.

Anyway, we finally left the house with a full entourage of crap and baby in tow, and after bickering about who was going to drive, where we should park, which route to take, whether the traffic light was on red or amber, what his surname should be and who was going to push the pram, we finally made it to the town hall for our appointment, just in the nick of time.

(ooo Nick. You see, I like Nick.)

The office was a tiny box shoved to one corner of the huge and impressive building, which seemed to be full of busy and important people.

Feeling like something indescribable that heaved itself from a swamp maneuvering my three wheeler pram (I won that battle) in to the tiny cupboard office, the lady behind the desk greeted us with a short official smile and went back to staring at her computer.

'Mr. Braonáin and Miss Ellis, yes?'

'Yes' we both chorused quietly silently praying Addison would remain asleep for the entire interaction.

'Please take a seat' she motioned to the two chairs wedged in front of her little desk and began click click clicking on her keyboard, while we shuffled around trying to fit in and I managed to knock numerous photo frames over with my swinging pendulum belly and thunder thighs.

'Sorry.' I muttered embarrassed by the sheer size of me wedged in to this cubbyhole, re-arranging them as she continued to ignore us.

We were finally sat down, our knees touching the edge of her desk and the pram wedged in at a jaunty angle between us, sweat pouring from us all from the over exertion, (did I say us? I meant me) and the atmosphere sticky when she finally spoke.

'So, I am sure you know how this works, you tell me his name, I put in to the system and your son is registered. What was his date of birth please?'

Wow. Memorable. Thank you for making this so special for us.

'9th of April' we both interrupted each other before scowling and trying again, we really should have organised who was going to be speaking.

'And name please' she asked without looking up.

The Irish One was about to respond when I, completely predictably had an attack of nerves.

'Listen,' I whispered to him 'are we definitely sure we like it? What about Nick or Sam, or James, or Harry, or the Pleb? Are we sure we are sold on Addison? Does he sound like a rock star? I need him to sound like a rock star! Myleene Class says a name should encompass a rock star, lawyer and poet all rolled in to one, I like Myleene Class, she is a good mother, what do you think?'

'Addison Jake Ó Braonáin' the Irish one relayed to the lady, brushing me off with the palm of his hand and smirking apologetically at the lady who was now not trying very hard to hide her impatience, 'Addison Jake Ó Braonáin.'

'Ellis.' I finished, not happy at being ignored but knowing, at the bottom of my heart it was too late for last minute deliberation anyway, and I would shout at him later for it.

They both looked at me.

'Addison Jake Ó Braonáin Ellis' I clarified glancing at the Irish one to check he was fine with this and continuing before my overtired mind could read too much in to the daggers he was sending me telepathically 'He hasn't proposed, or even inclined he wants to marry me, even though I just gave up my entire life to have his baby, so I want my name on there too, and besides, if I don't, my dad may actually kill me.'

She shot me a funny smile while the Irish One made himself busy, mentally ringing my neck and snarling in my general direction.

'Ó Braonáin with a hyphen?' She queried 'That way you can always remove the Ellis when you *do* get married.' she looked at him pointedly and I had to restrain myself from leaning over the desk and snogging the face of her.

'Yes.' I said, as he remained quiet 'why not? You never know, miracles may happen.'

She laughed and so did I.

HA! That'll teach you to face palm me.

So that is it, it is official.

He is a fully-fledged, pooing screaming *insomniac-ally* mental member of society.

Addison Jake Ó Braonáin Hyphen Ellis.

Nice ring to it doesn't it?

Although I do still have a penchant for the pleb.

We travelled home in thick silence, or we would have done if it wasn't for Addison screaming blue murder in the back.

Apparently he doesn't like the hyphen either.

Actually losing the plot here...

I miss my heels, I miss pissing people off at work, I miss making decisions and I miss my pencil skirts. I miss the laughter and the gossip and popping out for a cheeky smoke. I miss the thrill of a challenge that doesn't feel insurmountable, but these baby days... Is it wrong to admit they just seem to drag on like a dead body and I hesitate, as I don't want to sound pathetic but I think I am a little bit lonely.

I do genuinely want to try and be a high achieving mum, but I don't know where to even start. What do I measure myself against?

If I am measuring myself against Gina Ford, Supernanny and Maria the organic mum who lives across the hall, who literally wears one baby in a massive hemp wrap, while breastfeeding the other, makes smashed carrots (apparently they are 'healthier than regular 'mashed ones') with one bulging bicep and uses the other to shave her smooth and slim legs, then clearly I am failing anyway.

So I can't be *arsed* starting anywhere.

I am fairly sure my son doesn't want me to anyway.

Failure failure failure.

It plays on my mind constantly.

Failure based Tinnitus.

I am failing so I am being petulant and I have stopped trying.

He only sleeps for his daddy, will only burp for his daddy and will only smile at his daddy, even though I am the one who sits with him day in day out trying to keep him entertained, feeding, burping, mopping up yellow poo and losing my damn mind.

I joke about this with people, I update Facebook with how goddamn funny my baby is and how adorable he is, but secretly? I hate this. And really how funny can a two month old *actually* be?

His daddy says I *must do nothing all day* and he is right.

All I do is ... nothing important.

So I decided to be completely and brilliantly useful yesterday. I decided to do something I was good at, that I just knew would solve absolutely everything. It would stop the arguing, make The Irish One love me again, give us something to look forward to, it would even include Addison and teach him so much about the world.

I don't know why I didn't think of it sooner!

I sat for most of the day, organising and booking us on to an around the world trip!!!

Leaving Friday this week!!!

We need to get away.

I spent hours on Expedia and I tried really hard to include all of the places I know The Irish One would like to visit. I made huge lists and tacked them on the walls, things to do and places to visit scrawled across the paper under the city and country title.

I paid with his credit card but I knew he wouldn't mind.

It did cost a lot but I thought he would be happy.

Turns out he wasn't.

He had the cheek to look at me with his face all screwed up and red, like I was insane.

He then called me crazy.

To be honest looking back now I can see his point of view.

And when I look around the living room at the debris from the day, I don't even remember writing and booking most of it.

I remember thinking about it... but, what was Addison doing while I did all of this? Was he asleep? I really can't remember.

I tried to deny booking it after about 10 minutes of shouting but he won the argument, definitely on this occasion, because I clearly did book it.

MasterCard called him at work 'for security reasons' and now the upshot it, we aren't going to Goa on the first stop of our whistle stop tour of the world, in two days' time.

Probably for the best.

I am going to buy a new pram instead I think.

There is nothing wrong with the pram we have, it's just, if I can't be the best mum in a loving way, and I can't think outside of the box and solve problems in a 'high performer way' then I definitely need to have the best pram and buy him everything I possibly can, that he *obviously* deserves, so that when other mums see me coming, they believe I am doing the best for him.

I need them to believe I am a good mum who smashes vegetables in to mush while also maintaining a loving home.

It is unrealistic though as I can't afford a new pram.

I literally don't know what I am thinking right now.

Every now and again I keep getting these moments of clarity.

What the Hell am I doing? But they vanish pretty quickly.

I wish I had bought the I-candy pram, I wish I had chosen a dishwasher instead of a wine rack when we first moved in here and I wish my tumble dryer didn't leave the house as humid as a steam room. My mullet is taking over my life.

The mums I see pushing their silver gleaming buggy's always look so well put together, and well, then there is me, in comparison, pushing my mud and vomit encrusted three wheeler looking like something the dog just threw up, with Kate bush hair and black, sleep deprived eyes.

Will I ever be good enough?

Maybe I should ask some of these amazing perfect mother specimens if they can come around here and do some stuff for me.

Maybe I could just be honest?

Would I be stoned like a witch if I was? Would they take Addison off me?

The Irish one was concerned but I think I have managed to hide it all beneath pretending to be ditzy and a bit thick.

I am not thick though.

I will need to learn how to do crafts and shit soon though.

Will The Irish One ever realise that 'sitting around all day' is actually exhausting in ways he will never understand?

When will my vagina stop stinging?

I have managed to assure him I am fine, because I am fine.

I just need to keep swimming. Just Keep Swimming.

Dear Mother Nature...

I am writing to you today, as I am unable to get through on your 24 hour helpline. I am growing increasingly annoyed due to having been placed on hold countless times, before being connected briefly and then being cut off, as you ensure something else goes a miss, usually in the form of a screaming baby, a shitting vomiting dog, or this morning (thanks for this one by the way) both at the same time. As you are no doubt aware, I then have to hang up my praying hands and call back later. (The middle finger at the sky is unnecessary; I understand that, however it is just a reflex at this point. You go too far sometimes ok?)

And besides, your automated system is awful. Continuously asking me to call back later (Magic 8 ball – seriously? If that is not a copout then I don't know what is! Who thought of that little triangle of frustration? A MAN! A MAN DID THAT'S WHO! AND YOU MADE THEM TOO!) When later is too late. I need to talk to you right this second! I have looked for an address for your complaints department but am unable to find one, another example of your shoddy workmanship, as of late.

I will not, however, be swept under the carpet like a discarded fish cracker. I will write this letter and I will bloody ensure you receive it on a wing and a prayer. (I will not send it with UPS who seem to LOSE EVERYTHING!!!)

Basically Mother Nature, my complaint goes a little like this.

I wee when I sneeze.

> I wee when I bend down.
> I wee when I laugh.

This used to amuse me.

TWO and a bit MONTHS LATER?!?!

Not so much. I am sick of buying Tena Lady.

Quite frankly I still feel embarrassed and uncomfortable at the checkout.

It's as though buying Tena Lady gives every checkout/new mother/granny an opening to tell you about how leaky they are too.

DO I LOOK LIKE I WANT TO KNOW THESE THINGS?!?

I just want to buy my gin and chocolate (The secret girls guide to a great night in... alone) and be done with it!

> I have no control over my fart reflexes and you know as well as I do, I am back at work soon.

I do not need to elaborate on this. JUST STOP OK? Just stop!!!

> I still cry at the Dogs trust advert/anything remotely soppy/tramps and every time ANYTHING sad comes on the telly.

Not good when you are sitting at a friend's house and Mr. Lopard (off Handy frigging Manny) loses his cat (although in fairness it was awful, he was desperate!! Even Addison was whimpering!!)

Do you not want me to have friends?? Well don't you?? Someone asked me if I wanted to sign a petition against child trafficking the other day. It took me 9 minutes to sign it, what with all the tears and wailing about the poor trafficked children.

It was for the BODY SHOP! She was way out of her league with me poor PR girl, and kept offering me free lip-gloss. (Which I took, so thanks for that one.)

> BUT my hair is still falling out but now you have added to my embarrassment further by growing it back in tufts at the front. I have mentioned this before, the mullet? Not a good look on me.
>
> My stretch marks seem to be going nowhere, I appear to have been run over by a sixteen wheeler, or mauled by a tiger in the dead of night.
>
> My back is buggered. I am like a geriatric. I wince and groan and *oof* whenever I stand up.

I am 30 for god sake! And now my fingers and wrists seem to be seizing up too!?! What is all *that* about??

> I have no control of my anger. If I throw the remote/full bottle of mile/poodle at The Irish One, one more time he will leave. (Hopefully. I don't mean that..... Ahem..... Oh poor Irish One... here come the tears.... Let me go hug him... poor soldier.... Wanker said he was too busy for a hug!!!... I'll BATTER HIM!!! .....See no control!!)

And finally,

> Why have you removed my ability to say no to chocolate??

I used to be able to say no?! Now I find myself sweeping my arm along the confectionary aisle in Morrison's. I have no self-control!!!

You're a bitch is what you are.

Forgive my anger and disappointment, but really, I am sure, even you can understand my utter disbelief at these, simply disturbing and horrifying games you seem to be enjoying playing.

So my question to you Mother Nature, are you taking the piss? What happened to the customer is always right? As mentioned previously I cannot express in words my disappointment with your recent service.

And before I go on, please rest assured I have not always felt this way, hence my current disappointment. At one time I found myself in wondrous awe at the magnitude of brilliance you seemed so easily to fulfil.

I have watched trees blow in the wind, snow fall in April, and little lambs playing with their sheepy mothers in May. I have seen kittens take their first steps, watched in awe at waterfalls and all manner of beauty over the last 3 decades. I have constantly respected and sang your praises.

However, at this juncture in my life, I have to ask you again.

Are you taking the piss?

What the hell were you thinking when you created childbirth?

I can't even enjoy sex anymore.

You ruined that too. I know how it ends!

I am waiting with NO anticipation for your reply. Although I am sure it will come. I am sure you will rain it down on me in your usual un-adultered and tremendous way.

I will not be wearing white trousers tomorrow. Just so you know, so you'll have to think of something else! I know I am three days late, but I know the minute I reach for those white trousers you will ensure it arrives!!!!

I may be unable to poo without wincing, but I am not stupid. I see you coming.

Yours sincerely.

Lexy Ellis.

PS –OHMYGODIAMTHREEDAYSLATE!!!

Period of adjustment...

I don't know why I was worrying about not getting my period because it isn't like we are having sex, you know?

It has been over two months now and although I know he must be gagging for it, I am pretty sure if I was to give him a full frontal body shot, he would scream like a little girl and then liken the experience to what the SAW victims went through.

Well, he is a man, so he'd probably still be up for it, but I just couldn't put him through it again.

We did try a little while ago but it felt like I was being shagged with an overzealous stapler gun. It was absolute agony and I imagine shagging me again at this moment would be like shagging an enormous sack of jelly with a mullet, nipples as dark as the night and a grimace which would be off putting at best.

I just can't bear the thought of him touching and seeing my body. The very thought of it makes me want to cut my skin hard.

Of course he is saying all the right things.

I am beautiful, I am gorgeous, I am the mother of his child... but to be honest, it just turns me off more.

Because when I look in the mirror, I do not like what I see.

I do not like who I am.

I am a selfish, ugly germ.

How do you have sex when you are a mother?

I mean, even if I could put to one side, the fact I am still in agony and am absolutely terrified of what will happen should anything ever be *placed gently* down in that area again, how do you have sex when you have no idea who you are anymore, and the only thing you seem to be, is a crap mother?

I can't be raunchy! I am a mother.

I can't be romantic and sensual (*shudder*) I am a mother.

So basically it is not happening again yet, but I have a feeling I will have to give in soon.

But happily, I now have my period, so that is ~~5, 7,~~ 12 guilt free days of saying no. (15 if I push it.)

It is a bloody minefield. Quite literally.

I thought having a baby was the point of sex with someone you love?

Well we have one now!

Give it a rest and leave me alone!

My libido must have been removed with the afterbirth.

It's been a hard day's night...

I opened my sweet and simple, pink and bobbly valentines' day card yesterday to find the message;

'I love you baby. You are definitely the one.'

Now don't get me wrong,

The 15 year old inside me began to jump up and down and scream 'he lovessss me, he really lovessss me! Before ringing every one of her friends and repeating the message down the phone in to the early hours, daydreaming about marriage and kids...

The 20 year old inside me tilted her head to the side and muttered 'That's so sweet! Margarita? Acid tab? Come on, let's dance!!'

The 25 year old inside me read the message twice, looking for a hidden meaning 'Has he typed the wrong name? Did he spell my name wrong? Does he really mean it? Is this card one of a pack? Just *how* many women does he *have* on the go?'

The 30 year old pregnant woman inside me tutted and thought 'I should hope so too, I am having your baby in 6 months.'

But in the present day and time, upon reading the handwritten note on the card, while boiling the kettle with one hand and burping the baby with the other, my first thought, if I am honest, was;

The one what? The one you want to maim with a blunt gardening tool?

The one you want to bury under the patio?

The one you want to attach a gag too? (To shut me up, because of my *constant nagging* – not because of any kinky sex game, (the 21 year old inside me just sighed in disappointment).

The one what? I am the one, what? I AM THE ONE WHAT IRISH ONE? THE ONE WHAT? I BLOODY HATE WHEN YOU DO THIS, JUST BLOODY TELL ME WHAT YOU ARE THINKING! YOU THINK I AM A BAD MOTHER DONT YOU? NO? NO? YOU DON'T? WHAT EXACTLY IS THAT *NO* SUPPOSED TO MEAN? I'M NOT A BAD MOTHER BUT I'M FAT? AM I? IS THAT WHAT YOU THINK? NO? NO? WELL WHY DID YOU RAISE YOUR EYEBROW? WHY THE HELL DID YOU ....' (Insert any mental meandering here.)

Because let us just be honest here.

This year so far, mostly the weeks since Addison's arrival, have not been easy.

So *hard,* has this been on the both of us, especially after my meltdown last week putting clothes on, that I did wonder at one point whether I would *even receive* a valentines card, and thought perhaps a death threat would be more fitting.

Don't get me wrong (again) I love him to death, I really do. There have been times in the last month I have *literally* wanted to pummel him (*with how much I love him)* to death, but seriously?!?!

This first 'trimester' of being parents, (Other than the *obvious total joy* of being parents and confirming our love *yada yada yada*) had been fucking tough!! (There is no polite way of putting that, I searched. There really isn't. And '*bloody tough'*, makes me think of an old man in a cap with a sheep dog. I don't know why. Maybe because of my Uncle David... he doesn't have either. But he does say 'bloody tough' a lot. So I used *fucking* ok? It just has more emphasis. More *boom.* And the kids should be in bed by now, so I hope it's ok. I hope its *fucking* ok, ok? I hope it is. For Fucks Sake.)

When I was up the *duff* (or when I *had an excuse for being a lard arse* – yes thanks dear) *anyone who was anyone* and *every man and their dog* would rush to my huffing puffing (and usually food –a-stuffing) *form* and with great glee, mirth and delight, gaily inform me of just how *'hard'* having a new born baby was.

I would (continue to stuff my face while) whole heartedly agreeing with what each *busy body all-knowing patronising idiot,* sorry, sorry, I mean, while whole heartedly agreeing with everything *they* said while *ummming* and *ahhhhing* and faux listening to all the *cobblesworth* (an Uncle David word) that every random stranger over enunciated in my direction.

'Oh yes I know it will be hard,' I'd say in between bites of lard *'sleepless nights and all that. Yah!'* before slowly and precisely thudding my way back to the burger van.

Seriously? If a random stranger has the nerve to walk over to a 'heavily' pregnant woman (I was 4 months at the time – cheeky bitch) and inform her with a huge grin, I may add, of just how *hard* it is going to be, why couldn't she just go the whole hog and be more *PRECISE!*

'Not only is it hard but you will feel a surge of irritation for your other half, at times, that is unbridled in its devastation. You will speak all manner of ugliness to one another in the early hours of the morning. Sleep deprivation will ensure you forget your wifely duties with ease and when he does look amorously towards you, you will find yourself looking for something to hit him with.'

There I said it.

'Oh and word of advice? Remove anything from the home *pre-birth,* that is too light in consistency or too *precious*, to be thrown, as the likelihood is, it will be sailing through the air towards his Irish head before you know your hand has even moved.'

'Yes that includes the dog.'

I also wish I had been told that *even* when I lost weight, my body would never be the same. I am a TOTALLY DIFFERENT SHAPE!? I tried on a pre pregnancy *pencil* work skirt today just for kicks, just to properly examine the damage, and I can't even get it over my thighs. I can zip it up, around my knees, but I am pretty sure that even if I had managed to huff it the rest of the way up, it would now be *baggy* on my stomach and seam split-tingly tight on my arse.

So basically, I wish I had been told;

'You will want to throttle The Irish One at times, this is normal'

'During the aforementioned *surge of irritation,* you will attempt to throw a high chair and a poodle at him. This is also normal' (Nail that high chair down, *seriously*. I was shocked at how high I got it off the ground.) (Er, the baby wasn't in it – don't worry.) (Honest.)

'You will lose weight from everywhere but your arse and upper back (I look like hulk Hogan from behind!) This is normal.'

Is that what you meant by *hard* little old woman? WELL IS IT?? USE YOUR WORDS!!!

Anyway, as it turns out, the card doesn't mean he wishes I were THE ONE who was dead. (Over analyse? Me?) It means (and I quote)

'One day I hope to marry you, I love you so much, I know this few weeks has been taxing (PAH! Taxing?) On us, but I seriously love you for every day, for giving me a son and for being as sexy as the day I met you.'

Which was pretty lovely to hear. (Nice try with the sexy. It isn't happening. I've been up since 5am and smell like a mixture of Calgel, Calpol and puke. Maybe next year babe. You know, if I am still the one by then.)

It *has* been hard times. (As well as wonderful and beautiful and we are still so in love *yada yada...*) But now we have another month to go, and then another and another and another.

Apparently that's when it'll get easier. *Relationship wise.*

I Hope so, or I don't hold out much hope of us growing old together.

Because I will kill him.

That's what I wrote in his card.

'Man up or sleep with one eye open.'

What? At least I was honest.

Forgotten...

I am not sure what I am supposed to be doing with Addison.

I know what I am *not* supposed to be doing with Addison.

I am not supposed to be playing airplanes, if he doesn't have a god damn nappy on that's for freaking sure.

I learnt that the hard way.

'Irish One! Irish ONE!! I HAVE BEEN SHOT!! I CAN'T SEE, OH MY GOD I AM BLIND! I HAVE BEEN SHOT WITH SHIT!'

I have had bright pink eyes for the last 3 days and nothing but the occasional snigger off The Irish One, but anyway, surely Addison should have seen the doctor or the health visitor again by now?

I called the Drs. Surgery again this morning (more shit in your eye Lex? *fake laugh* no no not this time!) And they seemed surprised I hadn't had any communications about jabs for him or anything.

Apparently he should have had some by now.

They said they would contact my local health authority office and get somebody out to see me straight away.

I hope it isn't the same health visitor as last time because I could really do with talking to somebody about a few things, and Helen having experienced me inexplicably passing wind through my 'front bum' while she was staring in to my innards, I am not sure I could retain eye contact.

I would be quite happy never to see *bouncy* Helen again, ever.

I need to tell someone who hasn't had a poke around inside me, that I feel a bit like, well a bit, a bit like this isn't just the baby blues and I need to discuss that if it is Postnatal depression, what can I do to make it go away?

Plastering a smile on my face is getting harder every day.

And also.

Yesterday when we got home from the supermarket there was a girl stood in my kitchen.

I saw her as clear as day but when I blinked she was gone.

I saw her AS.CLEAR.AS.DAY.

I am frightened.

And I am telling nobody.

Am I going mad?

Bat Shit Crazy...

I must live in the moment.

I don't want to end up in some mental hospital with Addison having been taken off me.

That just can't happen.

I would die without him. He is my best friend.

I must live in the moment.

I must take deep breaths.

Think rational thoughts.

I must not freak out.

What can I hear if I close my eyes and take deep breaths?

Yes everything is ok.

I can hear the sound of Doodle licking his bollocks romantically in his bed next to me.

Over my ragged breath, I can also hear the clunky clanky tinkering of The Irish One fixing his bike in the kitchen (because why do it outside? Outside makes no sense!!!) While muttering expletives under his breath and faintly, if I focus, I can hear my Barmy and adored, sweet smelling boy snoring, mouth wide open, in his cot.

All is as it should be.

Deep breaths. Do not freak out. It will not happen. Don't freak out don't freak out don't freak out. I do not want to end up in a hospital.

It has reared its violent head again.

I went for a lie down at 8pm 'to rest my eyes for five minutes' after loving every moment of snuggling with Addison, telling stories of tractors who could talk and dogs who could fly.

I lay down peacefully, promising to rest for only five minutes.

What must have been hours later I found myself sitting bolt upright in bed, my heart hammering and dripping with hot tears and sweat. I could hear gunshots.

'Irish one!' I screamed in to the darkness after reaching out to grab him and with a huge sense of dread realising he wasn't't there. 'Oh my god, Irish one! Where are you?'

He burst through the bedroom door like a shocked and panama cladd warrior.

'What's the matter?' He shouted racing towards the bed in what I thought was panic and worry for me. (Turns out I was screaming like I was being stabbed and he was worried the neighbors may think he was bludgeoning me.)

'Stop screaming woman!!'

'Are we at war?' I whispered clutching his shoulder and grabbing the PlayStation remote from his tight fist in case I needed to brandish it as a weapon later on.

'No you idiot,' he laughed, 'I am playing Assassins Creed on PS3 I will turn it down.'

As my heart began to slow, I scowled in his general direction mentally digging him a shallow grave and handed him back his remote.

I was intending to go back to sleep. But I couldn't't sleep. I knew it was back. I recognise the heaviness in my head from the day when I booked that 'holiday.'

I felt as if I had invited it in. Immediately I was disappointed in myself and anxious. Don't freak out. Don't freak out.

Something had crept in to bed behind me, and was now spooning with me, breathing its hot breath on to my neck, making all of my hair stand on end.

Psychosis. This must be psychosis. I googled it. These are the symptoms.

Go away. Please go away.

A feeling of dread so worrying, I am now, a week later, still struggling to function. All I can think about is what if I lose my waking mind completely and accidentally drown Addison in the bath or something, believing I am washing pots?

Calm down. You are ok. You just haven't slept enough.

You are imagining it.

Things are improving. They have been improving over the last three days.

Doodle is slowly starting to realise 5 years after emerging from his doggy mother's womb that outside is where he must poo and the rocky start I had at motherhood myself, is just starting to feel lovely, like deep down in my bones, awe inspiring, heart rupturing lovely.

Everything is ok. Deep breaths. Don't freak out.

But no, I know it is there waiting for me, seeping in at my edges, the darkness, the paranoia, I can feel it, no matter how much I argue with myself. I see blinks of this girl I know can't actually be there.

She is there.

Has The Irish One spiked my tea? He repeatedly denies it, his brow furrowing with worry and of course, then I laugh.

Set his mind at rest. Before surreptitiously creeping in to the kitchen and pouring my cup of tea down the sink. I will make a new cup of tea, and I will keep my eyes on it. He may be trying to spike me. You never know.

Ok. I think we have a problem. Do those girls hate me really? Will they follow me back to my car and throw bricks at me and my baby? Are they plotting to follow me home? Do they call me fat and see evil in me? Are they planning to steal my baby? I must tell them I made my baby up. I must pretend he doesn't exist that I am pushing a doll. No harm can come to my baby.

Ok. I think we may have a problem.

And then I am lost.

The deep breathing has not helped. I know with certainty right now it will happen. The moment I dread. The moment I am pulled roughly from the serene moment I am resting my lips peacefully on my son's forehead, or inhaling his sweet playful childishness as he smacks his lips together in his sleep, and everything will just... disappear.

I will blink myself from this life and find myself in a stark white room 30 years from now stinking to high heaven of hospitals and bleach, tethered to a bed with an old man leaning over me, his teeth yellowing and his complexion pale, begging me to come home and get better.

I will recognise nobody. I won't know what happened. I was putting my son to bed and I blinked.

The old man will be The Irish One but of course, I won't recognise him, having only seen him three minutes before when he was swearing in the kitchen and leaving greasy oil prints everywhere.

Now. I mean... just then! What happened? I want to go back.

'Lexy,' he will tenderly whisper in my ear, his salty old coffee breath gushing over my senses, 'I am your husband we have been married 30 years today, Addison is here to see you, can you remember him? Are you lucid?'

'You don't like coffee' I will whisper confused, 'You Can't be him' my eyes wide with fear, my heart exploding with every beat from my chest.

'Mike wazaouski' he will whisper our private joke playfully in my ear, and I will instantly know it is him and I will turn to ice.

'Mum.' I will hear his voice before I see him and I will sense his tears, his heartbreak at how his mother went Bat shit crazy 'Mum, it's me, Addison. Are you lucid?'

I will turn slowly, my head a dead weight filled with fear and disbelief and I will look at the grown up man stood at the end of my bed.

My heart will catch in my throat. Don't freak out. I missed it all. I missed him growing up. I missed it all. No.

'No!' I will want to scream long and hard.

'Mum' he will whisper, his little lopsided smile and cracked baby teeth, long gone, his baby blue eyes once filled with vulnerability now replaced by life experience I haven't witnessed, a life with his mother trapped in another world. A life where his mother abandoned him.

And I will howl in desperation, where is my son, where has his smell gone, his little milk stained pajamas? Where are our moments? The man at the end of the bed cannot be my son, he just can't, my son is not even a year old.

And I will black out.

Ok. I think we may have a problem. Don't freak out. Everything is ok.

Addison is asleep in his cot.

Concentrate on the now. But will now be the moment it happens? That my years will be violently stolen? I am still in bed. I can hear Doodle farting.

Concentrate on the now. It is all ok. The Irish One has come in.

He is shouting at me to calm down.

He sounds worried.

I must be freaking out.

I am trapped in my imaginary world.

Heart racing, panicked, mouth dry, and the room swinging in and out of focus.

I must live in the moment.

I must not freak out.

I must not get too upset and angry when I hear people off handedly label others, with mental health issues, funny names.

How can they know what I am going through if I haven't told anyone?

Wouldn't they still call me funny names though?

I must live in the moment.

A panic attack will only ever be a panic attack.

The Irish One is getting really concerned I can tell. I will lie, cheat and kill before I admit to this being anything other than a bad dream.

How can I ever aadmit I am 'Bat shit crazy.'

I love you but please don't bring a horse...

Choosing a godmother and Godfather has been something of a dilemma for The Irish One and myself.

Actually I take that back. It has been a dilemma for me. (The one with *DRAMA QUEEN* stamped under her passport picture.)

The Irish One picked one of his friends.

I don't know him very well yet, but he is fantastic with Addison and only lives half an hour away, so I am sure he will come up and visit him all the time and this situation of me not knowing him very well will be rectified over time. His girlfriend also seems to have a fondness for shopping and vodka I can totally relate to as well, so I was pleased with The Irish Ones choice.

See and that's where we differ.

The Irish One faces a problem or dilemma and he fixes it. (The Irish One with Jim stamped under his passport picture. - As in, *Jim'll fix it*. His real name is not Jim. Just in case you were wondering. The Irish One that is, not the godfather. (Cue freaky music and a dead horses head.)

For me on the other hand it wasn't so easy. Not because I am a lonely cow, who nobody loves *(cough cough lying cow cough cough)* But because I am hugely popular and desirable and everybody loves me. (*cough cough that's what you think cough cough.)*

In all honesty though, it was a tough call because I have so many beautiful and lovely women in my life, I wanted to choose them all. Which I very nearly did. (I got a bit giddy on gas and air during the labour and apparently was asking anybody who gave me an internal, to be my son's spiritual guide. Including the lunch lady. She didn't give me an internal. I just asked her if she wanted to. To be god-mother that is. *Not to give me an internal......* Ill shut up now.)

I am not religious. My understanding of god mother was always '*she who shall look after my child if I was to be hit by a bus*' and '*she who shall baby-sit at a moment's notice and guide my son through girls, smoking and the importance of using a condom.*' (When he is older, that is. MUCH *MUCH* **MUCH** OLDER!) and **obviously** -'*she who shall take a haggard mother out on the piss following a horrific birthing experience and hold her hair back while she vomits up three glasses of wine, a vodka cranberry and a dodgy chicken kebab*'

So who was the lucky woman?

It wasn't easy to decide between them all but I felt I needed to choose the friend I have known the longest in the whole world. The friend I made secret 'dens' with when I was five. The friend who's mum was allowed to tell me off for being cheeky. The friend who came with us on every family holiday growing up. The friend who got me in trouble. The friend who I got in trouble, and the friend who literally carried me through the death of my only brother in 2005.

I rang her walking back from the crematorium screaming with the pain of having just seen his beautiful face unmoving and very much dead. She sobbed and snotted with me, virtually held me as I broke down at the side of the road and responded to me with similar heartbreak having also grown up with him, and with an equal measure of tears.

'I am under my desk at work Lexy. I am crying as hard with you. I am crying with you from under my desk at work. It is only my second day here so I probably shouldn't be under my desk crying but I am, and I am here for you. I am sorry Lexy, I am so sorry' and in that moment she flicked a switch.

My hysterical crying was flipped to hysterical laughter at the mental image of her and although it was short lived, it helped me find a laugh.

That was following the single hardest moment of my entire life, and she provided, albeit inadvertently, an escape hatch from the break in my heart, and she provided the support I needed even though it put her in a compromising position. That is something I have never thanked her properly for.

She is more than my friend. She is my family. She is somebody I admire and somebody I want my son to love as much as I do. She is charming, gorgeous, caring, kind, sensitive, a total nutcase and most of all? She is a bloody great laugh!

If I get hit by a bus? I want my son to laugh.

(Not by the fact I was hit by a bus but later in life. I want him to have laughter *in his life.* But not directly after. A little bit of grieving would be nice. I mean, I held his butt cheeks apart to help him fart, for god sake. So yes son, laugh, but not straight away. You know what I mean right...I'll shut up now.)

So well done Lady! You are Addison's God-mummy! He loves you, I love you, we all love you!

Can you baby-sit Friday night?

Dory...

The Irish One has decided to start growing potatoes on our kitchen windowsill.

I paused there so that the full horror of what I am telling you can sink in.

The man has ultimately thought about it long and hard, and has evidently come to the conclusion that growing potatoes, in an already crammed two bedroom flat in the middle of industrial Hell Manchester, is a sensible and normal thing to do.

And it's not only potatoes.

It's tomatoes too.

I have started to gently contemplate suicide.

Although the two events seemed to kick-start around the same time, I am almost sure they are not related.

Almost.

'What in the hell is this on the windowsill?'

The windowsill, by the way, was the only surface in this godforsaken flat of Doom* that hadn't already been taken up by some form of clutter.

My windowsill was glorious. It reminded me of days gone by.

Half a meter of shiny white, varnished wood that on the one sunny day of the year would shine and glint, occasionally reminding me of sunsets in the Caribbean when I worked near there and of a life spent growing up in Spain free of the doldrums of this existence and occasionally in my darker moments, it would remind me of wood worm.

And then I would want to smash it to smithereens.

Because, seriously how can t*he very thought* of a worm that eats *wood* just not freak you out?

It cannot be natural.

Does the worm go hard?

And if not?

HOW COME? It is EATING WOOD!

"It's Potatoes! Addy and I are starting a mini allotment! Isn't it a great idea?'

'Addison doesn't even know what a potato is Irish One.'

'He does. I've been telling him all about the Famine.'

I had been out of the house for four hours finally getting the blonde put back in my hair.

4 hours.

This is how long it took for an indoor allotment to be created in my kitchen.

Can you imagine what would happen if I left them to their own devices for longer than this?

Doodle would be sharing his bed with chickens, that is what would happen.

We are only one step away from chickens!

And I have a phobia of EGGS! (Yes. Eggs. They freak me out. I don't understand how they can't freak everybody out?! Imagine you grew a shell around your period, and then someone fried it up? It is *farking* weird and gross and creepy. Eucchhh the shell. I can't cope with the shell.)

Anyway. I am so bored of what is happening in my brain at least this provides a little distraction.

Blah blah blah, I want to hang myself, or suffocate myself, or maybe tie bricks to my feet and go for a swim in the Quays, blah blah blah... you are not good enough, everyone would be better off without you blah blah *bloody* blah.

I am bored of having no control over my wandering thoughts, but I am even more tired and exhausted of feeling this way, of shuffling my dusty feet around and around in circles seemingly making absolutely no progress further than the occasional bout of euphoria, usually only caused by accidentally spotting Selfridges stock a new Marc Jacobs handbag, which I can no longer afford.

I am sinking here.

I am so bored of sinking.

Of being.

But what the hell is he thinking?

Potatoes?

Is he *trying* to push me over the edge?

Our flat is tiny and already has *four* heartbeats crammed in to it.

8 if you count the Guppy fish we inherited from the upstairs neighbour who randomly moved to china.

Do fish even have heartbeats? Wouldn't a heartbeat in something so tiny put them off their stroke? Annoy them?

I am not going to be as predictable as to regale you with how I feel I can relate to those fish if I stare at them long enough, endlessly swimming around their prison, stuck, being able to see what life is like on the other side of the glass but never being able to reach it, with no hope, completely reliant on a small pair of child bum smelling hands, to provide their happiness, their sustenance.

But I will be honest. Sometimes I think they may be communicating with me.

Boc Boc Boc Bo BOC BOC, basically means; 'Kill us now you miserable bitch, or at the very least shave your damn legs and get off the Sofa.

(Boc Boc Boc is how fish talk. I am also aware chickens talk like this. DO you see a pattern emerging here? BECAUSE I DO!)

But I can't. I have no energy left. And the energy I do have I am certainly not going to waste on getting up off the sofa and shaving.

And now?

The Irish One is growing potatoes on the windowsill.

And most of my time is spent trying not to take an overdose.

Although the two *may* not be related, they definitely kicked off around the same time.

A tale of Woe...

There were three things that my Aunty Olive used to say to me as a child, her face shoved directly in to mine. (Personal space didn't exist in those days.)

1) Enjoy your school days; they are the best years of your life.

2) Always wear nice underwear in case you are involved in an accident.

3) The dentist is terrifying, so brush your teeth.

And 4) save me all your orange Smarties.

Apart from the last one, because I agree, orange Smarties are the tastiest, I just put it down to her being a boring old *grown up* who was a little bit bonkers.

School days are the best years of my life? *Are you on glue* old woman? (I didn't *actually* say this to her, I was six at the time. But if I had it would have been that sticky glue you could peel of your hands an hour later. More satisfying than sex that!)

Have you seen my uniform? Do you think Grey is an *attractive* colour on me? Have you forgotten how *awful* school is?

Have you forgotten how *truly terrifying* reading out loud is, in front of the *whole class*? Have you forgotten how cruel kids can be, when you are a little bit chubby, have a bowl haircut and wear 3 inch thick glasses? Have you *never* met my Spanish teacher? Mrs. Chancellor was a five foot nothing, battle-axe with a short blonde ponytail and a gaze that could turn you to stone. Now she was *terrifying*! Get a verb wrong and you had to stand at the front of the class with one foot in the dustbin while repeating the correct one over and over again. Get caught passing notes and you would get *clobbered* over the head with a wooden parrot on a stick. School days aren't the best days of my life, Aunty Olive!! They are *horrific*!!

And as time has gone by, my views on this have **not** changed as every grown up at the time suggested they would. I hated every second of my primary and secondary school career and to this day the very thought of it makes me positively shudder. The cool kids, *shudder*. The bullying kids, *shudder*. Patrick and Tony (the school 'hot guys' who looking back were total losers) making my life a living hell, *shudder*. The woman was wrong ok? *WRONG!*

The nice underwear comment went *way* over my head and was completely forgotten about until I was *circa* the age of 24. I was working in a call centre attempting but failing miserably to sell ATM machines to news agents and other small businesses who really didn't need them, when the stress of dealing with Mr. Smith the butcher, must have got too much and I fainted and hit the deck. I was rushed from the office in the back of an ambulance to the local A&E department.

On arriving I awoke, a little dizzy and a little mortified to find I would need a scan and would be staying in overnight for observation. As they passed me an open backed gown to wear, the somewhat now haunting words of my Aunty Olive crescendo's around my head in surround sound, while a little bubble with her face emblazoned on it floated over my left shoulder. 'Always wear nice underwear' said her patronising voice. 'In case you have an accident!'

Damn it. I should have listened. It was washing day. I was going commando.

That was an awkward conversation with the nurse, *let me tell you.* (And paper knickers, are Impossible to sleep in!)

The last one, used to baffle me. I mean, how can you be scared of a dentist? All he does is look in your mouth and then you get a sticker and a lollipop. You also get an afternoon off school if you are lucky enough! How can anybody be scared of the dentist? I never really understood.

Now I do.

I have had toothache for a while but having never been scared of the dentist wasn't worried when on a preliminary visit the kind old dentist looked in my mouth, nodded and advised me with a kind shrug that I would need a root canal. 'Don't worry about it at all,' he said, putting me at ease immediately. 'It won't hurt a bit.'

'No Big deal,' I happily responded looking around, 'I will book my next appointment when I go downstairs. Can I have my Lollipop now?'

The weeks have passed and yesterday with my appointment looming, I realized that going to the dentist in the throes of the worst bout of stomach flu I have ever experienced probably wasn't the *best* idea. However, I was in so much pain, and as I am an idiot, I put these warning signals to the back of my mind and arrived at the dentist with time to spare.

As I sat down in the waiting room, I was surprised to feel a few butterflies in my stomach. Was this another bout of the runs? No it couldn't be! I had nothing in my stomach! It must be nerves! What is up with me? I thought. Root canal is nothing! That is what everyone has said. Compared to *childbirth* Root canal is nothing!

I sat pondering this for a few moments, until with a short gasp the penny dropped. Compared to *CHILDBIRTH??* Everything is a doddle compared to sodding *CHILDBIRTH!* Oh my god this is going to hurt isn't it?! I looked around, a mild panic culminating in my bowels.

'Ooo dentistssss are terrriiifyyyingggg, you should have brusssheeed your teeethhh' my Aunty Olive whispered in my ear, her head floating around in front of my eyes.

Oh shut up you old bag. I'll be fine.

'Pardon?' The receptionist barked, snapping her head up to meet my eyes.

Had I spoken out loud?!?!? 'Nothing' I laughed self-consciously 'just talking to myself again.'

She looked back down at her computer, thankfully but I didn't miss her rolling her eyes for good measure. Bitch.

What proceeded to happen over the next hour is honestly something I am **not** proud of and can only be truly understood and appreciated if you think back to those old *carry on* films.

No my breasts did not pop out of my top and no there was no Kenneth Williams camping it up in the waiting room, but as my name was called and I began my assent up the steep stairs towards the *operating room*, my heart began to pound and for every step I took, my stomach flu got the better of me, as a little *wind* escaped from my *over troubled* tummy. I was walking with a trumping soundtrack, totally against my will.

Reaching the top of the stairs, clenching like a mad woman with a red face, and dreading looking the receptionist in the eye on my return, I was met with an Italian looking model type. My mouth dropped open and I prayed I wasn't about to greet him in a *runny bum* scented cloud of perfume.

'*Cam* in' He said in an Italian, cockney accent. '*Itss Lexeeee*, isn't it? I can see from Dr. Hamilton, that you need a filling and a *raout* canal. He isn't here today, so I will be *piforming di proceeeddurrre,* which one would you like *mee* to *doo* today?'

His over pronunciation immediately reminded me of *Allo Allo* and my mind went in to overdrive. I cannot laugh at this man, for this man is *too sexy*, but how can I allow this man in my mouth, when I will undoubtedly bite his finger off from laughing if he speaks?

'Yes, *Ai* need both' I stuttered like an idiot, and for some reason in a god awful Jamaican *school of comedy voices* accent. What the hell is wrong with me? '*Noice* to meet *yao,*' I continued, sounding like a total eejit, while following him in to the room and smiling at the dental nurse. '*Ai* fink I need you to look *at my canal.* I mean,' I gasped flustered '*AI* fink I need you to take a look *up my canal,*' Oh the humiliation of being nervous! ' Ai mean I think I need you to *do my canal.* It hurts.' I managed to revert back to my normal voice just in time to catch his eyes widen and a look of total confusion pass across his features.

'*Where a youuu frommm?*' His eyebrows knotted, in confusion.

'From *ere,*' I laughed, now for some reason, speaking in the worst French comedy accent you have ever heard ' I just get a bit cuckoo when I'm nervuuusse' I giggled like a school girl.

This was not going well.

He looked at me like I was suffering with a brain disorder and the dental nurse, who must have seen this behaviour a hundred times off nervous women in the face of this dental *Adonis,* just smirked and turned around.

'Ok, *Lexeeeee,*' he sighed, having also clearly seen this a few times and probably thinking he should move back to Italy 'Pleaz lie back an open wide so I can ave a *looooek.*'

I popped my bag down on the chair opposite and climbed on to his operating chair like a dog would climb up on to a sofa. Why I didn't just walk around the chair and plonk my arse down before swinging my legs up, like any normal person would, I don't know. I had spoken to him in three comedy accents *against my will,* and now found myself on *all fours,* facing him on his dental chair.

All I can say in my defense is, I am a nightmare when I am nervous, I lose all control and my brain does horrible things on purpose to embarrass me. If you couple this with the fact I have been operating on autopilot for months, and *then coming to, in* the face of this model dentist, you must be able to understand? I had totally *sizzled* all the connections to rational thought and was now a rogue mother who was not *on* the edge, but who had fallen *over* the edge and was clearly losing her mind.

He watched me turn over and finally lie back with a confused expression before asking me if I was ok. Again.

'Not really,' I sighed trying not to look him in the eye. 'I have a terrible stomach flu and I am very nervous.'

He recoiled.

Up until yesterday I wouldn't have been able to fully describe what the word *recoil* actually looks like. But now I could.

'Ok' he said a little nervously, now clearly understanding where the smell was coming from 'let's get started, you aren't allergic to anything are you?' He added as an afterthought before pulling the biggest needle I have ever seen, from behind his back.

'No' I almost screamed, seeing the full girth of the needle for the first time. 'I'm not allergic, but I don't like pain and I hate having things *thrust* in my mouth.'

Yes I actually used the word *thrust.* Against my will I had turned in to a walking, talking Mills and Boon novel. But, hey! At least I hadn't said it in a comedy accent.

'You will be fine,' He smiled kindly as if to a child 'this won't hurt a bit.' (That's what they all say. I thought to myself.)

As it turns out, it didn't hurt *a bit.* It hurt a *bloody lot.* But after it was done he sent me back down to the waiting room for five minutes while the anesthesia kicked in.

Is this normal? Because, I have never heard of a dentist sending you *out* of the room before to wait, but to be honest I can't blame him. After an introduction like that, he was probably thinking twice about ever allowing me back in.

On the way back down the crazy steep stairs I went dizzy and felt my heart speed up. I had just had a shot of god knows what, and this woman probably heard me farting. 'I feel really dizzy' I gasped to the same receptionist, 'is this normal?'

'Have you just had anesthetic?' she replied *boredly* without even looking up. (Which means she probably hadn't heard me trumping. Winner.)

'Yes' I said hopping from one foot to the other, trying to stave off a panic attack.

'There is adrenalin in anesthetic so it is completely normal to feel like that. It will pass' she said before returning to her click, click, clicking. (Nails on a keyboard, not in a district 9 alien, *you fucking prawn!* type way.)

Now having spent the evening previous watching 'G*et him to the Greek'* (which by the way if you haven't seen, you really should. Not usually my thing, as I am not a big Russell Brand fan, but it was hilarious) I immediately thought adrenalin? I need a furry wall! Unfortunately for me it appeared I had also said this out loud!

'You need a what?' the woman looked back up at me with her finger undoubtedly poised on a panic button under the desk.

'A furry wall' I *stupidly* repeated. 'I've had a Jeffrey!' before cracking up laughing and forgetting myself again.

I would like to tell you things got better from here on in, and that I acted normally for the rest of the visit, but they didn't and I didn't.

When he called me back up, I walked back in and noticed he had put on some music. Funk soul brother was quietly playing from the corner of the room and as I lay down and prepared to open wide (oooerrr) the dental nurse passed me a pair of orange glasses which could easily have passed for *full on raver specs.* Do I need to tell you what I did next or can you guess?

Small box, big box, fish. That's right.

Nobody laughed except me.

He had just reached for the drill a while later, when there was an almighty crash of thunder and the room was lit by a bright spark of lightening. I had a mouth full of cotton wool and spit sucking equipment, and both the hot dentist and the nurse were peering over me and in to my mouth. In other circumstances this may have been funny, but all that came to mind was some horrible horror film, especially as he then proceeded to start up the drill.

My heart started to pound as I imagined him butchering me on the chair, and my mind began to lose it when tubular bells came on the radio. (I really need to stop watching horror films!) My mouth started twitching, my heart was racing out of control and I ended up grabbing his wrist, which was attached to the hand holding the drill, making its way towards my mouth and blinking furiously.

I was on the verge of a panic attack, the hot dentist was a murderer! He was going to drill my brain open!!! (He wouldn't find much in there to be honest.) But who would look after Addison? Who would drive my car home? (The things you think of, honestly!)

It was only when I caught the dental nurse starting to snigger that I got a handle on myself and let go of the poor man's hand.

He checked I was ok again, to which I nodded and shut my eyes just in time to feel a huge movement of air in my lower abdomen, as the drill began vibrating my head like Jelly on a dildo. (*I* haven't done this, but I saw Heston do it, ok? And believe me, if you put a dildo in Jelly. The Jelly wobbles... Anyway. Moving on.)

Panic and stomach flu? Evidently *not,* a good combination.

The rest of the appointment was spent clenching my butt cheeks in an attempt not to fart.

I came home with a root canal in place and my dignity flying around somewhere in the wind, on Salford crescent.

I have to go back next week to get it checked. I seriously hope that A) my stomach is better and B) the hot dentist has decided to move back to Italy and it is the nice old man again, or god knows what I may end up doing to embarrass myself.

My Aunty Olive, it turns out, was right. The dentist can be a terrifying prospect.

Now, where did I leave those romantic *laxatives?*

I used to be Cool...

Will there ever come a day when I sneeze and don't involuntarily piss myself?

That's it.

That's all I have to say today.

Except...

I used to be cool you know, even if it was only *I* that deemed it so.

I used to spend hours perusing the fashionable handbags in Selfridges on a Saturday and then go out and get 'funny drunk' with my best friend.

I used to have untamed passionate sex and lie in bed until noon lazing the next day away with a cup of tea and a good book.

I used to have wild parties with fantastically drunk drag queens. I used to wear high heels so tall and make up so elaborate, I would sometimes be mistaken for one myself.

I used to pump the volume up in my two seater convertible car, step my foot on the 'gas' and speed down to Blackpool, wearing huge shades, for a day on the beach with the Poodle and 11 of my closest friends.

I used to stand on the very edge of the ocean, my hands thrown in the air, the elegant dance of freedom lifting the ends of my hair and the salty sunshine in my lungs. I used to believe anything was possible, that my life could be as big as I chose it to be, that time was never ending.

I used to laugh from deep within.

I used to go out on a Friday night after work, just spur of the moment 'yeah I will come for a drink fuck it!' Imagine that!

I used to go to Festivals and know the words to catchy songs. I used to wear my Doc Martins in the sun and dance like I didn't give a fuck, covered in mud, face-paint and sweat.

I used to have money in my purse and a spring in my step.

But I *didn't* have Addison.

And although he just shoved his finger up my nose and sneezed, and I feel like my eyeball *may* have *actually* popped out of its socket for a moment or two there, and I am typing this with my eyes still streaming (with what feels like blood) I wouldn't change it for the world.

OK, maybe I would change it every now and again just for a bit of a break, flit back to Vodka at V fest just every so often, but yeah, it is all definitely becoming more worth it.

He is becoming more interesting to me every day.

My love for him kind of explodes out of my heart and grabs him by the face occasionally now.

I feel like a tiger. If anyone every hurt him I am pretty sure I would rip the skin of their face and stamp on it. (Too much? I apologise.)

Seriously what the hell has he done to my eye?

I swear I can now see a panoramic view of the bedroom, facing forwards.

Is my eyeball actually swinging about on my cheek like a ping pong ball on a shoelace?

Just another day in paradise.

I need to put some slippers on, my feet are freezing.

I used to be cool you know.

Amelie...

It is the hallucinations that are the hardest to deal with.

They come thick and fast now. I don't have time to panic about them anymore. I am kind of just getting used to them.

Imagine your brain as a half-eaten pot of strawberry yoghurt, you know the big silver spoon will soon reappear and hungrily begin scraping and scooping out the final remaining blobs of your sanity, and there is absolutely nothing you can do about it.

That's how they feel.

They eat you from the inside out.

That's not to say that when I am in them, I don't enjoy them.

Well I don't know if I do or I don't.

Ok, that is a blatant lie.

I love this one.

I am an empty pot of yoghurt.

Profound escapism from the mind, caused by the mind.

What woman wouldn't't enjoy that feeling? Like they say, sometimes the fear of something awful happening, is much worse than when it actually does happen. I have no idea where I have come from or where I have been, no recollection of my journey, no idea what I am wearing or how fat my thighs are, whether the dog has been fed or whether Addison's sleep suits will be dry in the morning. I am completely unaware of everything and anything.

I do not know, or seem to care who I am, and whether I am still in fact, behaving as I would allow myself to when consciously making choices. I am unable to remember my name and I have no graspable thought patterns, only feelings. And yet, I remember them wholly, in their entirety.

I am unable to process rational explanations and nor do I feel the need to.

I am, simply put, a cloud of particles, clumped together, made from only what I see before me.

Amelie. Amelie is one of my favorite hallucinations. She is the girl in the kitchen.

Dark skinny jeans on short skinny legs finished off with enormous lace tied black boots. Her frame is delicate, fragile, but you would know instinctively she is anything but. Huge elegant black eyes and under her pond green hooded sweatshirt, hidden away, is a completely hairless head. I do not know why she is bald, but I envy her. Funny, or perhaps not, that I can think of nothing and yet feel with the intensity of heat from a dancing flame.

We meet, at 3am, usually in my grubby and chilly kitchen.

My feet are always bare but I do not feel the cold.

She requests food in a voice that betrays the gentle look of her, like a ravenous street girl. She always asks for food, seems to always be hungry, and yet she never eats. I make her whatever she wants, I don't have it in me to be paranoid about my lack of cooking skills, the fact I haven't done a shop.

I don't know any of these things.

She asks for sustenance and I set about to provide, just like I would do with any of my closest friends. We talk at length, about nonsense. Long drawn out conversations about roller coasters and theme parks, the sticky and yet melt in the mouth delight of candy floss and where deluxe paint colours get their names from.

We giggle in to the night.

I feel vivacious and effervescent, I enjoy the animation in me, the lightness she brings. I could stay with her forever like that, her biting what is left of her scraggy nails and snuggling her wrists under enormous comforting sleeves. Her jumper is too big for her.

I always mean to ask, but I know I will never be able to.

I adore the sound of her laughter, throaty and deep, as if she holds not a single part of her back.

Does not care for judgment.

We feel whole somehow, the two parts connecting.

Is she a fragment of me, perhaps caught in time?

A part, maybe I am desperate to connect with, and yet am unable to?

Or is she nothing to do with me at all, and is simply a smattering of electronic sparks misfiring in my brain while I should be asleep?

The latter is more likely, and this makes me sad.

Or.

Or, is somewhere else in the world, a young bald girl having midnight hallucinations about a fat thirty year old woman with two tone hair and long acrylic nails, wearing her husband pajamas?

It always turns though.

It goes off, like I suppose most things do.

A children's party that has run on too long, the kids all sugar high and fighting, the wedding guest that holds the brides hair back at 4am while she drunkenly vomits in to the toilet bowl, a once beautiful, but now manipulative trophy wife, who peaked too soon.

It all eventually turns to pain.

What is that song? They burnt down paradise and put up a parking lot? She slowly and methodically, almost catatonic, begins to pull her eyelashes out one by one, the salted anguish dripping from her eyes, and although I hate it, I am unable to stop her.

I am transfixed. It is always the same, we laugh until we can laugh no more, and then the harm starts. The more time we spend in each other's company though, the more reluctant she seems for it to end. Almost as if she is never quite ready anymore, to turn off the light. Maybe she needs me like I need her.

It is the nights I spend with Amelie that I am usually awoken by the smoke alarm, or a banshee like Irish one, prodding me and interrogating me as to why I am making sandwiches using unopened Gas bills, badly cut cheese and fairy liquid.

I am an empty yoghurt pot.

I thought I was making Bolognese.

I am often found, he tells me, his eyebrows all knotted together, sniggering in to the washing machine, twirling pasta around in an empty pan, ironing his pajamas while still wearing them.

And when he pulls me out, I am bereft.

Injured sometimes.

Then there follows the migraines, the sickness, the unimaginable struggle to raise my lips in to an upward half crescent, the disbelief that none of it ever happened.

That she doesn't exist.

I remember all of our conversations for a short while, and how she made me feel, but then the memories disperse.

I know they happened, I know how I felt, just like I know how it feels when you give birth, I just can't connect with the feeling anymore.

The memory is there of exactly how I felt, I just can't remember it.

Does that make sense? What would I ask her if I could? This friend that doesn't actually exist. Who are you?

Where have you been?

Do you know my brother?

Whose jumper are you wearing?

How do I know your name?

Can you stop asking me to cook as I am destroying our kitchen and could possibly end up poisoning myself in the process?

She is not real.

I know this.

Except sometimes, she really is.

Some Secrets are too big to share.

The Iron the Bitch and the Wardrobe...

Every time I open my wardrobe I can hear my size 10 jeans calling me a fat arse.

'Soon' I used to whisper to them at the start, fingering them idly *'Soon!'* and then I would proceed to torture myself rotten with guilt, anytime I put anything in my mouth. (Food I mean, you smutty lot!)

Now though, I ignore them completely.

I don't whisper anything. I just grab my one pair of size 16's from right under their snooty little noses, and shake my love handles at them, as I turn around to get dressed. They might miss me, but the truth is, I don't really miss the pressure of them.

'BITTTCHH!'

Sorry about that. They can obviously hear me.

But the truth is I don't miss them. **AT ALL.**

'BITTTCHHH!'

Sorry! - For the love of god shut up!

Body image is something I have always struggled with, that I will admit.

But to be honest, at the moment, I am struggling more with *mammy image* than body image. I am, for the first time in my life, and I am being totally honest here, at one with my body.

This is not because I am content, or have suddenly developed high self-esteem overnight, and am no longer picturing my body in front of a train, I just feel like OH FUCK OFF intense pressure to be skinny!

I just had a baby and I have too much other stuff to worry about! Like looking after a little boy that is literally my heart on legs, and hearing voices that are not limited to the size 10's in the wardrobe. Worryingly I am now also hearing dogs barking and starting to 'recognise' people in the street I have never met or seen before.

At first I thought it was coincidental 'Oh my god! It is you! Where do I know you from again? You are the third person I have run in to today!'

But when every person I 'recognise' stared at me blankly, I started to notice a trend.

So with all this very real fear, because it feels so disorientating, and all this real heart stopping love I am now also starting to feel, I am past caring about how big I am.

Which is odd considering I am probably the biggest I have ever been.

Maybe I have finally listened to my friends and accepted that I *should* be so amazed by my body and what it has created (yes, yes the sperm was there too darling, what ***WE*** created...) that instead of feeling disgusted in myself, I should forgive myself the cow udder breasts and pendulum belly.

I do sometimes wish I didn't have these issues.

I was, as well you know, *disgusted.* Which is ridiculous as I would never ever judge anyone larger than myself and yet I set myself impossible standards.

On the first morning after his birth, as I limped off for a shower to clean off the 'magic of labour' I have this overwhelming memory of being mugged by a full length mirror.

(Which begs the question, WHY NHS, ***why*** in god's name can you not afford to give relatives visiting newborns a cup of tea but can afford to hang full length mirrors in antenatal wards?? Priorities people! Just take it down! Is it any wonder I literally went from *hero to zero* in 2 minutes flat! Are you trying to push us over the edge?)

'LOOK AT WHAT PREGNANCY LEFT BEHIND!!!' I shouted and sobbed at The Irish One as I wobbled back in to our curtained cubicle having gotten naked in front of it, been scarred for life and then completely forgotten about the illusive shower.

So worked up was I, that The Irish One kindly told me he would watch the sleeping child for a while longer while I shuffled off to ask for a sweet tea to anaesthetize myself from the shock.

On my very slow and painful return down the long corridor from the tea cart (THAT RELATIVES ARE NOT ALLOWED TO SHARE) I noticed my bearded Irish man stood pressed up against the bathroom door gently murmuring sweet nothings to whoever was inside.

'B*aby you are amazing, your son loves you, and I love you. Come out and give us a cuddle.'*

Imagine his shock then, if you will, when I accusingly tapped him on the shoulder and questioned just who the hell did he think he was talking to?

He was mortified, and I was elated by some real life comedy.

He had heard crying from inside, (SEE! Just take the damn thing down!!) And had assumed I had gone back in, to continue my hissy fit!

As he sprinted back behind our curtain and I limped behind him guffawing, I overheard a young girl being consoled by her other half.

'And as if things aren't bad enough, I now have some weirdo outside calling me baby!'

But anyway I digress - Maybe I am slowly coming to terms with my body and all of its changes.

I can even admit to occasionally feeling proud of my body for what it has achieved, especially when I look at this little boy, who has changed everything shoving his finger up his nose and wiping it on his own cheek.

So, my size 10 jeans can just *fuck* right off. (They can't hear me now, its ok, they are being suffocated by the gusset of my size 16 tights.) And when I look at all my old clothes, the fact they are all too small, well in the middle of this, it seems redundant.

Also these pre pregnancy clothes, they seem......well..... Not me.

They just aren't me anymore.

Do you know what I mean?

I am not the same woman I was. Mentally and in shape.

I don't want to wear butt cheek skimming skirts and tank tops (god forbid) with a push up bra. (I was a right tart.) I don't want to wear ripped jeans and tiny t-shirts. (I was trying to stay young) and I don't want to wear leather chaps and nipple spinner corsets. (Joking! Or am I?) I want to wear..... Well that's just it. I have no idea what I want to wear.

All I know is, I need to give in, and buy a few more clothes that fit.

I am quite excited really as I love to shop!

Bargain hunting is a new thing for me since The Irish One has me on a strict budget to avoid a repeat of the 'round the world trip fiasco' but you know, I am up for a challenge.

If I can have 23 stitches holding my rectum together and still poo, I can find a decent outfit for £30.

I am a *mother* now. I can do anything. I can *rule the world* if I so choose.

So will I be ***stylish mammy?*** (I doubt it.)

Or ***flowery skirt mammy?*** (I could braid my hair and call myself Inga! HALLO! I am Inga from Sveeeden!)

Or ***biker mammy?*** (I'll buy a red and black thriller leather jacket with matching leather pants! I could get a tattoo! I could get a Doberman! Call it butch!)

Or ***pajama mammy?*** (This is blatantly, what I will end up as. *(Cough cough continue to be you mean, cough cough)* Not used the iron in months, dried Rusk in my hair, spit up down my top, last night's make up crusting up round my wrinkles...)

Or ***Greek mammy?*** (I could buy a toga and a gold headband! But then I'd have to shave my legs... no, forget that one...)

Or ***Holiday mammy?*** (All I need is a towel, (for the sun bed) and some socks and sandals! I am up at six every morning anyway!?!)

Or ***Disney mammy!*** (I would love to be Disney mammy. If I could I would dress like Cinderella every day and flounce around singing about the washing up and the amount of hair on the carpet, while Doodle the Poodle did the Charleston in the background and the local wildlife changed the baby's nappy...)

So much choice!! I am just not sure!

One thing I am sure of though, I am going to try really hard to stop beating myself up and accept the way things are now.

Tena-lady included.

The midwife once recommend I stand in front of the mirror naked (having just done this I also recommend whacking the heating on first) and giving a memory to each and every stretch mark.

All of mine now have a memory attached.

For every thigh wobble I have a smile off my gorgeous son to match it with.

For every cellulite pimple I have a new experience to remind myself of.

And this angry red stretch line here, spreading the length of my gut, will always remind me of the day my boyfriend acted like a crazy stalker.

Post-natal body? You and I are going to try and work together.

Which Mammy image to go for?

How's about ***Pirate Mammy?*** (I can buy a parrot to go with my eye patch then!

And meet Johnny Depp!! And take Addy on a rowing boat! And teach him about booty... oh no wait, forget that.

Romeo oh romeo... Pass me that spade...

Relationships **are hard.**

Why do none of the pregnancy and *'let us prepare you for motherhood and the ensuing torture'* bibles, warn you about the **fact** that at some point you will no doubt find yourself, *in the misty haze of after birth glory*, wanting to maim your other half with a blunt object, over the head? Several times. Repeatedly. Again and again.....and just once more for good measure.

At no time during my experience of gobbling up *'what to expect when you are expecting'* or *'the best friends guide to the end of your life as you know it'* do I remember reading or even touching upon a chapter which explained to me, that post-birth, not only would my relationship change indescribably overnight, but that on a day-to-day basis I would be using the restraint of a saint, to *not* go down for murder and enjoy the peace and quiet of a life sentence. (They have telly's in women's prisons you know! And some one cooks *for* you!!)

Sitting in a well-known family venue this afternoon (we needed to leave the house!) I found myself distracted by the couple sat next to us.

'You are a lazy bastard' she whispered venomously at her other half as she turned her changing bag upside down and began searching for something manically, her breath coming out in gasps.

'I can't believe you didn't put it in! How hard can it be, to just follow simple instructions? You are an idiot and I hate you. I really do! You don't listen!!'

I glanced to the left surreptitiously to get another quick look, and was soon pretty much gawping, even though The

Irish One was having a go at me about it, I just couldn't help myself.

It was like listening to a recording of me and The Irish One from just this morning, and sure enough, as well as an empty changing bag, she also had a tiny baby wriggling on her knee. Her hair was *upside down* and her crumpled features spoke of many a sleepless night and a *whole heap* of misheard, ignored and unhelpful situations between her and the man *who gave her his sperm and therefore, in a way, I suppose, helped her create* ***her*** *child.*

'Stop shouting at me.' Came the angry, badly whispered reply from her disheveled husband, after a pointed glance at me to shame me in to looking away (It didn't work.) *'I can't be bothered listening to you anymore! Give me my son, you boring cow.'*

It took **all** of my strength not to slap him for her. Boring? Does he know what she is going through??? Outrageous!! I gasped and shook my head in solidarity.

This *discussion* between them went on for the entirety of our visit, and by the end I have to say, as awful as it sounds, I was just glad we weren't alone in our misery.

I tried to shoot her a knowing glance on the way out but The Irish One's head got in the way of my potential eye contact, a fact I cursed him over all the way home. He is always in the bloody way!

An old work colleague of mine, who I have not seen for years, but she wanted to visit anyhow on account of the 'new arrival' visited on Monday.

Can I just say that I still don't get how babies send people as mental as they do!? She has *just* got back from traveling around the world, but her excitement at seeing my son was unbelievable!

I was like "Grace, calm down he isn't the Taj Mahal!' but she just looked at me a bit funny like I was a complete twat and got on with the job of picking him up and talking to him using the same voice I use to talk to Doodle and other cute animals. He clearly isn't used to it but he seemed to like it. Maybe I will try it.

Anyway, we were her **first stop** on the home tour and I am hard pressed to remember *where* it was we even worked together. Babies. Mental. She even brought me a cheesecake.

So during a tour of the *babyfied* flat which she has never seen before (as usually she would have had no interest in coming to my home, all of which took about 30 seconds) we arrived at our bedroom. As I opened the door, she gasped.

Thinking she was physically appalled by the cot bed shoved up against the bed, the wardrobes overflowing with unwashed clothes and 15 cold and stagnating cups of tea slowly fermenting on the windowsill I hurriedly tried to shut the door in her face.

Well, I can't have her slagging me off for my uncouthness to all and sundry. She is single you see, and now she is back she is no doubt going to be very much a girl about town. The last thing I need is my perfect Facebook persona being dirtied! (Which reminds me I must update with what a perfect time we had during that family outing later!)

'Aww' she cooed, to my surprise, pushing the door back open. 'It's so *romantic!'* and as I carefully tried to rearrange my facial features to wipe the bitter grimace off my face, I witnessed a funny smile spread across her features, and then her eyes only went and glazed over. Next thing I know, her hand is absent- mindlessly rubbing her uterus.

'NO!!!!!!!!!!!!!!!!!!' I screamed, grabbing her face in my hands and gritting my teeth together 'DON'T DO IT!!!! IT'S HORRENDOUS!!!! DOOOONT DO IT!!!'

Ok not really.

But romantic?

Romantic was not how I would have described the faint smell of puke and baby trumps coupled with the lingering aroma of man sweat and stale formula.

Romantic?

Can she not sense the *atmosphere* in the place? It is heavy with discarded anger and forgotten dreams.

The last event to take place in that bedroom on that morning was about as far away from romantic as you can possibly imagine. World War 512 had erupted out of nowhere, or maybe World War 513, there are so many right now I can't keep up and who even knows what started it?! But I know how it ended, the grand finale resulted in me stood in my knickers and bra screaming at him down the hall.

'You are venomous SNAKE and I wish you would just leave!!!'

I honestly have never felt anger like it.

Moments later I was crying and he was slamming doors.

Why do the books not warn you about this!! SERIOUSLY!!!

There are SO MANY BOOKS about babies and birth; I just can't fathom why women aren't *warned* about the impact on your relationship in detail!

I am sure it would help me and The Irish One, to know that the turbulence is all part of learning to live as a three. It isn't it?

I have wasted *so much time* over analysing the failure I thought our relationship was, when I could have been asleep!

But clearly, other couples go through this too right?

So from now on, I shall make a concerted effort to put down the spade. Take a deep breath and walk away from his constant nagging.

We are normal.

This could be considered 'Romantic.'

I need to stop plotting his murder.

Radio Silence...

Radio silence commenced last Wednesday morning.

I heard the birds outside gearing up for a full day of worm hunting and squirrel taunting, and knew *instantly* the moment I had been dreading since bedtime was upon me.

Damn it! It is morning!

As my ears tuned in, searching for the usual bedroom noises, trumping, yawning, scratching and Doodle McPoodle treating himself to a morning lick, I realized all was not as it should be. No morning noises were filling my ears, *maybe I am wrong* I thought, *maybe it is just a bad dream!* Maybe morning is *still two weeks away!*

But then I heard it.

The unmistakable sound of giggling.

I prized my eyes open to see my child manically grinning down at me while attempting to maneuver his ankle, think of a shoe that is too tight, backwards and forwards and side to side, in an attempt to get his full foot in to my *overworked and underpaid* and unsuspecting slightly dry, mouth.

My mouth is big some would say, (yes thank you Irish One) but not big enough to fit a size 2. (If I do say so myself.)

From the outside looking in, this could be seen as quite funny. And on a normal day I am sure it would have ensured I *came to* with a smile on my face.

However, unbeknownst to me, somewhere between the hours of 4am and 6am radio silence had commenced without prior notification.

I was covered in cuts.

I lay there looking at my beautiful son with a sinking heart.

I had been hallucinating again.

I was no longer in control. My brain had once again been invaded by the post-natal *bloody* aliens and my mind was unable to communicate. I liken it to somebody who has been possessed (but without the green vomit and the head spinning, no that wasn't Wednesday, that was on Tuesday after a drinking session on Monday night...) I was no longer able to function normally.

As soon as radio silence commences, it feels like my mouth has been clamped shut against my will, my heart has been shut down and all the little men that live inside my body making things work (I was never very good at biology) have gone on strike and normal service delivery is brought to a complete halt.

I am unable to speak.

I am unable to think straight.

I am unable to *snap out of it*.

I am unable *to feel* and I am unable to function.

I am a zombie.

The post-natal depression Zombie.

I can scroll down my twitter feed and I long to join in.

My fingers cannot type.

Nobody would want to speak to me anyway.

I am worthless.

I can plaster a fake smile on my face, but why should I smile?

I am not worthy of anybody's care or anybody's love.

I am worthless.

I long to go to the supermarket and buy my son a delicious *(and nutritious)* meal.

But how can I leave the house and let anybody see me like this?

They will take one look at me and they will know.

I am worthless.

I am a terrible, horrible person who deserves nothing but terrible horrible thoughts and terrible horrible happenings.

I am worthless.

I am trapped in my mind like a prisoner.

I am claustrophobic, I am frustrated and I am tired of fighting back.

Every little comment made is a mountain to climb. Every little issue raised is a mountain to climb. I see evil looks and hear horrible comments where there are none. Every spill or break or fall is a mountain to climb. Every morning, afternoon and evening is a bloody mountain to climb. Getting out of bed each morning is a mountain to climb. I just want to die.

I am *so tired.*

Today marks the end of this dose of radio silence. I think.

I can feel it draining away.

No one can help me fight back and I am so tired of trying.

Post-natal depression 1. Lexy 0.

This time.

Maybe I will win next time.

If I had the energy to *hope,* I would say I hope so.

But can you hear those voices?

They are like Radio Chorley.

They come in my ears.

Is there a therapist in the house?

'Have you been thinking about doing something silly?' the GP asks me as I present in his office, at the end of my line, desperately needing some sort of support.

{Support. Definition = that which enables.}

The edges of my universe have once again become blurred by blunt uncontrollable, unexplainable misery.

Once again; I find I am having to restrain myself from escaping out of bed in the middle of the night and driving my car in to the wall by the industrial estate around the corner, at 70mph.

'Silly?' I cross my legs and lean forward in my plastic NHS chair towards him, 'Why, yes actually I have!!! It's funny you should ask, because I have recently *actually* been having thoughts of perhaps dressing up as a clown and joining the circus, abandoning my beliefs and running off in to the sunset with the bearded lady and her pet monkey.'

He nods at me for a paused moment before hurriedly scribbling something down on his pad.

In the silence that follows, the door opens, and in trundles my old boss, drunk and disorderly, a man I once held in high regard, glancing at me.

Without warning he then begins to repeatedly shout in my face. He tells me I am useless, and 'High maintenance.' He laughs about what a 'nightmare' I was to manage before eventually prodding me in the cheek and pulling at my hair viciously.

I close my eyes firmly and *will* the *prick* to back the fuck off, I tell him that his words are burning at my renewed courage, stripping out my remaining resources. I whisper that he is embarrassing me and making me feel ashamed. I beg him to stop. He smiles in my face and shakes his head when he hears this, and with patronising eyes, sits down next to me.

'Have you been having *suicidal* thoughts?' The GP asks this time, pen impatiently poised in thin air to mark my response on some useless scale.

'Oh, you don't mean *silly* thoughts then?' I respond angrily, worn out by my ex-boss *and* the stigma of even the NHS never using real words to describe symptoms of what feels like a very real illness.

'I meant suicidal.' He nods curtly.

'Is suicide *silly* to you then?' I retort petulantly as the door squeaks open again and my Aunt rushes in, firmly placing her feet next to my old boss, and shaking out her hair.

I bristle and wait for the hurt to bombard me.

'Oh don't listen to her!' she happily announces, embarrassed, before going on to tell him that he is not to listen to a thing I say, for I am a drama queen, and a liar, and quite selfish. She also explains to the 'lovely Dr.' that she herself would look after me but she has had a glass of red wine so can't be arsed, plus as I am only being attention seeking, why should she bother? There is nothing wrong with me really, you see, except the need for a few home truths.

Expect nothing, and always be grateful.

I place my head in my hands and signal her to stop talking, to go home.

She shuts up, acting injured, but goes nowhere, preferring to stay and chat with my ex-boss.

They both stare at me every now and again, between whispers.

The Dr. is speaking but I cannot hear him, as someone else has bowled through the door to join the party.

'Depression is like giving up smoking;' she says waving her newly thin hand in the air 'you can choose to stop feeling miserable. It is your choice to be like this Lexy. How very annoying you are.'

My aunt and my ex-boss nod their agreement.

I look down.

I will not let a bully see she has got to me, no matter how many games she plays.

The three of them stare at me for a while, and then start giggling.

'Miss Ellis? Are you suicidal?'

'Yes.' I whisper, the waves of insecurity rattling around my ribcage.

'How long have you been feeling like this?'

'Suicidal?' I respond distracted, as I catch sight of my brother waving at me from outside, through the window. He has a disappointed look on his face, as he slowly vanishes, taking the baby I never got to meet, the little girl I will not allow myself to talk about, or feel anything for, because the loss would kill me, with him.

I clutch my heart and take a deep breath as my soul vanishes and I am finally, fully depleted.

A conquered army.

'A while.' I whisper, as my son appears out of nowhere and grabs hold of my face begging me not to die, to not leave him like I did last time, that he needs me. My aunt, the bully and my old boss shake their heads at me in disgust, as a debt collector, the teacher who called me a bad egg, the popular girls at school who told me I was fat, the boy who said I looked like a whale and then continually abused me, the ex-boyfriend who cheated on me, my first therapist and a teenage version of myself walk through the door and fill the room to bursting, around us.

'Are you on medication?'

I can barely hear him now over the chorus of bile being spewed in my general direction. All of the insults I have ever received are burned in to my being; they are all I can hear. All of the faces flashing behind my eyes, the guilt, the evil, the misery, the hurtful words, the insecurity, the shame.

It is all being piled on, I am stuck in some sort of hideous loop.

'No.' I stutter, losing my voice again, 'is that not on the system?'

I raise my head up to meet his eyes.

I *am* high maintenance.

I *am* lonely.

I *am* annoying.

I *am* ashamed.

I *am* bombarded.

I *am* struggling.

I *am* a failure.

But come on!

I *am* here, and I *am* asking for help.

'Oh, yes.' he says glancing at the screen, 'you refused medication, of course.'

I sigh.

'And you self-harm!'

He is looking at me intently again. I raise my hands in question to him.

'I am aware of all of this Doc, it is *my* record.'

'It started after you gave birth!'

I roll my eyes.

If I wasn't't losing the will to live before the cast and chorus line of 'Lexy's worst hits' arrived in to the Dr's office with me, I was now.

'Yes.' I sigh again.

He looks at me for a while, considering something, no idea what.

He shifts in his seat and coughs.

He looks scared for a split second.

Scared.

'Well if you still don't want medication' he pauses 'the only thing I can recommend for you to do at this stage is go home and relax.'

I am open mouthed.

'I have a baby!'

I am enraged.

'Well go home and keep busy. Do the washing. Do you face your problems Lexy?'

I don't answer.

He mistakes this for acceptance of the crap he is spouting. He puts his hand on mine.

'I know it is hard. You, go home and keep busy, maybe then have a nice long bath. You will be ok.'

'Doc,' I pause 'Can I have some medication please?'

"Yes. Take one of these daily,' he says brandishing a prescription in victory 'And if you feel desperate, have a think about visiting A&E, or talking to someone, I have also referred you to the Priory...'

He smiles abruptly and rests his hand on my shoulder as he ushers *us all* out of his office with a wave and halfheartedly spouts some advice to call back if I still feel the same way in a few weeks and haven't heard anything back yet.

I am open mouthed, but hopeful.

I didn't appreciate the go home and relax part, I wonder if he would say the same to somebody else who was potentially showing signs and experiencing symptoms of a different terminal illness?

[Stigma. Definition; That which disables.]

I better go put a wash on. Or join the circus, maybe. That would be super relaxing!

Now.

Do I really need to start on this medication?

It scares me.

Follow the Yellow Brick Road ...

A week after my brother died I booked a plane to Florida.

I planned to run away from the grief, sadness and pain that I was surrounded by and have a little holiday in a place, which had always brought me feelings of happiness, joy and love.

Ever since I was a child Walt Disney World held special meaning to me, it was a place of family unity, a place of laughter but most of all it was the place where I was sure I could run away to, and the grief wouldn't find me.

When I arrived for therapy last Tuesday, after a tense 25 minutes on the motorway getting completely lost and ending up on the ring road for Terminal 2 car park at Manchester airport (my sense of direction is absolutely terrible, I could get lost in my own living room) I was absolutely frazzled and unsure of whether this journey would be worth all the effort.

I shouldn't have waited so long really, as it turns out my medical insurance covers me.

I drove past a golf course *internally screaming* about my inability to listen to even the simplest of instructions, and *screaming externally* at Vivian (my Sat nav is called Vivian, on account she sounds like an anally retentive, posh school teacher) who was now insisting I 'make a U-turn, make a U-turn' on a one way road. I banged my fist on the steering wheel in frustration and prepared to throw Vivian out of the window, when all of a sudden, like the illusive light at the end of the tunnel, there it was in front of me. *(Screw you Vivian! You make a U-turn you clapped out whore bag! Update your software!)*

'The mental hospital Altrincham' was written as clear as day on an understated sign surrounded by a backdrop of sweeping green, perfectly mowed fields and majestic, beautiful oak trees. 'Huh?' I thought to myself. Altrincham? I thought I was in Hale. (Story of my life.)

I put my foot on the brake too quickly in surprise and stalled the car.

So much for my celebrity entrance.

Nobody seemed to notice though. Teenagers and adults combined were mooching across the lawns in a relaxed manner, holding folders, and chatting, there was a woman sat to my left, cunningly hidden (but not very well as I saw her) between the trees having a sneaky puff on a no doubt elusive cigarette. I smiled at her as I passed and wondered what her story was.

I wound my window down to let in some air (I still have stomach flu and my air-con is broken) and noticed immediately how peaceful it was. It was like a blanket of calm had descended over the entire place. The sun was shining, the birds were singing, but still somehow, this place held an atmosphere that was so tranquil and still, it was almost eerie. Maybe I have just watched too many films.

I located the car park with moments to spare before my appointment, and in my panic to park, duly knocked off my wing mirror maneuvering in, next to a great big mucky, yellow skip. (I wasn't even reverse parking!)

It's typical really, that amongst all this beauty and expansive open space, I would be the person to locate and destroy a material possession on probably the only *eyesore* in a 500 mile radius. I see now why nobody else had parked there. Would you park a *Porsche Carrera* or a Range rover *sport* next to a skip outside a loony bin? No? Me either, but hindsight is a wonderful thing. (My car is a shed, but I was still gutted!)

After having a quick puff on my inhaler, picking my mirror up off the floor and trying not to cry at the lack of peripheral vision I now had for the journey home, I slammed my door shut and headed towards the Manor at the top of the hill, looking for reception.

I walked through the sparkling double doors just as two girls were making their exit whispering to each other conspiratorially. They had their heads down and their hands shoved deep in to their pockets. Smuggling out food? Smuggling out cigs? Sneaking off for a cig? The nosy person inside me was desperate to know their story too.

They glanced in my direction but looked away quickly. They probably thought I was one of the counsellors; such was the age gap between us. Although, come to think of it, I am probably giving myself way too much credit there. I had just been on my hands and knees next to a skip. But anyway, very quickly I started to feel very old and very ridiculous.

Surely I was too old to need all this guff? Surely self-harming and crying one's self to sleep is for the emotionally unstable youth? What the hell was I playing at trying to stay young by being a total fuck up? I didn't have time for this. I needed to get a grip and move on.

Every fiber of my being was screaming at me to get back in the car, and go home. Stop wasting everybody's time, it shouted. But my feet kept going and before I knew it I was in reception.

I walked in, to what can only be described as a *grand hall*, to the sound of silverware clattering against silverware, (food smugglers those girls then I reckon...) and as my feet sank in to the ridiculously lush carpet, I looked upwards towards the most beautiful double staircase and my gaze caught on to an impressive mosaic painted ceiling. It was like a house you would see on cribs. But tasteful.

I stopped in my tracks and just stared for a while, agog. I am used to the NHS. The words poles and apart would be appropriate here. I once was booked to have psychotherapy on the NHS in Salford. The reception was behind bullet proof glass and the woman actually locked the consulting room door behind us when we went in. 'Never be too sure' she had laughed nervously before spending 20 minutes trying to unlock the barred window to let some air in. I never went back, fearing for my safety never mind my sanity.

'Hello,' the receptionist said kindly from behind her huge mahogany desk 'How can I help you?'

I heard her, but couldn't respond. I was lost in the moment.

'The suuuun will come out tommorrrrroooowwwww, bet your bottom dollarrr that tommorrowwwwwwwwww, come what maaaaaaaayyyyyy' If I had been wearing a red dress and not my lumberjack Dr martins, I would have been prancing about and singing. True story. As it were I can't dance in those boots, so just let my imagination run riot.

This place was *incredible,* I was orphan Fanny (because, well, why not?) and Bupa medical Insurance had become my Daddy Warbux. Damn it! Why hadn't I worn that spare ball gown I keep lying about the place?!

The moment overwhelming me slightly and completely lost in thoughts about changing Doodle's name to Sandy and searching on the internet for a bald rich man, I took a step forward and nearly catapulted myself over a very well camouflaged, amongst all the grandeur, reception desk that the kind, jowly old woman who had spoken earlier, was sat behind.

'Hello,' the receptionist said again kindly, looking up at me, undeterred by the fact my face had just made contact with her bosom. 'How may I help you?

'I am here to see, Dr G' I stuttered out the unpronounceable surname, mortified that I had only been there two minutes and had already managed to nearly inflict injury on both myself and an unsuspecting other. If she had been bent over the desk, (not in a kinky way, as in, if she had been writing or something) I probably would have chinned her and she would have been knocked out. My life is never straightforward.

I straightened out my top and cursed my stupid big boots with their stupid big laces for planting me in such an uncompromising position.

'Who?' she asked, attempting to make eye contact and looking only slightly amused and just a tad concerned by me.

After my humiliation at the dentist last week, I'd just about had my fill of making an arse out of myself so instead of continuing to attempt to pronounce the 64 (or thereabouts) lettered surname I sensibly began to rummage in my bag for the letter containing the Dr's name to just show her. Unfortunately my bag was still filled with formula, a bottle, 3 nappies and 7 empty biscuit packets, so this took a while.

'Ah' she said, when I produced the letter in such a flourish of triumph that I nearly took her eye out. 'Dr. *Supercalifragilisticexpialidocious*, I will tell her you are here, please rest your weary bones over there on those amazingly squishy and luxurious leather sofas by the window.'

(She didn't *actually* say this, but this is what I heard.)

'Would you like some champagne? Maybe a little caviar to tempt your over sensitive palette? Maybe a canapé?' (Pronounced '*canap*', for comedy value.)

(Again, she didn't *actually* say this, but this is what I heard. I think she *actually* offered me a brew, in all honesty. But I don't like Earl grey so declined politely.

I sat down and as my oversized pillow bottom began to sink in to the heavenly cushions I closed my eyes for the briefest of moments and was immediately transported back in time.

'Santaaa Claus weeeee nevverrr seeee' my internal monologue sang 'Santa Claus, what's that, who's he?'

Oh how I used to love the rags to riches story of poor orphan Annie, and *oh how* I thought I could relate to the poor little darling with the hugely curly hair. (For the record I came from a loving home, and my hair is bone straight.)

I must have been sat there for a while because the film, in my mind, had reached the part with the evil (and now I see, clearly fabulous) Miss Hannigan.

'Er, excuse me?' A voice bluntly interrupted my reverie.

My eyes flew open and I realized with a start I had been tapping my feet and swaying to the internal beat of Mrs. Hannigan's drunken gin fuelled symphony. When I was younger I used to *hate* her, what a horrible woman, I used to agree with the orphans, simply terrible, what a villain.

Now, by the way, I totally get it. 'Little boys, with their little toys, night and day I eat breathe and smell puke and poooooo, little cheeks and little teeth, everything around me is little!! Some women are dripping with diamonds, lucky me, lucky me look at what I'm dripping with..... PUKE!! (For the record I love my son to the moon and back, but if I had 75 of him, I reckon I would be on the gin too. Which reminds me, I am out of wine...)

'Er yes hi!' I coughed out groggily.

'Who are you and what can we do for you?'

It was the receptionist I had given my details to only about five minutes before. I was instantly confused. She was looking at me like you would look at someone you had just caught trying to wake your baby up during your well-deserved five-minute period of peace and quiet. Murderous.

'My name Is Lexy Ellis and I, err, I am, err' I stalled, a bit scared she was holding an envelope opener or some other *girls interrupted* type of weaponry behind her back (shoe laces maybe.)

'Yes?' She asked again rudely.

'I saw you a moment ago,' I stuttered, 'at least I am pretty sure I did, I told you I am here to see Dr Gidumdumdumshawadada...'

Was I going mad? Surely I didn't just walk in here and sit down? I am *sure* I spoke to her, surely I didn't imagine up the whole conversation? Thoughts of Russell Crowe in *A Beautiful Mind* flashed before my eyes and I snaffled a quick glance at her cleavage. Yes, yes, I did! I remembered, the relief washing through my brain instantly and slowing down my rampant heartbeat, I would recognise those boobs anywhere.

'Ah,' she rolled her eyes and backed down, immediately cursing herself 'sorry, have you already spoken to me? My memory isn't what it once was.' I was flabbergasted. 'The doctor will be down soon to get you' and with that she ambled away back to the desk I had been bent over, not five minutes before. Memory isn't what it once was?!

I didn't really get to process this random and clearly mental occurrence as literally 2 second later the kind doctor appeared in front of me like a vision in designer labels. She introduced herself as Dr Fabulous and beckoned me up the beautiful double staircase towards her consulting room.

I immediately warmed to this fabulously dressed Dr and her kind, accepting manner the moment I sat down in her *inner sanctuary*, as this is what it was, the term *'office'* does this welcoming and comfortable room no justice, and she commented on my handbag.

Materialistic? Maybe. But I am a woman who loves handbags. If she too, was a woman who loves handbags, we were going to get a long like a house on fire. Screw the delving in to my turbulent psyche; show me the lining on your Marc Jacobs!

She didn't council me. She didn't umm and ahh and cock her head to the side in a patronising manner as I sat down and spoke about why I was there. (She didn't show me her lining either, in case you are wondering.) It was a very matter of fact conversation, and I found it very easy to open up, as if we were talking about somebody else. (Gossip? Moi?)

She was absolutely lovely (and I really want her scarf) with a way about her that yes, although she was clearly loaded (I want her scarf) said that she was also down to earth and capable of empathising with those who weren't clearly loaded. (Did I mention the Chanel scarf?)

The appointment was incredibly personal and unbelievably effective.

I told her where I was at, what I was thinking most days, and all about the hallucinations and voices. I told her that that rather than things improving after counselling, they seemed to be getting worse. I told her about my childhood, as she asked. I told her about my twenties, as she asked, and I told her about the fateful week I spent in Florida after my brother died, because she asked.

It turns out I hadn't run away from the grief. I had just taken it with me.

That week, spent alone, in a world so far removed from the one I then knew, a world filled with smiling families and laughing children, a world filled with possibility and hope and love, was one of the worst weeks of my entire life.

I remember sitting in the middle of Magic Kingdom, totally alone on a bench, probably the only person who was alone, in the entire park, with a vintage greying film reel of memories playing out before my eyes. Memories from long ago, memories of me and my brother, memories of me and my family, memories of working there and all moments of happiness I had experienced when I was living there, a time when life had seemed like a fun game to play.

Screams of joy, peals of laughter and *it's a small world after all,* made up the soundtrack to my agonizing grief, that day, sat on that bench, in the middle of a theme park, a million miles away from anybody who knew me or what I was going through, alone.

As the sepia, frozen pictures, of a happy moments lost long ago, trampled across my soul, one after the other, my heart was slowly torn out and shredded, piece by piece, and then stamped on. Everything was lost, everything was irreplaceable.

In some ways I think I left my broken heart over there, lying under that sodding bench.

I came back a different person.

(Dramatic huh? I don't do things by halves, me.)

Ignored grief. Denial (which isn't just a river in Egypt you know! Fnar fnar.) And a metaphorical pick and mix of psychiatric terminology was thrown at me towards the end of the session.

I was exhausted. I hadn't cried. I hadn't wailed but I hadn't lied.

I hadn't missed the painful bits out. For the first time in my entire life, I had been completely truthful about where my emotions and head had been at, for the last decade. I thought maybe I should be feeling like a weight had been lifted off my shoulders, but I didn't. I just felt weird. Spaced almost.

I admitted slowly and steadily I had been having absences from reality, my confidence over discussing the numerous visions, hallucinations and voices growing as she encouraged me to be honest.

The Dr in Chanel, or Dr. Chanel, as I will now call her, put her pen down to mark the end of the session and told me something which I will remember till the day I die.

'When you're stuck with a day, that is grey, and loneleeeeeeeeey, you just stick out your chin, and grin, and saaaaaaayyyyyyyyyy, ooooooohhhhhh... the sun will come out tomorrow....'

Ok, she didn't really.

But it would have been fab if she had.

No, instead she very sensibly and softly advised me to start taking the medication and that said she wanted to admit me to the hospital effective immediately (ooo the drama!) and I thinking about it too, until she told me I would have no contact with the outside world for a week.

'Take my mobile off me? I can't live without my IPhone for seven days! No twitter at all? No Facebook? Are you insane??? I should get ***you*** *committed woman!!'*

I, I mean, *obviously* I would have missed Addison *way* too much, and I wouldn't have been able to bear it! That goes without saying! Which is why I didn't just say it first! It goes without saying *do you hear?* Of course I would miss him, I was just saying, you know that I err, oh sod it.

So anyway, I managed to talk her out of a Section 2 (which apparently means I admit myself by choice but am unable to leave until they say, which FYI scared the shit out of me) so Daddy Warbux willing, potentially I will be starting intensive day therapy instead, twice a week for a month.

Group therapy, no less.

Hopefully after which, I will be a well-rounded, happy individual.

Stop laughing.

It *could* happen!

And Lexy lived happily ever after.... She went back to that bench in Disney World with The Irish one, Addison and a photo of Doodle and got closure. She now lives the billionaire lifestyle after wining Euro millions and sharing it with all her followers on Twitter. The woman is an angel.

Not in to fairytales? Is that too cheesy and end for you?

Well how about this then,

Driving home with my left wing mirror riding shotgun in the passenger seat was horrific, and although I am sure I barely use it, I really noticed how much I missed it, when it was no longer doing the job it had been destined for (much like my third nipple) especially on a four lane motorway, in rush hour (unlike my third nipple.)

But needless to say, I did safely make it home and collapsed on the sofa in a heap.

Three minutes later I realized I had left my iPhone at the place.

Now that is irony for you.

One hot piece of ass...

Today is Tuesday.

I know this because yesterday while visiting a friend, exhausted and miserable after dropping Addison off at nursery for the first time, which I don't want to talk about because I will break down, I plonked myself down on her sofa ready for a good *heart to heart* when unexpectedly, within seconds, my arse felt like it was on *fire.*

Evidently it turns out, I had unfortunately sat on a freshly cooked and piping hot pizza, that my friend had slaved over a hot oven for, and left on the sofa (who puts pizza on the sofa?!) for me to find, as a surprise lunch for us.

It certainly *was* a surprise but not the kind; I think she was hoping it would be.

I could act like a *drama queen* and tell you I suffered third degree burns as I was running around the room trying to relieve the pain by attempting to grab behind myself at an impossible angle to remove *arse from fabric,* but that would not be true. As painful as it *was* (let's pause for a moment here, and give my arse the respect it truly *deserves,* after all it has already *endured* this decade) it is now recovering, and other than still being a bit hot and stingy, it looks like I will now survive.

I could also tell you that like in a *cartoon* there was a barrel of water in the corner of her living room which I ran towards and splashed myself in to, but that also, would be a lie. What I actually ended up having to do was much, much worse.

Over the screams of laughter coming from my other two 'pals' and her 'lovely' husband, the pain became too much. The cheese was sticking to my muffin top like shit to Sellotape, and the flimsy (fake) denim material (bloody bran new jeans) was not cooling fast enough and felt like molten lava on my most tender of areas, so in the end I just dropped my *kecks* (her husband graciously left the room, when he sensed what was about to happen) and twenty minutes later I was still standing in her living room in my knickers padding my angry bum with a sodden sponge, over a bowl. (Thinking back now, I have no idea why I didn't just escape to the privacy of a bathroom, to soothe my *under bits* when this seems like such an *obvious* thing to do. But I just didn't. Nothing comes *'obviously'* to me anymore.)

It was a while later, as we noticed her neighbors staring quizzically through the bay windows and sniggering, that the realisation hit; it probably would have been a good idea to shut the curtains.

Yesterday was Monday. Things like that can only happen on a Monday.

Today is Tuesday and even though I have not left the house at all other than to visit the Dr for post-natal depression related conversations, (nothing to do with my flaming cheeks I promise! I have to send sick notes in to work as I can no longer afford to be off on maternity) I have, however had a much better day than yesterday.

Which wouldn't have really taken much.

I am having Pizza for tea though.

The Mental hospital...

Wow, so it turns out, according to the mental hospital *Nork* scale (it may or may not be called that, although isn't *nork* another word for tit? So maybe it is.) I am 'severely depressed.'

So basically, I am a severely depressed tit.

It is 3.30 pm and my official assessment before starting group therapy, to assess which group they are going to put me in with, is at the midway point, stuck somewhere between the intake of breath just before the admittance of defeat and the catch in the throat just before the tears roll.

Just about finished with assessing the level of my crazy, the good doctor looks up from the dog-eared clipboard resting on his knee and fixes me with a solemn stare. He leans forward every so slightly preparing himself for what is about to happen, and in the hesitation of his actions, my heart begins to flutter. He is on the precipice of telling me something I probably do not want to hear. He senses my reaction may not be accepting and is selecting from the archives of his encyclopedic knowledge of the mind, the appropriate and suitable words to use, as not to cause more damage than necessary.

In his hesitation my mind races out of control. A smile is frozen across my cracked and sore lips caked under a quick flash of cheap lipstick and in my mind's eye I get an image of myself as the joker from Batman. My body is overflowing from my clothes, my lipstick is smeared all over my face, I am panting like an exhausted bulldog and my shoulders are twitching at random moments. I am not dressed like a penguin. I am talking about the *joker*. Jack Nicholson plays a huge part in my afternoon of craziness; he seems to pop up everywhere.

In reality I am sitting perfectly still as if frozen in the moment. This will be the photo I remember. A fly is repeatedly head-butting the window. It is the only sound in the room. Time has stopped and I am too hot. I am claustrophobic in my own clothes and the door is locked. The window won't open.

The fly is trapped. How frustrating it must be, to almost, be able to taste the freedom you once experienced on the other side of that thick glass but lack the understanding of how to actually reach out and have it once again within your grasp.

The good doctor stirs in his seat. I avoid his eye contact but can feel his intrigued expression burning in to my right cheek as I try to distract myself from the fly by looking upward towards the sky filled with puffy white, happy clouds.

'You ok?' his words shock me. Are these the words he has spent *all this time* choosing? No I am not ok. I am in the priory. If I were ok I would be shopping with my boy, or laughing with my friends, spending a Tuesday afternoon working my old nine to five. If I were ok I would be out *living,* I wouldn't be stuck in this glue like room, empathizing with an insect.

'No' the word splurt's out of my mouth against my will. I am instantly angry and embarrassed by myself. 'Did I tick a box incorrectly?' Images of a huge hotel on the side of a bleak and lonely mountain in the darkest of winter flash across my mind. Am I like Jack again? Am I all work and no play? My eyes dart nervously to the clip chart trembling slightly on his over caffeinated lap, I sprint backwards erratically in my mind, attempting to recall the questions or even the answers I circled on the quiz, which defines my mental state, but in my panic am unable to recall what I am even fearful about in the first place.

I remind myself, what if I had subconsciously and inadvertently scribbled 'poo *bum'* across the form several times without realising, instead of sensibly indicating the number, which corresponded with the level of my upset.

On a scale of 1-10 have you ever considered suicide?

Which end is which? How can you answer that on a scale of one to 10? Is 1 never? Is 10; I regularly jump off tram platforms, but so far have failed to die due to conscientious drivers and state of the art ABS?

Who came up with these questions? Professor *Nork?* Did he scale everything in his life? Did nobody ever tell him some things can't be scaled?

On a scale of 1-10 how inappropriate do you think this scale is?

I chose 5. Bang in the middle. I am not suicidal. I am not, not suicidal. I am just average. It depends on the day.

Or had I? What if I hadn't circled those numbers in the boxes, which we all clearly fit *like a glove* in to and instead written 'All work and no play makes mummy a total mentalist' over and over again without even knowing what I was doing? No wonder the doctor *was hesitating.*

Under all the plastic glitter and Arndale glamour was this woman carrying an axe? (LEXYS HOME!!! – note to self, must by plastic axe and try this level of crazy out on The Irish One. If only for comedy value.)

'No box could have been answered *incorrectly'* he breathes out a long shaky breath and his shoulders sag as he does so, his expression has changed, a sympathetic smile now plays on his lips. He is no longer intense. He is mellow.

I feel my highly-strung mind start to unwind and catch myself attempting to crack a joke about *one flew over the cuckoo's nest,* but he doesn't laugh. He doesn't respond *at all* except for a cough which triggers his glasses to slip down his face and away from, what I can see now are innocent huge brown eyes which have been previously hidden by rectangular thick, *I'm trying to be a geek,* frames.

His eyes surprise me. In them I can see a life outside of his job. It unnerves me and I feel foolish.

He uses his index finger to push the trendy frames back up his nose and looks me directly in the eye as he does so. I am young, I have my own life, but I can swim, he says to me without speaking, I know what I am doing here.

I look away uncomfortable that he seems to have gained access to my mind so effortlessly but impressed by his self-conviction. If he wasn't so blatantly gay I could probably fancy him, I think to myself distracted for a moment by the kindness and confidence in his features. It isn't that he is sexy, or *even my cup of tea*, he just has the token mannerisms of somebody who I would assume would be nice to me. In the olden days, this was all it took.

'You are severely depressed' Boom.

'Your treatment will be intensive for the first few weeks' Boom.

'I am worried about seeing you only as a day patient' Boom.

He slowly leans back against his chair not taking his eyes off me.

'I don't feel severely depressed.' Rumble.

'I have been quite happy these past few weeks actually.' Rumble.

'Inpatient treatment is not an option that I feel is necessary.' Rumble.

I laugh it off and fight him with every ounce of my being.

I am not depressed. I am FINE.

'We only know how *we* feel.'

The understanding of what he is saying smacks me hard across the face repeatedly all the way home and carries on beating me long in to the evening.

It is an answer for everything. His final word is a circle, which cannot be broken.

I do only know how *I* feel. Slap.

Maybe **this isn't** how everybody feels. Slap.

I am a total embarrassment and I thought I was just happy. Slap.

I have a label. Slap.

I am one of *those* people. Slap.

I am a failure. Slap.

I failed at life. Slap.

'Lexy are you going to wash those bottles?' It is The Irish One interrupting the self-abuse I am becoming extremely proficient at.

'I can't babes.' He knows what is coming 'I am severely depressed.'

'You are a chancer is what you are.'

'Get me a biscuit. I am severely depressed.'

'Fig or chocolate?'

'What do *you* think?'

My official treatment starts on Monday.

Six weeks of intensive training for the severely depressed with great medical insurance.

That is the name of the group.

I have group therapy all day Monday and all day Thursday for the next six weeks. I have passed all the requirements of the crazy test and am being admitted to the mental facility as a day case patient forthwith.

I am on a journey of self-discovery.

Vulnerability feels a lot like like fear.

Vulnerability, my Nemesis...

'My legs are hairy.'

Like really hairy.

Like hairy where you aren't't sure if there is actually skin under there anymore of whether you are slowly morphing in to a gorilla woman from the caves of the Outer Hebredi jungle. (Which is somewhere near north wales, according to my Satellite Navigation.)

The Irish One hasn't noticed, which basically tells me one of two things. Either he secretly has a penchant for cave women with furry shins, or it has been far too long since he got up close and personal with my knees. Probably a bit of both to be honest. But anyway.

I am telling you this because *apparently,* according to my 'key worker' (now Addison has one at nursery and I have one here! How bloody fantastic! We match!) I have this affliction where *apparently,* I put myself down in front of people and then laugh it off, because *apparently* I have this fear they will put me down first, and so if I pre-emptively strike and if it turns out I am right, they do *interject,* I have protected myself.

Are you following?

An *interject,* just in case you aren't't aware (I wasn't't) is when somebody will say something to you like;

'Oxo you look like you've lost weight!' and even if you **know** it **not** to be the case, you automatically believe it, as why *in the hell* would somebody say it if it wasn't't the case? And it impacts you in a good and positive way. You even start to feel like you may have lost some.

Which is great if people tell you are skinny all the time because who doesn't want to hear that? Unless of course, you are like me, and you then allow yourself a Bigmac on the way home, because their opinion has had such a huge impact on you, and has put you in *such* a great mood, you feel positively *waif like...* but not so great if someone says something like, oooo, I don't know....

'You are over sensitive.'

And here is where it gets me negatively.

I will laugh it off, cos **I know I am not**. I know I'm not.

But... *and this is the bastard thing about interjects...* while washing the pots an hour later....I will catch yourself...

Am I? Am I? Am I over sensitive? *Am I over sensitive?*

...I'll even put the sponge down for a minute while I have a **proper** think back...

'I must be. I must be!! Otherwise, why would *they have said it*, if it weren't't the case? Oh my god I **am** over sensitive! I am such a dick!'

I was convinced at the time they accused me of it, that I wasn't, but... the sneaky interject... it creeps up on you...

And by the time I have washed the knives and forks (that he *'forgot' again)* I have ultimately and concretely decided **nothing is ever allowed to upset me again**, because that person was right!!!! I just need to get a grip.

It happens to me all the time, they are right.

I am in a **great** mood, but then, out of nowhere, while I am busy thinking about how I may shave your legs tonight and maybe if he is very very lucky, The Irish One may get some, my bestie will ring and say;

'What's up with you today you sound miserable?'

'Hey' I respond, questioning myself immediately 'No, I'm not miserable! I'm having a great day thanks!'

And you fight the sneaky *interject...*

You **know** you **aren't't** miserable; you *even have lipstick on today!!!*

But...an hour later, after one other person, has said something similar...

I will put my iPad down and...

'Do I? Do I look miserable? DO I? Do I look miserable? AM I miserable?'

...I will even go to the toilet to get a look at myself in the mirror to check...

'Oh my god!' I think to myself, 'I *do* look miserable! I thought I looked ok today but I really do look miserable. I must do! Because why would they have said it, if it simply weren't't the case?'

And there you I was mistakenly believing I was feeling great!

The sneaky interject, it creeps up on me...

So, I plaster on a fake smile (which up until 3 minutes ago was real) so bright, I look like the village idiot and unsurprisingly... I am starting to feel completely and utterly **miserable.**

Shocking. How did I never notice this before?

It's ok though! I told sue the Keyworker.

Because I have a plan!! I can beat the interjects!!

Basically, by telling people I have hairy legs (and have my hair tied up with a pair of knickers right now – god The Irish One is one lucky man) I am essentially guarding myself from interjects by not putting myself down, but by being honest and proud!

'No Lexy.' she sighed softly 'that is exactly what you *have* been doing. Telling us you have hairy legs is not honest and proud. It is sharing your fake shame to stop others shaming you further. Try again. Be vulnerable. Tell me something real.'

Oh piss off Sue.

A Doughnut...

For a split second as I was shaking vanilla powder on to my extra skinny extra hot Extra shot Starbucks Cappuccino, my heart jumped up in to my throat, the unexpected adrenalin thudded painfully throughout my entire body and the sound of me gasping sent a shockwave through my previously silent mind.

The above statement basically explains perfectly where my headspace is currently residing. For a split second I had thought it might be salt.

Not gun powder, not a bomb, not the end of the world, as we know it, just *salt.*

Why I thought, in that moment as the ground opened up and I fell in a hole I struggled to climb out of, that Starbucks would have a jar of *salt* stood proud as punch next to the chocolate and other coffee flavoured memorabilia, I cannot tell you.

I am confused, I am exhausted from deep within, and I am one big twisted, angry, bitter, irritable, anxious, sad, hysterical, surprised, ashamed, unhappy knot.

My head is so far *up my arse* today; I am surprised the happy, spritely girls (who I want to punch) stood by the Krispy Kreme stand at Selfridges didn't mistake me for an anxiety filled donut. (I would definitely be in the *alternate*, summer collection, squeezed in between Mentalist mango and *Psycho* Surprise....)

The silence in my mind is *actually* not silence at all, it is white noise caused by too many thoughts jostling for position and assaulting each other in their attempt to be heard, with complete disregard for the damage they are causing to their surroundings, deep within my physic. (SURPRISE!!!... Sorry. I'm losing the plot.)

'Did you change the water in the Sterilizer?'

Maybe I should swerve the car while doing 60.

'Why don't you give Addison a kiss, he has missed you.'

Maybe I should just slice at my stomach where nobody will see.

Physical pain is *easier* than mental. Physical pain I can handle.

Is that too deep for a Tuesday morning? I am sorry. Here, have a biscuit.

Group therapy is like being given a donut laced with arsenic. (You just put the biscuit down didn't you?)

I am desperate to feel the light, delicious powdered piece of heaven on my taste buds but am terrified of the horrific, gritty powdery badness and how it will affect me, which it is surrounded by.

Inside good. Outside bad. My choice.

My choice.

I was stood in the courtyard, after having marched out of my first ever group session in *a fit* of defiance and a cloud of *rather pathetic, weak arse* drama that I made the decision.

Every part of my being was resisting this change.

Sent in to fight or flight mode at the first inkling of trouble, all the thoughts, negativity and resistance to accept change, that had been nestled safely and comfortably inside me for so long, began to rise up in an angry panic towards the surface.

I became a walking talking cliché (a movie version of crazy) and a sitting duck all in the space of an hour.

My feet were tapping, I was picking at my fingers, my eyes were darting from the door to the window and back again, my back was *killing* causing me to *jerk* randomly, and very slowly my agitation building, and my mannerisms and quirks now out of control, it became all too much for my heart and brain to handle.

'Lexy, please tell the group about your trauma.'

I refused to look at him, like a stubborn child refusing food, I turned my face away from him. I knew what I was doing and I didn't want to, but the teenage me had taken over, I had no choice.

'I don't have any.' I stropped.

'Yes you do.'

'No I don't.'

'Yes you do.'

'Fuck off.' An explosion of agitation, and I ran.

Stood in that courtyard, the sun too hot on my arms, my face burning and the realisation that nobody was going to come after me dawning, I cried the first real tears I have cried in over ten years.

No drama, no present circumstances. These tears were for me, from deep within me.

Who the hell, was I fighting against?

I did have a choice, and at that exact moment, I made it.

In my second session, defying my defiance, and telling the teenager and silent army of insolence and denial to be **brave,** I opened up.

I will be going back Thursday.

I am no longer *intrigued to see what group therapy is about*, it isn't something *I am doing for material, or just because I can, or for the experience,* it is something I am choosing to do for me.

And as I sit here (in bloody Starbucks!) with tears rolling down my face and my heart on a plate in front of me for anybody to have a stab at, it finally dawns on me.

[In the words of Chandler Bing] Could I beeeeeee anymore scared?

Moaning Bitch...

At 9.15 pm last night, with my toes slowly turning blue and wrinkly from too long spent doused in soggy socks nestled in to even soggier 'all weather' Ugg boots (which will now undoubtedly stink until the end of time) I did wonder for a moment if I had somehow been transported back in to an alternate universe that was still trapped in the 1990s, and if the teenagers wandering past wearing tiny skirts and tank tops, swaying to 'rhythm as a dancer' while the rest of us were frozen solid in mattress type attire, were actually mental alien life forces from planet 'Annoying' and if potentially, I was the only person in the crowd of over 3000 silhouettes that thought perhaps this whole 'standing in a field and watching stuff burn-*celebration*' was a bit, well a bit, *random!*

I mean I understand the reason why we do it.

But I just don't understand the reason *why* we do it.

Do you know what I mean?

Maybe my disappointment over not being American, and therefore not being able to go over the top with absolutely everything (have you ever been to the cinema in America? They laugh **out loud!!** It is amazing, and shocking and I love it!) Means that I have always felt why bother? If you can't go the whole hog then seriously, WHY BOTHER?

I am renowned for being a miserable cow around this time of year amongst my family and friends and seriously? I am fine with it.

If I had a seasonal smell around the 'holidays', that smell would be '*fusty.*'

I am like the human equivalent of a damp squib.

There are many things in this world I love; Show tunes, Britney spears, shoes, sunglasses, handbags, good friends, hot chocolate, Grey's Anatomy, Ryan Reynolds, Disney World, Square Crisps, things that make you go hmmm and The Irish One's home made hummus, (and no, that isn't a synonym for something else, his chick peas are perfectly sized) but this time of year, will never, ever, ever, ever, ever, make it on to that list.

I hate Halloween because I hate dressing up. If I want to wear a witch outfit, or a zombie costume or a pair of plastic fangs, I shall do so at my own leisure you know? I will do so on a random Tuesday in February, and certainly not when everyone else is doing it. Where is the fun in that?

I hate bonfire night because every year I have to listen to my elderly neighbor bleat on relentlessly about how the local kids keep trying to nick off with his shed which then leads him unceremoniously on to how many cars are on the roads in comparison to when he was *my* age, and eventually on to the price of petrol.

I don't know how much petrol costs and I don't get the whole *litre to the gallon to the mile* thing. All I know is, Starbucks is next to a petrol station, so that's where I fill up.

I need coffee more than I need petrol; especially with the speed Doodle releases his bowels after each and every bang from the blessed fireworks that will go off from now until Christmas, so how many litres do I get to the gallon? Who cares? I get home don't I? And in case I don't, I have one of those spout things in the car.

How many shots do I get to see me through the day? 3. And make them DRY!!! (When I ask for a DRY cappuccino I do not want a latte!!!)

I hate Christmas because it's always a big 'who are you spending it with' drama and seriously? Turkey? Ergh. I would rather have Pizza. Which I have actually eaten on Christmas day in the past, and no it wasn't topped with stuffing. (Ergh.) Christmas sucks bum. I hate it. Even ketchup is banned.

Also, while I am on this subject, I never understood why we eat chocolate eggs on the day Jesus was re-born and I don't like summer because my thighs rub together. But those two are *by the by* I suppose.

I would even say bah humbug. But I don't like mints.

But you know what?

This year, as Halloween approached I thought sod it, I am starting therapy so how's about I actively encourage a new me.

I have to make an effort for Addison.

Mammy sort your head out and let's sparkle some glitter over the end of this year.

Let's see if I can 'live in the moment'!!

Yeay! Doesn't that sound fun???

Embracing the now and being open to trying harder for Addison is the reason Addison found himself at nursery last Tuesday dressed as Dracula.

I thought *he* could make an effort on *my* behalf and to be honest, he did look really cute, and a part of me, as I went to drop him off, if I am completely honest, was a little excited for him!

His first costume party!

The nursery had been advertising a 'spooky and fun party where all the kids need to be dressed up' for weeks.

I spent 8 quid on that Halloween costume from Morrison's, but I am sure the therapy he will no doubt need as a teen to help him understand why his mummy dressed him up as Dracula and sent him to nursery when NO OTHER CHILD IN THE WHOLE BUILDING was dressed up, will cost more.

I got the wrong day.

And I forgot to pack spare clothes.

He will be fine.

I am sure.

Although I have never seen a 6-month-old Dracula look so pissed off.

They should cast him next to Tom Cruise.

He has his smolder *down*.

This 'making an effort' is also the reason why I found myself stood in a field last night holding The Irish One's hand and muttering under my breath as Addison slept through the longest fire work display in history and my feet slowly sank in to the mud and dog poop surrounding the bonfire, which actually, now I come to think of it, did look suspiciously like my neighbours shed.

Everybody was saying 'ooo' a lot, so you know, I made an effort.

'Oooo....' I bleated. 'Can we go now?'

'No shut up whinging.'

The Irish One just doesn't get my misery. He is a strong believer in doing random things with wet feet, in fields, and dressing up as a pumpkin and I hate him for it.

Why bother?? (We have to now we have a son, I understand that but he is not even 1! Surely it can wait a bit!)

I could have been at home, setting my neighbours *actual* shed on fire, saying Oooo a lot, from the warmth of my living room with a hot chocolate!!

My boots are ruined, the pram is caked in crap and doodle's bowels have become so loose from the repetitive strain of all the loud banging that my back is now buggered too from all the bending over with the poop scoop.

Christmas next.

Can't wait.

Maybe I will get stuck in the chimney.

That's something to look forward to I suppose. (It'll get me out of eating turkey!)

Although, apparently, (*childish mimicy voice* ‘Ra raaa- from The Irish One) that is **NO** laughing matter. (GoD! It's not like someone getting stuck in a chimney caused the Potato famine, calm down!!!)

Addison will be dressed as Santa on Boxing Day though, I like the idea of the 'day behind' tradition.

It suits my disorganisation. (And yes that is a word, I looked it up.)

Second verse same as the first...

Here we go again...' I reluctantly swing my legs out of the parked car and plonk with considerable effort, my feet on to the hospital grounds.

Right in to a bloody puddle.

Watching the water soak up my trendy flares, so it will now look like I have decided to wear waders to my therapy session, I take a deep shaky sigh and close my eyes. Today is day 2. Everybody has wet legs on day 2. (The things you tell yourself to calm yourself down when you're anxious are weird. Moving my legs *out of the puddle* probably would have been a better idea but I couldn't.)

I re-open my eyes and sit motionless, staring at the denim on my shoes slowly changing colour before grasping on to my thighs and attempting to blow out all the anxiety through my mouth and calm my shaky core.

As I do this I look away from my shoes, which seem to also have some sort of blobby white stain on them, and up at the foreboding Victorian building sitting on the top of the hill like a majestic sturdy Grandpa who has seen it all.

I clamp my eyes closed for a second, feel around for my belongings and begin an attempt at preparing myself for what is about to happen.

'I am henry the 8th I am, henry the 8th I am, I am' I mutter to myself through gritted teeth in a failed effort at smiling, while remembering the advice The Irish One had given me last night.

Smile lots, he says. Smile lots and you'll feel calmer.

He also thinks, that if that doesn't work, in a separate and desperate bid to overcome my nerves I should go back to the courtyard where I was hysterically crying on Monday morning, and run around in circles clasping my head and singing I am Henry the 8th at top volume.

I told him last night that when I am here, I feel like a fly trapped under a thick drinking glass on a hot and sweaty summer day. Everybody is watching the fly for signs of madness and all the fly wants to do is fly away and go and party with its *fly* mates. (And, obviously ignore all of its issues and never come back to this place ever again.)

The Irish One believes behaving like this will get the *nerves,* over everybody watching me and thinking I am mad, out of my system, as it will convince everyone that I am in fact ***not mad.*** His logic being, that a *mad* person would never run around in circles in an institute, they would *zig zag.*

I am not sure about this, but I will see how today goes. (By the way, talking about *zig zagging,* if you ever find yourself being chased by a crocodile this is how you should run... take my word for it. This isn't relevant. I am delaying the inevitable. I know this.)

I slam the car door, now managing a shaky and somewhat manic smile to myself and sing 'Second verse, same as the first...'

'Pardon?' A woman on her way to work pauses and looks at me questioningly, 'Did you ask me something?'

'Oh, er, no, nothing sorry, just er, talking to myself again' I step towards her forcing myself to laugh loudly and therefore coming across like a deranged monkey. 'I am just a bit nervous' I say before turning towards my car and pointing my key at it, in an attempt to lock it.

This does **not** work as my key isn't electric.

It is just a key.

My car has no central locking and I am an idiot.

I am hoping the lady behind me has walked onwards and up to the reception but unfortunately she seems to be waiting for me. I mention something about leaving something on the passenger seat but still she just stands there. Waiting. Looking puzzled.

What I should have done at this point is walk calmly to the car, stick the key in the lock and turn it. But I didn't. In my anxious and idiotic state I thought I would try again to lock it with an imaginary button. God knows what I was hoping would happen. Maybe the gods would smile kindly on me and inject me with *the force* or something. Needless to say it didn't lock.

Eventually I accept defeat, shrug my shoulders and walk over to the keyhole.

'Don't know why I bothered, it doesn't even have central locking. I feel like a wasp you know?' I say without pausing for breath 'No not a wasp, a fly, I get all nervous and I do stupid things and now you will think I am mad, and maybe I am, have you ever heard the song henry the 8th? Well maybe I should tell you about this because The Irish One, well actually his name is...'

'It's Lexy isn't it?' She interrupts, her voice crisply cutting through the brittle morning air and in to the circle of craziness taking place in my brain.

'Yes,' I reply too brightly and run in to her personal space. I was expecting her to start walking but she hasn't so now we are almost nose to nose. 'Sorry,' I gasp and step back in surprise, I thought you were going to move.'

'I'll see you later today. Go and get yourself a cup of tea' and with that she gives me a tight smile and wanders off in the opposite direction to where she was initially heading, probably to the place where sane people are protected from people *like me.* (If a gorilla is chasing you, don't run in a *zig zag,* just fucking run ok? Don't go confusing a gorilla with a crocodile; I am not getting the blame for that one....just be aware is all.)

My bloody nerves!

You see, this is the thing; this is *exactly* why I didn't want to come back here today! Monday was exhausting; all that indecision about whether to open up or not and when I finally did, and I had exposed my core and much much more (not in a rude way, it isn't naked therapy or anything) before I could *process* what I had done, it was time to go home.

For the past two days, because of this, I have found myself over examining everything. I am over examining myself at a rate of knots! (Again, not in a rudey got my kit off way, it really *isn't* naked therapy!)

What if I don't put the washing in the drier now, and go for a wee instead, what does that say about me?

What if I only kiss Addison on the nose, and realise he tastes delicious so lick his cheek, what does that say about me?

What if I eat a full packet of fig biscuits, a bowl of ice cream and then some minestrone soup, what does that say about me?

Why do I know how to escape from random jungle animals when I live in a city, what does that say about me?

Coming back here today just amplifies this tenfold. After my run in with the lady in the car park, I am even more aware of the fact I am coming across Bonkers.com completely against my will.

If someone shouts 'Act Normal!' for some reason I grab my left tit and whistle the grand old duke of York. This is just the type of person I am.

The minute I get here I have this sense that all the doctors, psychologists and therapists are secretly examining my every little movement and metaphorically pulling apart every word that comes out of my mouth, searching to find the an underlying reason for my behaviour, so they can truly analyse just how mental I am.

This sends me in to a state of total panic and I end up behaving like each and every character from an episode of Winnie the Pooh in just under 15 minutes. (Eyore being my default setting.)

The day doesn't end there either.

As I was walking up to grand old house at the top of the mountain, I noticed a uniformed member of staff walking towards me and out of nowhere I seemed to develop a dodgy gangster limp.

All memory of being able to walk like a normal person was immediately wiped from my mind the instant I spotted the gangly, brown haired doctor walking towards me and I was instantly, and against my will, switched in to Lexy *demo* mode.

Gangster limp, normal limp, skip, hop and back to gangster limp.

AND then to make it worse! (Yes it got worse) I had a light bulb idea moment.

Remembering what The Irish One had told me the night previous about reverse psychophysiology (I've given up trying to spell that word now), I thought the good doctor would *obviously* be able to see it was just nerves making me act random, and so decided to try and make light of it.

As he walked directly past me to my left smiling slightly and avoiding eye contact, I all but bellowed (bloody nerves) 'Yo!' and flicked my fingers in that annoying way teenagers do, except I have never been able to do it, so it came across as a swipe, and I accidentally caught his hip bone with my nails.

He stopped and turned to look at me startled as I stood there finding this complete balls up hysterical, and doubled over laughing. I was about to gasp my excuse for the behaviour but sensing I was about to speak, he interrupted quickly before I could.

'It's Lexy isn't it? I'll see *you* later.'

I decided to brush it off and walk onwards and upwards.

Spotting a young girl from my group pouring herself a coffee I shook off the gangster limp and managed to stumble towards her in a desperate bid to make a new friend and in a frantic hope to quell some of the nervous behaviour that was taking over my bodily functions.

My opening gambit?

'Hi, how's your crazy this morning? Mine is out of control.'

I thought she'd laugh. She didn't.

She said she was fine and then very sneakily escaped while I was trying to find the button for black coffee.

Walking out in to reception carrying my cup and saucer I spotted both doctors I had seen this morning, chatting behind reception.

Immediately reverting in to *hill Billy* mode I wave and shout howdy.

Unfortunately I use the hand which is holding the fresh brewed and very delicate (posh) cup of coffee.

I wince as it runs down my sleeve tracing a trail of pain from my wrist to my elbow, but trying to ignore the fact it has happened at all. (Much like someone who falls over in front of a group of people and then denies it ever happening by getting up and walking off on a broken ankle.)

'Are you ok? That looks sore' the one whose hip I thwacked jumps up 'I'll get you some tissue.'

I plaster on a smile and dig my own grave.

'It's ok, I like the pain.' I proclaim proudly 'And it smells lovely.'

They look at me with their mouths hanging open. I am a walking talking gangster loving, imaginary star trek car locking coffee self-harming crazy crocodile quoting mentalist.

I turn to walk outside.

'Lexy?' The therapist shouts.

'Yes?'

'Your key worker wants to see you at 3pm.'

I bloody bet she does.
I walked out singing 'I am henry the 8th I am...' in response.

The image of Depression...

There comes a certain point in a woman's life where she has to break the silence.

The past few weeks, in and out of the Priory more times than Amy Winehouse during the drug years (and with very similar hair, much to my disappointment) has left me feeling locked inside my head with no escape.

Alcatraz holds nothing in comparison to the self-imposed confines of my radio silence let me tell you. Swimming through all types of nauseatingly smelly and putrid emotional mud has left me feeling both emotionally drained and exhausted, and now on top of that, we are all suffering from a pretty horrific stomach bug.

Therapy is hard, there is no two ways about it, but what is harder? Not being able to escape over the border to Mexico when one really needs to. I look online at all these images of supposedly depressed people. They are all sat in corners holding their heads and I have to be honest, it's so very not real life. I would love a spare 2 minutes to sit in a corner holding my head but my fight to not book an escape online came to an abrupt and shocking end at approximately 8pm on Saturday night.

I had just received a text from a friend requesting my company at the local pub.

'The mum's are out partying, we are at the cinema, we miss you. Where are you?'

I felt; *'I am currently trying not to machine gun poo while violently throwing up, enjoy the film.'* would probably have been a slight over share on my part, and more than likely would have put the girls right off their half pints and chocolate raisins, so I chose instead to not respond, and direct my full attention and maximum focus to the task at hand.

The task being emptying ones stomach without opening ones bladder against ones will, while moaning erratically each and every time the wave of nausea crescendo's up in to my throat, as well as, at the same time groaning 'I've been siiiiiiiiick' at a volume the entire neighborhood can hear in a bid to ensure each and every person in the vicinity has a full understanding of what I am having to endure and can completely agree and attest to the fact that I, Lexy Ellis am a brave little soldier who is being poorly but really should win an award for her blatant courageous vomiting.

The sweat was rolling down my forehead, my stomach was cramping, convulsing and contracting and I was doing my damnedest to hold on to consciousness while at the same time cleaning up the rim of the loo with a wet wipe (is there anything worse than sick on the loo rim? See? Even in times of trouble, mother nature calls to me, singing words of wisdom... hang on sorry, that's not what I meant, I am clearly still delirious...I am still conscientious of others that's what I meant!) When like a demon of stupidity whispering in my stressed to fuckety ear, from behind the bathroom door came a little voice, filled with fear.

'Darling, I am sorry to trouble you, but the dog has shit everywhere and Addison has been sick all over the sofa, do you know how long you will be? I could really do with some help out here.'

I honestly think that this simply horrifying and nightmarish experience deserves a moment's silence. I really do. We should totally give it the respect it deserves.

But to be honest, having had enough silence over the last 3 weeks, this was the prick that broke the camels back, the cherry on the ball shaped cake, the stone being thrown in the big glass house and the icing on a big hairy poodle shaped turd.

My silence has been broken.

Can you hear me screaming?

I cleaned up dog poo while running to the toilet to be sick.

Addison has a tummy bug too you see and although The Irish One was amazingly helpful in other non-sick related ways, I had to clean up doggy doo doo while wiping a nappy one can only describe as a swimming pool of murky green poo at the same time. I then had to be sick myself and it was at that point I noticed there were bits of sweetcorn everywhere, but nobody even ate any sweetcorn? Also why did I then think eating a bag of salt and vinegar Disco's would settle my stomach when the all they did was take what was remaining on the roof of my mouth off with their vinegary torture!?!?

Why the hell do I have to catch everything Addison catches and then Why the HELL does doodle have to catch everything I catch?

I had to clean up poo while cleaning my own sick up! Weeing when you sneeze is one thing but following through when you vomit? That isn't funny at all! Not at all. It may have scarred me for life! Doodle witnessed it! He will never be the same again. Ever. Motherhood isn't magical! It is tragic. Tragic. My friends were all at the cinema living some sort of dream life and meanwhile I was stuck in the little flat of horrors. There was no need for a talking plant or a woman with bouncy red hair, I had a dog with gastroenteritis and a baby who in between all the vomiting and wet farting, thought it was fun to try and lick a glass window, resulting in more bruises on his forehead and more screams of anguish than you would see on the *hills have eyes.* If you wanted to play connect the dots on Addison's forehead now you totally could and you know what you would spell? THE HORROR THE HORROR.

It wasn't only my weekend that got me here, it was last week too! My bag got nicked, my phone screen smashed, my car got a flat tire... the list is fecking endless!

SO yes. I would love to sit in a corner with my head in my hands acting 'depressed.' I WOULD LOVE TO.

Today at the mental hospital I intend to talk a lot.

Just woe betide, the person who politely asks how my weekend went.

The mosquito effect...

It was while I was driving to McDonalds for a sneaky Drifter Mcflurry at 8 o'clock on Tuesday evening that I decided I would probably hold off on the whole *killing myself* thing.

I hadn't put much thought in to the actual event other than thinking perhaps I would leave a note describing how I would like people to behave and what I would like people to wear at my funeral (big shades and lots of random dramatic hysterical sobbing please. And then a disco that goes on all night.) And yes, ok. Maybe I had thought *a little* about how I would do it, but I hadn't set a date or anything.

The very idea of it was tiny. It was just a little niggling mosquito at the very back of my head that would occasionally flap its wings, buzz and fanny around. At first it would annoy the hell out of me and I would fight tooth and nail to swat it away.

I have to admit though, there were times during the worst *days* when I had become so lethargic in both mood and physicality that I would allow it to bounce around joyfully and my struggle to wave it away would become very lackluster, preferring instead to lie back and watch.

It was during these lonely and hidden moments, filled with self-loathing and internal sadness that, I suppose, if I am truly honest, I thought perhaps it might be a good idea.

That the world would be a better place without me in it.

I also spent an inordinate amount of time planning the disco for my funeral.

There was going to be a disco ball and vodka fountain, where instead of dipping fudge in chocolate you dipped lemon in vodka. Fabulous Drag queens would belt out a load of sad tunes but with a glittery and marvelous twist and once all the old fogeys had retired to their own homes and just the giggly girls were left, I would organise some sort of hilariously naughty camp ra ra show involving Sinitta singing a whole host of 80's tunes in a Hula skirt bonanza.

It was during my second week at therapy in a moment of madness, I admitted I *had* been planning to jump off a train platform.

I surprised myself by knowing which station.

So it turns out I had put some thought in to it after all, without even realising.

Enjoying the peacefulness of sitting alone in the car, swirling cheap half melted ice cream and liquid gold around a big white plastic spoon, while staring out at the grimy grey tower block in front of me and above it at the almost translucent yellow, orange and pink, tranquil and yet somehow angry, sky, I finally swatted the mosquito and allowed myself to consciously acknowledge what was going on.

Those thoughts aren't healthy to entertain even on a subconscious level and if I was planning anything of the sort then why the hell bother putting myself through all the therapy in the hope of getting better? Surely putting oneself through hours of torturous ruminating and reminiscing over some quite traumatic events would be totally futile if the end result would be me; dead.

I have an illness. The priory hospital has helped me understand this. It is an illness just like any physical illness except it is in my brain.

It is not my fault, it does not make me a bad person or a terrible mother. It does not make me disgusting or ugly or evil, or even unworthy.

It is not my fault.

The illness is Post-natal depression and I am *not* going to let it beat me.

I have a support network of friends and family, and it is time to come clean and *fess up*, thus allowing them to help, however hard that may be.

And most importantly I have my beautiful, angelic, gorgeous, tottering, wobbling, giggling, slobbering son who I bloody brought in to this world, and who needs me just as much as I need him.

He is my fucking everything, and even though this 'chemical imbalance' has robbed me of some of the most precious moments in his first year and is still attempting to steal each and every positive emotion from me I will not let it win the war.

The occasional battle maybe, but never the war.

Did I tell you about my Drifter Mcflurry moment?

The machine was broken so the guy made it by hand. It was my idea of heaven in a cup. Far too much topping and not enough ice cream. I still feel all warm and gooey thinking about it now.

It was one of those once in a lifetime events. (Stay with me here.)

It's funny how sometimes a tiny action made by a complete stranger, an accidental flick of the wrist, allowing too much sugar to fill up a cup, can effectively change somebody else's life path forever, without either of them even ever realising.

Last night a Drifter Mcflurry saved my life. (The lesser known In Deep song.)

Oh and, FYI– if I ever get married, one day (cough cough, M-A-R-R-I-E-D Irish One, that thing where one person gets down on one knee and then you go to church and profess your love for one another....) my reception is now going to be bloody brilliant!!!

How do I get hold of Sinitta?

Eh?

Listen now, this is important.

If you cannot picture me dressed up as a giant root vegetable running around Manchester city centre, then I suggest you skip this chapter and come back another day.

I wouldn't mind either because some things just aren't meant to be.

Like, World Peace for instance.

Or even, my last set of false nails.

You think that's a bit far-fetched? That my extremely glittery, bombastically special talons couldn't possibly have anything to do with the state of the new union, Rupert Murdoch and some bearded dude in Iran?

Well you would be wrong.

What? Where the hell am I going with this one?

I honestly do not know but seriously stick with me; it'll be worth it in the end.

I just know it.

(Obviously I can't promise this and don't sue me if you get to the end of this bit and feel like a) wringing my neck or b) demanding your internet provider refund you the 7 minutes air time it will undoubtedly take you to decipher the insanity of this chapter or even c) digging up the back garden and planting a marrow. I take no responsibility for what is about to happen.)

This week the obligatory therapy sessions have left me feeling a little like I have been jumping on an emotional trampoline.

Wahhheyyyyy look at meeeeee I'm sooo hiiighhh I feel like a teenager againnn!!

Oooooooooo fucking hell coming downs a bit hard on the old back oof!

Waheeeeeyyyy look at meeeeee I can do a star jump it feels so goooood!!

Waoooof was that my ankle that made that breaking noise? Campumf eck, my necks gone all tingly.

Wahhheyyyyy I'm going to try a sitting jump! I can do anything I'm amazinggg!

Awhaccckkk good god somebody help me up, my back is *actually* broken and im pretty sure I just bit my tongue in two!

Oh what the hell Waheeeeeyyyy one last go can't hurt, I'm higherrr than everrrrr!!!! I am the QUEEEN OFFF THEEE WORRRLLLDDDDD.

Er, yes. That *is* wee running down my legs. Do you have a spare Tena? Anyone?

Seriously, it is *such* a shame there isn't an Olympic sport for being a tit, because I seriously deserve an award. I would win it too.

'And the gold/diamond *Nork* trophy, sponsored by *tommee tippee* and *Lanosil angry nipple cream* for how many emotions can you tear through in a ten minute period, goes to Lexy Ellis for being a prize floppy and floundering, utter mammary gland!!!

Congratulations all around. You are officially a pimpled teat.'

Seriously. (In case you felt I hadn't already used the word seriously enough. I am totally serious. Seriously.)

Either that or someone should ~~seriously~~ consider casting me in an emotional version of Challenge Anneka. They could call it Challenge Knobby, and instead of dressing me up in a jumpsuit (because let's face it, this is tea time telly and no one needs to see *that* while they are tucking in to their reduced fat Bangers and Smash) they could dress me up as a giant cucumber and have me half run half waddle around shopping centers worldwide trying to find hidden objects stashed under 3 wheeler prams without anyone noticing. I can see it now.

'Mary, was that a giant cucumber that just walked past or are these sleepless nights getting too much for me?'

'No Laura, I think I saw it too. Actually, I am sure it stole a bottle out of my changing bag. But then again, it may have been a gherkin.'

And I would be filmed scuttling off dressed as a huge vegetable (that Addison clearly wouldn't eat) riddled with guilt about my thievery before doing an emotional 360 and coming back, bending over and battering them both with my elongated forehead because my mother never showed me enough affection.

Can you imagine?

I can see the headlines now.

Killer cucumber strikes again. Mr. Bloom involved in compostarium nightmare!!

First and only interview here!!

'It wasn't my allotment, there **was** fuck all to see!' He sang with his northern twang 'She was just a mentalist from up somewhere near me....'

BBC show gets out of hand!! Overtired mother finally loses the will to...

Anyway.

Moving on swiftly.

Dear diary,

Today I bought Addison some foamy letters for the bath. Ever since I first saw those two pink lines sat on the bathroom side (pink lines not white lines, those days are long gone!) I have imagined walking in to the bathroom post bath time and seeing my daughter's (oops I mean son's) name emblazoned on the wall in foamy letters. It would be so romantic. This would mean we had made it as a proper family. I would be a <u>proper</u> mummy. Limping around Mothercare today (two toes, one sofa, a great divide) I spotted a bag of alphabet letters and bought them! I cannot wait to give Addison a bath and make this simple dream come true! As soon as he gets up it is bath time! Can't wait to see what they look like! Will have to take photos!

Dear diary,

There are no fecking eses's in the bag. (Like the letter s. Not Esse like some Spanish mafia type. I'm bloody glad there are no Spanish mafia types in the bag! The last thing I need at bath time what with all the wailing and splashing already going on, is a little Spanish man in a straw hat holding a machine gun to my head. What the hell kind of pressure would that put on me? Why the hell would Mothercare do that to me? A B C D E F YO SOY JOSE!! And what if the mafia type got hungry? What would I feed him? Do mafia types eat paella?) What the bloody hell kind of alphabet doesn't have an S in it???? MY son's name has two BLOODY ese's in it. (Again the letter S. My sons name does not have two Spanish men holding machine guns and plates of badly made paella behind their backs in it.) So there goes that daydream. I couldn't even swear. All the swear words I can think of have an S in them! (Except the c word and although I was tempted, I was that angry! There is always a chance that grandma could call round and I'm not sure even I could make excuses and get away with having the word c*nt written in bouncy letters on the bathroom wall with a one year old in the house.) How does one make paella?

Dear diary.

So pleased with my sparkly new nails! They look wonderful. Feel a little more human again after the nightmares of weeks gone by. Sarah did such a good job on them and I feel proper glam.

Dear diary.

Within 2 days of having my nails done, the plague hit. I broke 4 in a terrible car door accident following on from shit up back –gate, and then managed to not only get **my** puke under the remaining 6, but also had a feeling there may have been some of Addison's and Doodle the Poodle's puke lodged under them too. It was a chance I couldn't take. I ripped the remaining 6 off in a fit of fury and disgust. My hands are in tatters. (And so is my arse but that is another story altogether.) I officially resemble Fagan from Oliver but with less britches and more swearing. Damn stomach bug spreading like wildfire. Bloody motherhood!

Dear diary, I actually met the real Jo Frost. She was amazing. She gave me some great advice.

Dear Diary, I got too excited and screamed in Jo frosts face. She was covered in spit.

Dear Diary, I am writing this from the naughty corner.

Dear Diary, I have met some truly lovely and amazing people this week.

Dear Diary, I dropped a red-hot fishcake on my foot. It hurt.

Dear Diary, The Irish One and I are going to spend some quality time together tonight.

Dear Diary, Was forced to watch Planet of the Apes. What a load of guff! How can you be romantic after watching that? For the love of god.

Dear Diary, Had a dream I was being attacked by a monkey in a smoking jacket. Woke up sweaty.

Dear Diary, Blame Tim Burton for full night of unrest.

Dear Diary, Took Addison to see the planes at the airfield. We had a great time.

Dear Diary, until he shit up his back while I was talking to a pilot. It smelt like somebody died. The guy clearly thought it was me. Addison found this hilarious. I did not.

Dear Diary, The council say I can't build a compostarium. I only want to grow shoes.

Dear Diary, Must find other ways of enticing Mr. Bloom. I think I fancy him. What is wrong with me?

Dear Diary, Therapy is supposed to regulate my moods.

Dear Diary, Just laughed, cried, sneezed and weed in the space of twenty minutes.

Dear Diary, Have put on 5 pounds.

Dear Diary, The Irish One said that 'compared to the empty water balloon' my stomach resembled after giving birth I have done really well. He said he was a 'bit worried' it would never go and said he thought 'what the hell is that?' when he saw me straight afterwards 'sitting with it plonked in front of me.'

Dear Diary, Have dug a man shaped hole in the back garden.

Dear Diary, Will this week ever end?

Dear Diary, Will I ever be an organised mother?

Dear Diary, Some things just aren't meant to be.

Like Monkey's ruling the world.

Or Being the perfect mother.

I think you must just have to let go and enjoy the moment.

But I see these other mothers and they look so restrained and in control! Surely they aren't having secret rumblings for a northern man in wellies who owns a talking cabbage? Surely they don't forget to clean dishes and end up eating soup out of the pan? Surely they aren't scared of turning in to Nanny from count Duckula?

Oh well.

Think I will retire my plans and settle down for a while, in the here and now. I am what I am, que sera and whatever will be will be. Once a brick always a brick.

(I may have made that last one up.)

But **seriously**, if you happen to see a giant cucumber toddling down the road looking a bit confused and carrying and Aldi bag, keep an eye on your belongings sure, but don't write it off, maybe give it a wave. Or maybe a hug.

But be warned, it may swear at you. Or cry. Or gush, or laugh, or dance, or potentially bend over and get in to fight mode.... you just never know with those root veg.

They can be a bit unpredictable.

Just like new mothers.

Footprint in the sand...

It was all going *swimmingly* well.

I had decided over a Mcflurry not to kill myself and was managing, on most days not to flirt with the idea of driving at 80 miles per hour directly in to a brick wall.

Things were looking up.

And then they weren't.

It was as simple a shift as that.

Everything was going wrong. Even the small things I used to be able to manage with ease, even the small pleasures I would take for granted, became un-climbable mountains.

My pizza was burnt, my socks didn't match and no matter how hard I tried to enjoy it, my coffee was tasteless.

The world lost its sparkle, my life lost its meaning and I just couldn't run any longer.

There was no hiding, around every corner, behind every task, the horrible truth was staring at me in the face.

It would jump out at me with every breath I took.

I didn't want to be a mum anymore.

I don't want to be a mummy. I just want to be me. I don't care about life anymore. It has no meaning.

In my little boys eyes I was supposed to see meaning, but there was none. In my little boys smile I was supposed to feel a soaring, but there was none. In my little boys hand I was supposed to find the strength to protect him, but there was none.

I couldn't be bothered to live my life anymore, not even for him.

What kind of horrible awful person thinks such thoughts? I deserved to be dead. Nothing more. Nothing less.

One by one, all the spinning plates I had been struggling to hold up, while keeping, of course, a big fat fake smile on my face, came tumbling to the floor, one by one and me? I allowed myself to fall down with them, finally.

I lay there for hours, in the dark with the scattered remains of my life laying in shards around me.

Nothing mattered. Least of all me.

As far as I am aware, the car drove itself to the hospital.

I have since been told I was at the wheel.

I found myself sitting in a group therapy session supposedly centered on self-esteem.

One last shot to tell somebody. One last chance to see if I matter, one last chance to prove I don't.

'Lexy, how are you today?'

Be honest Lexy, this is your last chance to be honest.

'Well Paul,' I spoke slowly avoiding eye contact, staring at the wall and trying to make sense of what was about to happen 'I have told numerous people I want to die, have admitted to countless friends I no longer want to be alive... But the thing is though Paul. Nobody can hear me, I won't let them, nobody can care, I won't let them.... But the thing is Paul...' I repeat, looking him directly in the eye, the tears coursing down my cheeks 'I want to die today... and nobody is allowed to care, not even me.'

And in that moment, I saw somebody staring back at me who may not know me, but who had heard. Not just listened, but had heard, and had understood finally, I hadn't had a choice in the matter.

Salvation.

And with his kind words, direct action and understanding smile, a man called Paul saved my life.

Thank you Paul you are one hell of an amazing person and I will never ever forget what you have done for me. You are precious.

And in that moment, life as I knew it was over. Forever.

Is that a little dramatic? Well come on now, give me some credit here, I am building up to the big finale.

I've just been admitted in to a mental hospital for the utterly depressed and the criminally insane.

Ok. No, not really the criminally insane, but it sounds beefier doesn't it?

What follows over the next few weeks will be my story, and mine alone.

My journey.

Searching for that illusive light, at the end of the sewage tunnel.

Check in here...

As the wheels of my car crunched over the gravel drive I paused for a split second, frozen by the magnitude of what was about to happen.

I stumbled erratically to locate the right gear, switching from third and back down to first and eventually manically settling on neutral, my logical thought process completely stolen by the bleakness of the morning.

With my heart pounding out of my chest, the only reminder I was still alive, my little black family carrier, with the backseat holding little more than an empty, crisp spattered car seat and a small bag of my clothes, rolled pathetically in to large space and eventually came to a stop.

I don't know how long I sat there staring at the big Daddy oak tree, I suppose it doesn't really matter, I was as numb to the ticking of the clock as I was to my son's kisses.

When I did eventually manage to climb out in to the cold air of the morning, I spotted a friend I had made here, a girl I had been having therapy with across the car park. She smiled kindly in my direction and that kind smile, knocked me sideways.

The numbness I had so carefully cultivated over the months to protect me from the searing pain, was wiped out and destroyed by a tsunami of icy panic, which engulfed me from the tip of my heart to the bottom of my toes.

'I don't think I can do this' I cried to her, my knees threatening to give way, my bottom lip actually shaking and wobbling as I spoke, the pain and the fear becoming unbearable 'I Just don't think I can.'

She helped me carry my bags and with her arm around my shoulder we crunched over the pebbles towards reception.

We both knew I had no choice.

It was the unspoken elephant between us.

I was to be admitted in to hospital or I would be dead soon.

I had just dropped Addison off at nursery, he was expecting me to pick him up in 3 hours.

Would I ever be picking him up again?

I am so so sorry my boy.

So so sorry.

Ann Glummers...

What does one pack to stay in a lunatic asylum?

The answer all though you may think simple is actually a recipe for disaster.

Let us examine the evidence.

Your head is west, your soul east, your mind north, and your boobs, as always... pointing south.

Couple this with having to put ones case together in the dark to avoid waking and therefore sobbing all over a small boy you are not sure you should leave, not actually wanting to go, a hefty amount of denial that anything is wrong with you in the first place (other than being a drama queen) and you quite literally have created a situation that I would have to liken to letting go of a social hand grenade in a heavily populated crazy house.

Also, let us not forget you are still two stone heavier than you believe you are and the climate has been temperamental to say the least.

Are you dying to know what I brought?

I honestly was.

I had absolutely no recollection of packing at all and was shocked to see the sheer volume of luggage waiting for me, piled dangerously on the single bed when I arrived in to my room.

2 heaving pale pink mucky rucksacks, one snowboard sized (body bag felt a little inappropriate an adjective here) sports bag, a bursting glittery river island 'hand bag' (Aka cargo

carrier) and the age old and ever present plastic Aldi bag (you can take the girl out of Eccles...) were all sat anticipating my arrival.

'Are these the bags you packed Lexy?'

I walk towards them slowly trying to banish thoughts of running home and back in to the arms of The Irish One and Addy. This is too strange a place. My head is too strange a place. I do not live here. I do not know if these are the bags I packed.

But I must have done.

'I think so yes' I whisper, moving over to the window and looking outside. Completely lost and yet feeling a little bit found.

'Ok honey,' the young nurse continues kindly from behind me 'are you ready for your bag search?'

'Bag search?' I gasp turning around, my breath catching in my throat, my heart beginning to hammer in my chest.

'Yes, we have to check your bags to ensure you have brought only relevant items, this may seem a little over the top but I am sure you can understand' she declares snapping on a pair of plastic gloves and looking nervously at the mountain of crap still piled precariously on the bed.

Flashbacks of the night previous scream through my subconscious mingled in with movie stills from Sandra Bullock in 28 days. (Jeremiah was a bullfrog....)

What the hell did I pack??

I am struggling to separate the two mangled thought patterns when a single memory pushes to the forefront of my mind and my bowels audibly turn over in a fit of horror.

Jesus Christ.

Please tell me that in my fog induced state, I haven't packed my dildo.

Wading through my muddy memory banks trying to recall the last time I saw my neon pink rampant rabbit, a man walks in to the room and I almost pass out.

'I hope it is ok Lexy but I need to be here to process everything too, it shouldn't take long and then we can leave you to make yourself at home...' Nick the ward manager fiddles with his handlebar moustache and feels out behind him for a chair.

'Ok, no problem' I whisper praying my bowels don't release all over the floor and hopping from one foot to the next.

There is a lot to be said for 'living in the moment' but to be honest at this point; *dying* in the moment seems more applicable.

Trying to vanquish thoughts of Nick in leather chaps from my mind (it's the 'tash, I keep wanting to call him Kenneth,) I turn towards the window, leaving my back to the room. My very own metaphorical escape attempt, and believe me, this is the kind of room, led to by a deserted and lonely corridor, you would really want to escape from at the best of times never mind when you have the cast of 'carry on the crazy' stuffed in there struggling for breathe with you.

My home for the foreseeable future is a cramped and murky cream carpeted quadrangular room tagged on to the end of an eating disorder unit on the upstairs ward of the hospital. It has an adjoining triangular bathroom off to the right, which can be accessed through a heavy and vicious swinging door.

(Mental note to self; when desperate for a wee, do not **PULL** door out *towards* you, walk in to the bathroom *and then* grapple for the light switch back on the *outside* of the wall as this will clearly leave your arm exposed to the downright sinister and *hit man-esque* rebounding door. The pain you will feel as it crushes your radius (posh word for arm bone) is in no way similar to self-harm. It is just ruddy painful and you could really do without it. Follow this process *dick head,* and you should be fine. Flick light switch, **PUSH** door *in* and then wee. Simples.)

There are two bay windows beside the single bed which look out on to the communal garden (occupied with nutter's lounging around on bean bags - I should fit right in) which give the room a light and airy feel even though the room itself, even without me in it, is quite cluttered with stuff.

A giant mahogany wardrobe, a matching wooden and outsized desk fitted with lockable draws, a slightly bigger than single bed and two large bedside tables have also been crammed in to the room, along with a hardback desk chair and a deceptively comfortable (but not at all) armchair by the door, which Nick himself is now perched in, flip board balanced on his crossed knee, and pen poised and awaiting instruction.

Hopping from foot to foot in the corner, and trying not to make eye contact with either of my un-welcomed guests I attempt to open the window.

Unfortunately, as I then find out, the windows do not open very wide; presumably to stop you from committing dildo induced *Harry Carry*.

'Ok, here we go. Nick, if you can make a list, I will start with the first bag.'

From behind me, I hear her as she unzips the full length of my horribly kitsch bursting at the seams hold all and is accosted by an explosion of fabric. She takes a deep breath and dives in.

- **1 long cardigan. Beige.** I think what she meant was; could have once been described as white but now resembles the colour Dulux would probably label 'Ingrained dirt.'

- **1 pair of trousers, size 10** she looks up at me dubiously before continuing **Navy blue. Half a powdery white tablet in the pocket.**

My heart stops beating.

'Lexy, I am hoping this is a paracetamol but either way' she sighs, turning it over for examination 'it will be confiscated and put in clinical waste'

'Umhum.' I reply, returning back to watching the mentalists out of the window while beads of sweat congregate at the base of my spine. 'It will have been a Paracetamol, I don't do drugs. Not anymore anyway, I used to but only recreational, not like...'

'Stop talking.' She interrupts. 'You don't have to explain.'

'Yet.' I panic to myself, while enduring visions of her pulling out a swirling whirling mechanical cock from the bag and saying deadpan,

•**One penis. Hardly used. Size Large.**

I turn back to the window and concentrate on breathing. The stomach clenching torture continuing from behind me.

•**One pair of jeans. Size 12, light blue. Ripped.** Scruffy bitch.

•**One high-heeled shoe. Size 5. Green.** Yes, just one.

•**One hooded jumper. Red.** That stinks of vomit.

•**Another high-heeled shoe. Size 5. Blue.** Eh?

•**One seemingly ancient teddy bear with one eye missing wearing a dinosaur print baby-gro**. That's fat-tum. My childhood bear. *Cringe*

•**One packet of fragrance free Asda brand baby wipes.** Huh?

•**One pair of leggings. Black. Gusset torn.** Oh god I brought the old ones.

•**Two packets of new Asda knickers size 8.** Seriously? Size 8? For the love of god! What planet was I on? Wedgie.com! FFS!

•**One make up bag containing a shit load of powder covered crap.** She may not have said these exact words but everybody in the room was thinking it. Even fat-tum. (Who was probably also a bit pissed off to be wearing a baby gro. He is 31.)

•**2 wonder bras, one black one white.** Shhh! The secret is out. I no longer have boobs but *used condoms* hanging from my breastplate. Ahhh the magic of motherhood. Never mind empty nest syndrome. I have empty breast syndrome.

•**A single and lonely croc. Red.** I literally have no idea where this came from. I have never owned Crocs.

•**A laptop.**

•**5 Pampers size 3 nappies.** 2 things are wrong with this picture. Why the hell have I bought nappies? And Addy is in size 4's anyway...

•**More Asda own baby wipes.** We never have wipes at home? Where have these all come from? Poor Irish One, he is in charge of a child and has been left *wipeless.*

•A hairbrush, hidden under a wigs worth of dead hair. Gross. But... fuck off. It's motherhood. Not my fault I am now the proud owner of a mullet.

•A pair of black Ugg boots. Size 6. Prized possession. At least I brought something right. She thinks, sweating in a t-shirt.

•3 t-shirts with various designs on them. All dirty.

•One little black dress. What night is vodka night?

•One pair of GHD hair straighteners' held together with gaffa tape.

•One pair of glasses held together with gaffa tape.

•One sports sock.

•One black sock.

•A mobile charger held together with gaffa tape.

•A hairdryer held together with gaffa tape.

'And that's it Lexy, so we will leave you to it...'

I turn around incredulously and stare at the empty bags. 'Is that all?' I stutter? '2 odd shoes, knickers that are going to stop the circulation to my upper body, but no willy? Thank god for no gaffa taped willy! There is No Way that would have passed the Pat test!'

I am too overjoyed with the outcome to realise what I have just spluttered.

She laughs and winks at me as Nick shuffles out of the room coughing and spitting in disbelief. (What? I'm crazy! Your bum hangs out of leather pants at the weekends! I'm almost sure of it! Sod off.)

'There are a few articles we will need to take with us to be pat tested, I would imagine that most of your appliances held together with gaffa tape will not be returned until the end of your stay here, as they may accidentally set the building on fire. Please try and get some rest now honey, as your therapy will start in the morning. If you need anything just shout.' She quietly closes the door behind her and I am completely and miserably alone for the first time in 15 months.

'There is nothing I want to do more now or need to do more now, than go home.' I whisper to fattum silently. 'I want to go home.'

I think about my son and how I won't see him for weeks before lying slowly on the single bed. Oh god what have I done?

I am on a section 2.

I jump up from the bed.

No. I will not lie here. I will pick up my heavy heart and head for the mystic garden.

Surely I am not the only Glum Mum in the village...

One for Sorrow...

I am on fifteen-minute observations.

Or '*1 in fifteen obs*' as they say in the business.

This is because I have a history of self-harm and am currently seen, during the settling in period, as high risk.

Red alert!! Amber warning!! Mentalist moose on the loose!!

This essentially means that every 15 minutes no matter where I am or what I am doing, a head will appear from around a corner, under a sofa or behind a door, nod at me, check a tick box and move on.

I have no idea what is written on that tick box but I imagine it to contain the following;

Dead/not dead. *Delete as appropriate.*

The person, whoever it may be, will then piss off for another 15 minutes before returning once again like a turd on a bungee rope to repeat the same action.

I do wonder on occasion if as their shifts plod by they grow ever so slightly fatigued with the same monotonous task and have to resist the urge to write;

Lexy Ellis. 1.20pm - Not dead but found crying in the bath, left her to it.

Or ;

Lexy Ellis. 1.35pm – Lexy located in room 42, bent over her armchair panting and scratching like an overworked Alsatian with a nasty flea infestation. (My eczema is really playing up.)

Or even;

'I unearthed Lexy in her chamber decorating a noose she had fashioned out of a mangy old dressing gown cord; I have therefore removed any object from the room, including her dressing gown, which could potentially be used as a weapon. The bitch can walk around hiding her bushel with a hand towel as punishment for making me late for the next 15-minute ob's. In fact, I may as well just stay *here* and annoy her for the next 9 minutes. I am then, in effect killing (the happiness) of two birds (me and her) with one stone. (I have no stone.)'

Do you get the gist?

It is *trés trés* bothersome. And they are *trés trés* useless anyway.

It isn't like there is anything in this godforsaken padded cell I could attach a noose to anyway! Which was why I was *actually,* and *pretty innocently* just decorating my dressing gown with blue-tac. Honest.

There are no light fittings, not that I have been looking, the light just seeps in from the ceiling through pot holes and there are absolutely no prongs, knobs or spikes protruding from anywhere that I could do any damage with even if I was intent on doing so. Even the bloody shower is electric, meaning there are no taps and as with the lights, the water just magically appears through a hole in the wall.

(Just to be clear here, the lights in my room do not magically shoot water through a hole in the ceiling. They shoot light. Which is a relief as I would undoubtedly flick the wrong switch in the dead of night and end up accidentally exposing myself to some pretty horrific electric shock therapy on a very regular basis.... And think about the carpet. It would be soggy. No. The water is out of the hole in the shower, the light is out of the hole in the ceiling. Are we clear?)

So yes, my attempts at exposing myself to any kind of injury would be pretty futile.

Which does make me wonder what the point of '1 in 15 *ob's*' is actually for other than to create a situation of complete and utter frustration and annoyance for everybody involved.

Having to condense each and every action in to a 15-minute slot has actually resulted in me having to speed me up a notch, when I am sure the point of being in here, in the first place, was to slow me down a few thousand notches.

I am now officially known (by the plants and shrubs dotted around my room) as flash Gordon.

Shower in 15 minutes? With hair as long and greasy as mine? NO PROBLEM!

I can;

- Get naked

- Press button on wall 15 times so water heats up.

- Climb over and in to the bath (that incidentally I am sure has been created by the same company that makes the kamikaze type water slides) and slowly and precariously hot foot it, like one may when walking a tightrope, towards water *spitter outter*.

- Dry hump freezing cold tile wall to ensure water dribbles on to my back.

- Forcefully squidge bum against freezing cold tile wall to ensure water seeps on to my front.

- Splash about a bit for dramatic effect (while trying not to imagine it is actually just somebody stood behind the hole in wall ineffectively spitting on me.)

- Press button on wall 12 times to turn spit-like shower off.

- Try <u>not</u> to die getting out of death-bath.

•Get to towel rail on other side of slippery bathroom.

•Shiver myself dry using hand towel for 3 minutes.

•Remember have left clothes in bedroom.

•Make sharp naked exit from bathroom.

•Grab heap of clothes.

•Sprint like a *white female and naked* Linford Christie back in to the bathroom to dress.

•Nearly knock self out on savage swinging door as it spanks my rear as a reminder I am not the boss here.

•Heave jeans over gigantic love handles.

•Pull, huff and gyrate dry t-shirt with crow bar on to moist skin. Accidentally remove nipple in process.

•Place leg on to loo seat and lunge, in an attempt to stretch jeans. (This does not work)

•See clean knickers lying on floor, realise my mistake, scoop them up, shove them in my back pocket...

Just in time for Falalakalai, the bountiful and beautiful Nigerian nurse, to pop her head around my door (with a cracking 16 megawatt smile) and state;

'Lixy! Yis! Alive! See you in 15 minutes.'

I wonder if they ever play bingo with us. They could use a point system.

Half undressed – 15 points.

Naked – 90 points.

Foaming at the mouth like rabid rabbit – 113 points.

Maybe I should make it more interesting for her.

I could do naked headstands, and half-dressed handstands and the cross-dressed splits... actually. No forget that.

Although I am sure these actions would no doubt catapult Falakakakailii to the top of the league tables, I really have had enough of putting on a show to last a lifetime.

The real world quite literally spat me out and in to here with as much force as you would imagine a convict to be shoved out of a moving car, other than the above shenanigans, it has taken me a full five days to finally break to a halt and be in a position to have a look around and take stock.

I have to be honest.

There isn't much wrong with my surroundings (shower, bathroom door, the fact I am completely alone and terrified, and a few other bits excluded obviously) it is when I look inside that I can feel the terror bubbling up.

I do not like what I see. I do not want to look inside.

But there really isn't anything else to do. (Apart from maybe shave my legs, but I have to be supervised with a razor! I have done many odd things, and will no doubt partake in many more random things in my life but I am not shaving my legs and pits with someone watching! It is too weird!)

Therapy sessions are helping, but it is slow moving, and I miss Starbucks.

And Addison, clearly.

This afternoon I have a free afternoon with no group therapy and I want some time alone, and not just in 15 minute blocks.

I need time to sit and examine what I feel put me in here, other than the obvious 'not having the energy to, and not wanting to, live the rest of my life.'

I am going to have to channel Steve McQueen, dig a tunnel, escape, find a hidden tree and sit under it. I have my notebook, a picture of my loved ones, my iPod and a small packet of tissues.

Since I have been here I have felt unable to cry, even though I have desperately wanted to. I seem to have settled in numbness. So I am going to sit on my own, avoiding the **one** annoyingly lonely magpie which seems to be following me around conducting its own set of *Ob's* (I have named him Jeff, maybe I can be the 2 to his 1), and write.

I have to be brave. I have to fight for the right to be me, even from myself, if that makes sense.

It is terrifying.

I am starting with a letter to myself, in an attempt to forgive myself for being ill. I have been told to start it like this;

Dear Lexy.

It is not your fault.

The tears of guilt should not take long to appear.

I may even listen to a bit of music. (I want to break free, would be too easy a joke here... but fuck it. I'll use it anyway.)

Now, where did I leave my spade, sparkling white t-shirt and motorbike?

Mission impossible music clicks on and the voices in my head crouch down in preparation

I push the door open and stick my head around, as it creaks eerily I peer in to the long, dimly lit and decrepit corridor. Other than a few odd bods bouncing off walls all I can see is Falakalikalaka chomping on a dairy milk with her back to me, it is now or never Stevie. .. Go!

I make a run for it.

The tree is my goal. Any tree. Preferably with a chair.

Sanctuary (not sanitary, as I still have my knickers in my back pocket) is my light at the end of today's tunnel...the journey has officially started.

Dear Me.
Do I sound less crazy yet?

Grief is the Price we pay for Love...

There is gravel under my skin.

As I march up the slight incline towards the prehistoric building where my morning therapy session is being held, I can feel it biting and scraping at my skin, creating irritation from the inside out.

I want to rip my own skin off and shake it out.

I am seething today, and it is only seven fifteen in the morning.

I am bubbling over with hatred, struggling to contain my disgust.

If I were able to, I would vehemently spit *pure* bile in my own eye.

The dawn air is bitter cold on my teeth and as I grasp at gasp-fulls in an attempt to calm my racing heart, they begin to ache. I clamp my eyes shut and resist the urge to stand completely still, pull my hair out and scream in to the morning silence.

Create a ripple of angst in an otherwise numb millpond.

'*Where did I go wrong? I lost a friend, somewhere along in the bitterness yeah, and I would have stayed up with you all night, had I known how to save a life...*'

The Fray is pounding out of my headphones headed directly in to the last remaining corner of my soul which still respond to stimulus.

I feel like a teenager again, drawing similarities from lyrics in to my own life. Struggling to feel anything but numbness or anger for more than just a second.

I am the friend. Aren't I?

My eyes watering now from poorly concealed wrath which is burning inside me, I continue to plough ahead, onwards and upwards, as the stillness throughout the hospital grounds catches at my insecurities.

I flick my head around, my hair whipping my cheek for the third time in a matter of moments, once again for a split moment sensing somebody is walking with me.

There is nobody else around at this hour but me.

I am a lonely morning plodder in a world filled with Glum's, and yet somehow I know you are here. I wish you weren't. I do not deserve your company, especially not here, especially not now. But I can feel you watching me.

Is this a true sign of madness, or are you actually around me?

The sun peeps out from behind a bustle of angry black clouds which seem to be gathering in preparation for a stormy ambush, quickly and without even thinking I turn my face up towards it, trying, just a moment to feel the warmth, to feel some self- care in a lonely and agonizing world.

It quickly fades, giving up, and with it, so do I.

Like me, the weather is unable to decipher the way forward today.

Except I suppose I do know what is coming today.

That is why you are here.

Resisting the urge to shout abuse at Jeff, I push open the heavy metal door and stomp up the stairs, really settling in to 'angry teenager' mode now, and locate the correct room.

'Room B3. A room for being a right royal misery guts.'

12 spacious pale red cushioned armchairs are placed in a jaunty semi-circle against the back wall. In the centre of the room opposite, another lonely chair sits waiting for the facilitator.

The room smells of sadness, mould and morning.

Nobody is here; I am the first to arrive.

This is nothing new.

I plonk myself down on the only green chair in the room, thankfully located by the window, and turn from the Fray to Eminem.

Angry rap. Just what the psychologist *didn't* order. I kick off my wet shoes and fold my legs up underneath me, small comforts.

From here I can look down on all three therapy buildings, the garden and the back of reception.

From here I can watch the early morning goings on of a busy hospital ward, without anybody even knowing I am here. I like it. I feel like Jason Bourne.

But miserable. And without binoculars. And female. Obviously. (Maybe they could cast me in the sequel....call me Janet Bourne...)

Jeff perches himself on the windowsill, gives me a cursory wink and turns around to have a nosy with me at the madness which is sure to erupt from below. Against my will I have somehow become like that man from the Shaw-shank redemption. Woman and bird. No library though.

I begin to wonder if Jeff will follow me home when I leave, or if maybe he is a therapist in disguise. It wouldn't surprise me in this place. Either way, he has become my new companion, and I like him.

I don't think he is lonely or filled with sorrow either. That clever little *ditty* may read *one for sorrow* but we've discussed it and Jeff and I are thinking of writing a strongly worded letter to the Oxford literary academy. We want action. We want the *shitty ditty* changed.

One for Ice cream, maybe.

Yes. We like Ice cream Jeff and me.

One for ice cream.

Two for a dream.

Three for jeans that make you look lean.

Four for Prozac.

Five for (liquid) gold.
Six for a friendship to really behold.
Seven for coffee
Eight for tea
Nine for a lie down under the tree.

Or something like that. Yes we like that. Jeff is nodding.

My (completely normal in the grand scheme of things) thoughts are interrupted by the whirlwind arrival of my favorite therapist Barry.

Barry is a Scouser, a jolly Scouser, who speaks the truth and makes me laugh while doing it. He is friendly from the top of his head to the tip of his toe. I imagine his wife and children feel very lucky to have him, I know I would. I trust him with my broken heart. I trust him to go easy on me and I trust him to know when to stop.

7 other mentalists, none of whom I am allowed to describe, and most of who will probably never check this to ensure I haven't (but still), follow closely behind him and the session begins.

After a brief introduction, Barry takes off his anorak and gets comfy. (He must live by a train station.)

'Who would like some help today?'

'Oh fuck off!' is spat out in to the silence of the room.

There is an audible gasp from yours truly, as I realise that horrendous language had come from me.

I am usually such a *lady!*

Oops.

'Lexy?'

'I do **not** have an illness!! I just want to die!!' My legs bob up and down in uncontrollable annoyance 'I am not depressed. I just cannot be bothered to live the rest of my life! I am fine! I do **not** struggle to get out of bed in the morning, lord knows us mothers have no choice in the matter and I do **not** battle to put make up on or clean up, I do **not** find leaving the house particularly difficult and I **can** laugh until my sides hurt if something funny happens. It just never does!! I can play with my baby, I can make him something to eat, I can walk around Asda and I can take a bath and read a book, so surely, **so obviously, so clearly** there is absolutely nothing wrong with me really is there? You **can't** be depressed if you can go and get your nails done. You **can't** be depressed if you manage to smile on a daily basis and for the love of god, you **can't** be depressed if you have hope for the future. **CAN YOU?** So can I just leave now please? Can I? I do not deserve or need to be here? I am a fake!'

'What is making you angry today Lexy?'

(I bite down on my tongue hard. One fuck off I may get away with, but two would see me sent out of the group, my head hung in shame) 'I just am, I don't know why.' (If I knew why I wouldn't bloody be in here you Scouse Muppet!!)

'Try not to ask why,' Barry mumbles in his thick Liverpudlian accent grabbing the back of his head and looking at the floor 'it takes you inside yourself, instead ask what or who.'

I glare at him. If my eyes could speak they would be saying 'DIE!'

'Who are you angry at Lexy?'

'Myself, my brother, Jeff the magpie, myself.'

'How does this anger feel?'

'Brilliant. Like a hot sunny day!!! What the hell do you think it feels like???' I catch myself and pause....' Overwhelming.

'Do you feel guilty?'

'Guilty, upset, hurt, annoyed, pissed off, and fucked off, irritated, ready to cry.'

'What do you feel guilty about?'

'Being in here, I should be with my son. I don't need to be here! **I am not ill!'** I stamp my feet.

Barry sits motionless and stares at me for what feels like an eternity. I try very hard not to break the silence and am about to falter when he takes a deep breath and goes in for the kill.

'Lexy. Tell me what you loved about your brother.'

An unexpected blow.

5 years of anger crumpled in to hurt by one single question. 5 years of sorrow and guilt, racing to the surface. 31 years of grief rising up and suffocating me, extinguishing the fury like water on a flame.

An hour later when the group slowly draws to an end, I head back to my room on the ward.

I am broken, and alone.

You didn't follow me out. I assume you heard what you needed to hear.

Jeff did though.

So for the moment,

It is just my hurt, my magpie and me.

It's Lima by the way...

Somewhere in between being sectioned kicking, screaming and making jokes because I don't know what else to do, and this moment right now, where I am curled up in a ball on the bed catatonic staring at the bathroom door, I seem to have lost all capacity to think positive.

I can't even laugh.

Not even at myself.

Which is peculiar because even in times of trouble (when mother nature calls to me singing words of wisdom...) I have always been able to find the funny, even if I am the only person in the room sniggering.

Friends and family 'on the outside' keep insisting, when they hear my hollow, tinny and tired voice, that 'this place' is making me worse.

I am maintaining and explaining on a regular basis that they are mistaken, that being in here is like taking a packet of antibiotics. Sometimes you have to get worse before you can get better.

'It is a process. I will be fine. I am on the mend. Honest. I am. Don't worry about me. I'll be better in a week.' At least that is what the therapist's say.

I battle through the dialogues, summoning the strength from god knows where, trying to keep it jolly and bright, all the while the silent tears running down my face.

Are they right though? *Is* this place making me worse?

I have now been an, isolated in my own brain, and yet, friendly outgoing and maybe even quite popular to the rest of the world, inmate for 168 hours and 15 minutes.

It all started to go a bit pear shaped (like my bottom) about 21 hours ago, to be exact.

I was fidgeting with my knickers again, trying to get comfortable in my regular seat by the window (seriously, a size 16 rump in size 10 pants is just not comfortable! Sitting down actually hurts!) Waiting for the start of another session of group therapy. I was sharing this information, and the contents of my badly packed suitcase (That is not a euphemism!!) with the rest of my fellow inmates and they were all laughing at me...

No, hang on.

I mean laughing with me.

With me.

Right?

When Barry sauntered in, took a look around, and began attempting to quieten us down in preparation for the start of the session.

Yes. I told him about my knickers. (And explained perhaps this could be the reason why I hadn't cried recently, they were *obviously* cutting off the circulation to my tear ducts.)

This didn't even raise a smile. (Miserable git.)

I had supposed up until this point, I had been *managing* on a day-to-day basis pretty well. As far as I was concerned I was an A* student.

I wasn't wallowing in my depression, I had let my walls down, or so I thought, I was talking in group about real honest issues, pushing out the odd tear, allowing people to witness me sad, grabbing tissues, blowing my nose and then lightening the mood for everybody and having a laugh before I left.

Surely this is what they want us to do? Surely this constitutes 'working hard on ones trauma.'

Apparently not...

According to the Scouser/miserable git, nobody had seen me 'vulnerable'.

I hate that word as you know.

Vulnerable is a big word in here. It means you are making actual progress, not just surface progress. (Does that make sense? Because it has taken me a week to figure it out.)

This is the only place in the world where telling somebody you are feeling fragile, or running to your room in a dramatic flood of tears gets you a pat on the back. (And all your weapons of self-destruction removed.)

I argued with him until I was puce and exhausted.

'I **am** being vulnerable. I am, I really am LOOK!' I stopped talking, pointed at my eye and pushed out a tear, my legs bouncing up and down like a jumping bean on a pogo stick 'Look I am, I really am!'

He cast a glance around the rest of the group; all seated silently in their semicircular placed red armchairs, declining to make eye contact and looking at best; uncomfortable.

'What do you all think, other random inpatients with absolutely no identity? Have any of you seen Lexy Vulnerable?'

The answer was a resounding no.

Treacherous bastards!

I didn't get it.

There was too much to laugh at in here, how could one not laugh? Is that what they meant? That I was to stop laughing?

On the Thursday morning I had arrived the weather was scorching, I had dropped Addison off at nursery and had nearly changed my mind and given up then.

I don't need hospitalization! We could go to the park.

As he waved goodbye to me with the usual 'buoy bouy!' I had turned towards to the door, tears coursing down my cheeks.

'Are you Ok Lexy?' the nursery lady had asked me, a funny look brewing on her face 'he is only on a half day isn't he? Are you picking him up in 3 hours?' The 3 hours pronounced slowly as if to remind me to 'get a grip.'

'No' I struggled to keep my emotions under some ordinance of control 'his daddy will be picking him up and dropping him off for the foreseeable future.'

'Ah right,' she said, a look of delight passing across her (thick bint) features 'are you going on holiday? How exciting? Somewhere nice?'

'Actually I intend to spend the next two weeks on the set of 'One flew over the cuckoo's nest!' did not seem an appropriate reply, so I just nodded and fled to the sound of Addison screaming and the nursery assistants shouting

'Have a great time on your jollies! You deserve it! Addy will be fine! BYE NOW!! Don't get burnt!!!!'

I was a shaking snotty and grotty mess by the time I finally arrived at my 'holiday destination' and was met on my arrival by a nurse called Samantha.

My legs were threatening to give way underneath me as I handed over my car keys and watched my bags disappear.

'When do I get my car keys back?' I asked, my heart racing.

'How long is a piece of string?' came the reply.

Eh?

168 hours later and I still can't fathom this riposte.

My head was royally and firmly placed up my arse, which was why I didn't push it any further, as she gently ushered me in to a poky side room just behind the huge reception desk, and began to explain the admittance procedures, of which I have no memory.

I do however; remember cheering up considerably as she began to ask me a serious of completely random and obscure questions.

'What colour are my eyes?'

'Pardon?'

What colour are my eyes?'

I lean forward to get a better look 'Blue, why?'

'What is the date today?'

'The 11th of June I think, why?'

'Can you hear voices?'

'Pardon?' (Seriously starting to consider that she isn't a nurse *at all* by this point, and is instead an escaped lunatic playing a joke on me.)

'Can you hear voices?'

'Yes.'

'Really?'

'Yes of course I can! I can hear your voice, I am replying to you. Look if this is some sort of joke then I don't really need this...'

'No I mean, can you hear voices in your head?' She interrupts.

I rock back in surprise and bellow 'Not right now, no!'

'Good. Who is prime minister?'

'Is this some sort of test?'

'Can you just answer the question please Lexy? Who is prime minister?'

Now that I fully understand that this is a test of some sort, my nerves kick in to overdrive.

I must pass this test! I must pass this exam! IT IS A REAL LIFE CRAZY TEST!

Who the hell is prime minister?

As per sodding usual in these situations, as my nerves kicked up to *warp speed*, my mind emptied all useful information out, and I was left with a big fat blank.

'Erm, I can't remember but I think there are two of them. Some sort of collaboration, association, alliance, agreement, DAMN IT! What is the word?'

'Coalition?'

'Yes coalition!' I shout, pointing in her face convincingly.

'Can you remember their names?'

I couldn't.

Complete. Mind. Blank.

'No. But I usually can. Honest.'

She smiles kindly. 'No problem.'

'Can you recite the five times table please?'

'No.'

'Why not?'

'I am numerically dyslexic.'

'Oh, ok.' She sighs, noting something in the margin. (Probably '*bullshitter.*')

'What year is it?'

'1999.' I pronounce, shooting her a big confident smile.

'Pardon?'

Oh god what did I just say?????

'2009!' I shout, quickly correcting the mistake and then falling over myself in the realisation that I am still wrong 'Shit! Sorry....'

'That is ok.' (Clearly it wasn't.)

Her final question *should* have been **'What is the capital of Peru?'**

Now *that* I would have been able to answer.

I have been keeping that tiny morsel of information for a rainy day, crossword puzzle, IQ test, pub quiz or test like this, but the question, unfortunately has never materialised. One day it will though and everyone will rue the day, do you hear me? They will rue the day!!

The remainder of the 'assessment for mentalists' did not improve much from that point, and I suppose in all honesty I have spent the majority of my time since then trying to convince the staff I am not *in fact* fully insane, just a *bit* sad.

Which is why it comes as a shock to me to hear the friends, colleagues and *compadres* I have met and been completely honest with, since I have been in here agree with Barry and state they haven't seen me vulnerable.

'So if I laugh I am not being Vulnerable?' I ask Barry haughtily.

'Lexy, who the hell *are* you? Really try to **hear** me now. Your laughter is a coping mechanism; you don't have to tell jokes in here. It is ok to feel anything and everything you feel. People will laugh with you. Not at you, with you, because I know you must sometimes wonder about that.....'

I curl up in to a ball on my chair, my forehead resting on my knees.

'... But we are here to listen to **you.** The you that has been forced in to hiding for the last 10 years, you can drop the walls. You are finally safe. And we will look after you.'

As the meaning of his words sank through the very many levels of my consciousness, like sand through an egg timer, the weight slowly lifted from my shoulders, the quiet settled on my heart and the tension vanished, muscle-by-muscle from my body.

The *proper vulnerable* tears started not long after.

What does one do with one's self when the coping mechanisms you have learnt to rely on are pulled down, joke by joke?

What does one do with one's self when the coping mechanisms you have learnt to lean on, become completely redundant?

What does one do with one's self when the coping mechanisms you have learnt to trust, can no longer be found?

I walk out of the room emotionally buggered and feeling very much like a frightened child.

Fear of the unknown.

I can just *be*.

Wonderful.

I can just *be*, **who?**

Counting crows blasts out from my iPod, as I remain, feeling like a teenager, curled up in a tight ball on my bed. It is 3am but sleep has long since evaded me.

My eyes are open but I see nothing, lost in a world so far removed from the world I have been living in. An unrecognizable, unprotected world.

'This circus is falling down on its knees, the big top is crumbling down... These trained conversations are passing me by, and I don't have nothing to say.... you get what you pay for, but I just had ***no*** *intention of living this way...'*

It is like a packet of antibiotics, and mine have just kicked in.

Right?

It is like a packet of antibiotics and mine have just kicked in.

RIGHT?

Thieves will be prosecuted...

Don't steal my chips.

I won't *even* add an exclamation mark after the above statement because it is clearly an unwritten rule, and therefore, there is no need for one. Or twelve.

Star date, captain's log.

288 hours in to my stay. God knows how long remaining.

Ordered a Chinese with the other inmates in a bid to 'cheer' us up, and it all went tits up... which is a surprise... as it was all going so well for us.....

I may have been duped in to believing that as an in-patient, once I had overcome the first week and was feeling a little more at home in the institution, that I was safe from negative influences, all responsibility, accountability and even at times the weighty burden of obligation.

I may have even be conned in to believing that the blatant disregard for my well being shown by some predators on the outside, the topsy-turvy emotional roller-coaster I have been on for a good while and my touching yet troubling turmoil over the simplest of mishaps, cannot lay a hand on me while I am beneath the metaphorical *bubble wrap* the hospital has me enveloped within.

The claustrophobic, prickly and anonymous walls that at the start felt like they were used to imprison my soul, my beliefs and my ability to exist as an actress (the show being 'I am not depressed let me go home!) have slowly converted without me even really being able to lay a finger on when. The walls have metamorphosed, and I feel like a caterpillar, patiently waiting in a cocoon, in this secure, sincere, encouraging and supportive environment.

The walls no longer seem oppressive, they reassure.

Dreams of escape have slowly drained from my mind, like cow pat off a shit slide.

The walls have become my liberator, allowing me to heal with no deadline.

I am beginning to embrace and depend on them as I imagine Castle Folk did a moat, keeping out the demons.

I am wrapped in loving conversations, which feel like emotional cuddles, and gently they have begun to darn my twisted heart.

Yes I remain disoriented and distressed, not used to having my pain completely exposed for the entire world to stare at, but from somewhere far above the realms of what I thought was possible and yet undeniably from beneath the horrific injuries and the internal damage, the sun tenderly begins to warm my back.

As the suns heat creeps throughout my soul, lighting up even the darkest, dampest and forgotten corridors of my history, I retreat to my now comfortable silence to bask in the much welcomed thaw.

Breathing in. Breathing out, leisurely and with discomfort almost forgotten.

Breathing in. Breathing out. Relaxed now and approaching the place which feels like home, somewhere between consciousness and sleep, where there is no evil, just weightlessness.

A feeling of floating, of flying, of freedom.

Of being safe.

Before long, in the company of others I am throwing my head back in raucous laughter without faking it, and truly for the first time in months I am genuinely enjoying the company of those around me.

There are no stages here, no predetermined dialogues, monologues and interactions.

These precious people, I want to call friends and can, need no explanations and offer support without boundaries.

They choose Courage as a means to exist.

People I never knew could exist in a life so dragged down by drudge, accompany me along the dusty and arid road to recovery.

We are each other's network, sharing emotional supplies and touching insight between us.

There is no punishment for 'plodding' here.

'Hey Tara, you alright?' A greeting of hello.

'Hey Lex, no I'm fucking shit you?' An honest response.

'Feel like I've been run over by a 16 wheeler actually, coffee?'

'No tea please, leave it on the side, catch up under the tree yeah?'

'Yeah, see you later Cow bag.' A touching farewell.

'Later's misery guts.' I get it.

Friendship salvaged from the mangled wreckage left behind by months, years and sometimes decades of despair.

I may have been hoodwinked in to thinking that if I could just stay here forever, if you and I could just never leave, if I could just exist in this place indefinitely we all might be ok.

Imagine a life not bogged down by an illness that nobody seems to want to understand.

Imagine never having to hear the words 'You just need to pull yourself together.' 'You just need to smile more' or even my *absolute* favorite; 'Stop being selfish!'

'Just smile more Lexy and then your face will tell the rest of your body!!' (Brilliant.) 'You haven't got an illness at all, stop calling it that for goodness sake! You know what you need? You need to stop acting strange and just be yourself. The person you used to be!'

Because without fail, I have heard them all.

I like to call it 'Therapy by dummies.' (And wankers on occasion too, let us not forget about the humble wanker, he who knows it **all** but understands nothing.)

I may have been fooled in to thinking that within the boundaries these walls provide, I have actually found the perfect world.

Nobody says 'You can choose to be happy!'

Nobody tells me 'You NEED to get back to work then you will be ok!'

It would be very easy for me to believe I have found the perfect world.

But I haven't.

Because I don't want to live in a world where I just *exist*, instead of actually living.

I have come to realise, that as comforting and reassuring as this co- dwelling nut house can be, it really is just the start gate from where the shotgun fires you in to the race, for **living** the rest of my life.

Would you be interested in knowing how I came to this realisation and stopped pestering the over tired night nurses to let me apply for some sort of equity sharing mortgage, so I could stay forever and ever and ever?

An inmate I don't really know stole **my** chips off **my** plate when I went to get water.

And now I want to go home.

All those descriptive and magnificent words I just used to describe this 'sanctuary' can be ignored in their entirety!

I am sorry for wasting your time.

It is a bloody mad house and I want to get back to my boy.

They won't let me leave though.

I spent 2 hours sobbing and begging to leave at 'reception' tonight.

'Please, please give me my car keys. PLEASE.'

My eyes were red raw, I wanted my little boy so much, and there was no way of getting to him. I was out of control and lost in a moment of sharp pain. I was on my knees as they rubbed my back and patiently explained over and over again why they couldn't let me leave.

'But please. I want my bed and my slippers, my Irish guy and my house. I need to go home. The Irish One has painted my son's room red, he can't have a red room. I will never see his baby room again. Please please please pleasssse just let me go home.'

Nick eventually sedated me and got me in to bed. (He didn't get me *in to bed* in that way, you know what I mean!)

'Who the fuck was it that stole her fucking chips?' I heard him mutter to the nurse as they walked out, closing my bedroom door behind them. 'Write that on her patient file: Doesn't share food.'

I smiled as I drifted in to blankness, off my tits on Diazepam.

I used to be cool.

Forrest slump...

Drum roll for the crazy person please!

For the past 2 weeks while I have been existing (not living) in '*the facility for the mentally incompetent*', and all the while delving in to the deep, dark and destitute corridors of my recollection banks and unearthing some pretty horrific memory morsels (or canapé's if you will) from years gone by, I have also been managing to uncover a few forgotten activities that I thought were now completely redundant.

Yes for the last 2 weeks, as I have been living the celebrity dream, crying daily, feeling shards of glass in my heart *relentlessly* and wearing big shades constantly (to keep up the superstar image!) I have also been indulging in a few activities that I really had forgotten I enjoyed.

Stop being rude.

I'm talking about listening to music, reading a book and just pottering about.

Although, while we are on the subject of rude stuff. (Because you know how much I love it.)

Do you remember when I told you I was on 15-minute observations?

Well I still am.

And do you also remember when I admitted to you I self-harm?

Well I still do.

(Yes I am in hospital but no; being in hospital doesn't magically make you better. It'll take a while before they'll manage to rid me of that age-old coping mechanism. I like self-harming, see. It makes me feel human. It is like anesthetic for my heart. Is it wrong to admit that? Does that make me weird? I don't care. Self-harm is better than self-dead right? Right.)

Well Last night as the clock struck 12 and Fahalarki the night nurse was prowling the corridors with a Twix looking for some poor unsuspecting anorexic to torture, (I'm setting the scene here so bear with me) and while I was busy doing a 13 minute poo (from start to finish, just in time for my next check) and after a particularly bad day involving somebody painting a picture of my favorite handbag and then purposely drawing rain heading towards it (therapy is hard yo!) I was overcome by the emotion of it all and with flashback images of wet Gucci and ruined leather screaming through my psyche, I took to my stomach with a paper clip.

OK.

Took to my stomach with a paper clip, isn't *necessarily* true.

But either way, let us just say I *harmed* my stomach, and this new wound combined with old scarring starting to heal, created a social hand grenade that the likes of Pol Pot (or even Kinga from Big Brother) could never have imagined.

Disaster.

I had jumped in to bed at the sound of heavy footsteps approaching my door and was having a good old scratch of the insistently itchy and semi healed scars under the covers, when who should bob her bedraggled and sometimes freaky, floating head around the door without knocking, but Fahalarki.

I was startled she had arrived as soon as she had and was concerned she would realise I had self-harmed so jumped at the sound of her voice.

'15 minute check Lixy.'

As her eyes widened and she quickly started to back out of the room I realized the sheer atrocity of the level of her misunderstanding.

She had clearly been mortified at the sight of my elbow bobbing about at stomach height under the covers, a fact further heightened by the fact I was now acting like a rabbit caught in headlights and had now automatically and INCORRECTLY assumed I was erm... giving myself a treat? Starting to feel better? Finding my happy place?

You know what I'm on about right?

EX.CRU.CIATING.

Shouting protestations but not actually being able to explain what I had actually been doing (for fear of being caught self-harming) got me absolutely nowhere but Shames Ville Arizona.

'Look Falahraki, I cannot tell you what I was *actually* doing but I wasn't doing *that* ok?? There are a lot of things I can do at hyper speed in a 15 minute slot, as I am now finding out, but let me tell you, *THAT* ain't one of them ok?'

I was wasting my breath. She was sniggering behind reception with Clarke the intern and I was now forever to be known as the 'MUST KNOCK ON DOOR BEFORE ENTERING WOMAN.'

Not good, really not good.

But anyway, Can we move on now? (I don't know why I share these things I really don't!)

'Sometimes you need to walk a mile in a man's shoes before you could fully understand the extents he will go to, to hide the pain. Welcome to the Hotel California, please check your car keys, your sanity and any weapons of mass destruction in at reception and follow me to your room. You may notice the bedding smells of cat piss, but let us assure you, that is your illness, there are no cats here.'

I am pretty sure there must be but whatever.

I cannot believe I have been in here two weeks.

It is nothing like I expected when I first arrived all those moons ago.

There are no straight jackets, there are no wide-eyed, straight-backed *shufflers* scuffling about reciting the Lord's Prayer and there is no nurse Ratchet. (Although there is one nurse who is a complete bitch. I think there always is, in any hospital setting. The token hag that nobody likes and who likes nobody, but the less said about her the better... JUST GIVE ME SOME DIAZIPAN COWBAG...sorry... moving on...)

Did I ever tell you that on the very first day I arrived (which now seems like 12 years ago), I spent so long meaninglessly ambling up and down the corridors, they assumed I was a pissed up alcoholic searching for booze and I was breathalyzed. And clearly, as I haven't drunk in months (ahem right) I was completely affronted!

'But you look drunk Lixy.' Fhalarkiiiii had assumed incorrectly. (AGAIN.)

I had just been admitted for god's sake! I had been sobbing for 3 hours straight as the realisation of what was happening, finally started to bleakly and sinisterly seep its way in to my consciousness. I wasn't going to be able to kill myself (I couldn't even be successful at that!) So I was imprisoned here, against my will, for the foreseeable future. I had shrieked and wept and prayed and pleaded, for them to let me go, I just wanted my son, my poodle and my own pillow.

Due to many a gushed tear, a heavily swollen face, the humidity in the air and eye sockets that could pass for boiled eggs, my contact lenses dried up and I was literally unable to see.

Now, clearly because of this I couldn't walk in a straight line, I was tired and I may have been slurring my speech.

I was not drunk. I was delirious and did not want to be alone.

'Oh you aren't drunk Lixy? **Ah well, sometimes you have to walk in a man's shoes....'**

The above condemnation definitely wins *most annoying saying I have heard in the recent weeks at the mad house.*

1) Because I don't want to wear another man's shoes I have my own, and have you ever actually put your foot in another man's shoe? They always feel wet! It is all kinds of wrong. Not going to happen. Like sharing socks. Gross. And 2) because it is a cliché and it completely redundant, in that no one would ever actually do this.

'Excuse me? Are you depressed? You are? BRILLIANT! Can I borrow your shoes? Apparently walking a mile in yours will help me understand my own pain. What do you mean no? Oh you are size 5, never mind, thanks anyway.'

Facetious me?

Well *I am* allowed to be.

I have managed two weeks as an inpatient (I am pretty proud of myself in case you haven't noticed.), and although I am slowly, as if wading through mud, making progress and maybe, somehow, possibly believing there may just be, potentially, perhaps an actual light at the end of the tunnel and that maybe, just maybe someone may have switched it on, I am still absolutely terrified of the future.

I feel as if I have been suffering with Post Natal Depression for so long, if that horrible debilitating illness is no longer *settled* in, and has been forced out, then what the hell will it have left behind?

Does that make sense?

Will it be like when a lodger leaves manky flooring, blue-tack stained walls and old apple core's in the drawers in the wake of their departure? Will my life be like a black and white still of a 1930's private eye's office? (Just go with me. It just came to me.)

I am absolutely shit scared of going back to normal life, outside of the confines of these walls. Back to the unknown, completely unknowing.

Which is unfortunate as next Friday I am being discharged, I hope.

They feel the time has come, to send me back out in to the real world as a fully rehabilitated, swinging from the chandeliers, in no way 'well' but certainly 'getting there' mother of one, wife of none and empty woman of weirdness.

It has been one hell of a journey. A journey I would not be keen to repeat, which is why I am going to try my damnedest over the next four days to learn some 'shit' to help me in the future.

Because I don't want to end up back here, I don't want to end up dead and I don't want to end up existing again, instead of living.

I suppose the up side of being released however is at least when I get home I can scratch my stomach in peace. (Ahem.)

When was the last time you listened to music **you** liked?

When was the last time you stopped running 100 miles an hour?

When was the last time you stopped torturing yourself and rested?

When was the last time you made time for you?

Am I cured?

.... And as the fetching *(and not even a little bit gay)* prince (*in his tight white jodhpurs and brown thigh high boots)* intentionally and carefully bowed his head down towards the blessed and fortunate princess *(who was more than a little bit annoyed he was wearing her boots)* and brushed his lips gently against hers (being *careful not to smudge her lip liner)* a concerto of salient song began to rise from behind them *(Ministry of sound presents the best of R&B 3)...*

...And as the music played on *(drowning out all thoughts of bronzed beach ready men, from both of their minds)* and as he gazed deeply in to her crystal white eyeballs romantically, grabbed her tiny perfectly manicured hand and whispered *(quite literally)* sweet *(FA)* nothings in to her shell-like, together they decided cheerfully and deliberately to toddle off in to the fawning yellow, orange and red sunset... *(Clearly for dramatic effect)...*

And of course,

The princess and the *(camp)* prince live happily ever after...

Yes, they lived **happily ever after...**

Er.

Hang on.

Did they though?

I mean, it is all very well ambling off in to the sunset on a nice warm day isn't it? Or, even, like in some of my favourite fairytales, splashing away in a rowing boat with a warbling frog serenading you with a Peter Andre hit, or even I suppose in a more realistic sense, driving away with tin cans suspended off the boot of your car and 'Just married' scrawled in shaving foam across your back window, but seriously?

Happily ever after?

What happens then, when twilight approaches and you realise that while you have been too busy hiking off in to the middle of nowhere, gawking in to one another's openings to the soul, not only have you caught sunstroke and are now beginning to feel distinctly frigid and nauseous, but that he (*the village idiot*), being the self- centered, tedious and irresponsible imbecile he is turning out to be, forgot to bring the bloody coats?

It is a bit more challenging to gaze devotedly in to one another's eyes, when your teeth are chattering incessantly and your nipples could cut through glass, isn't it?

It is slightly more arduous to remain with the feelings of *happily ever after*, when you are vomiting in to an ice bucket and he is holding your hair back while checking out your arse, isn't it? (Because let's face it. They probably do.)

What happens then, to the Happily Ever After, when you realise that while you have been too busy splatting about in the middle of the Atlantic ocean, enjoying the time spent with your singing frog and the man of your dreams, that you are actually in fact starving, miles away from the nearest Harry Ramsdens and that Prince *Fumble in the jungle* here, couldn't catch a fish in a deep fat fryer?

OOOO I'm on a roll now,

And what happens, to the (*spit it out now*) Happily Ever After, when you arrive half a mile down the road from the church in which you *just* declared your undying love and betrothed yourself to him *forever,* when he turns around with a look of glee etched on to his features, starts waving besottedly at a 6 foot, perfect figured, big boobed goddess and starts advising you that this is, in fact his ex, she lives next door, he absolutely adores her and that you and she, will, *no doubt*, get on like a house on fire.

What happens then ey? (EY? A spade that's what! A spade!!!)

AND what happens 3 months post Sunstroke-gate when she drunkenly forgets to reach for a condom, gets impregnated, tears her *Tupperware* from tit to tatters and ends up in a mental institute having spent too long chasing all her scattered marbles aimlessly around the living room floor?

What happens then ey? (EY?)

I tell you what I believe would help maintain the *happily ever after*.

I believe that if all men, *princes, paupers, kinsmen* and *blokes* came with a handbook, life would be a lot damn simpler. THAT'S WHAT.

I believe, that at the age of 19 there should be a mandatory handbook ceremony held for all men. (Mandatory like the army is mandatory in Spain. A civil service type agreement.)

From the ceremony until the end of time, they are to keep the handbook with them at all times. Through every relationship, through every argument and through every tryst, the handbook must be accessible for the female to read/use/study at any given moment.

The lady in question can then fill in the handbook as she goes along and when she deems it necessary, therefor preparing the next potential girlfriend for what is to come, and what she expect from this fellow without ever having to meet her.

PERFECT!! Don't you agree?

Very immature, laughs at his farts, never does washing. 01/08/1999.Annabel.

Great at cooking, very bad wind and total commitment-phobe. 02-11-2001.Jane.

Picks his nose & eats it, can happily sit on loo for up to 3 hours. 09-9-2006.Meg.

Cooks a lot, great in bed but won't wash knives and forks. 01-01-2008.Susan.

Generous, Lazy. Farts too much, moody, boring but great in bed. 07-07-2010.Lisa.

Needs another mother, never mind a girlfriend, also, pretty sure he is gay... 01.01.2016 .Princess Anon.

Charming my arse. 04.05.2020. Cinderella.

That sort of thing, do you see what I am getting at?

I honestly believe that if all men came with a handbook, our happily ever after's would be a lot more accessible.

We could window shop.

'OO farts a lot, no thanks! But hmmm Great in bed, may be worth the excessive farting, hmmm may give it a go... oh no! Doesn't wash the knives and forks! That's a deal breaker, NEXT HANDBOOK PLEASE!!'

(Wouldn't it also make life a hell of a lot easier if all ex-girlfriends were then transported/shipped/kicked off to another planet entirely with no reception on their *slutty* phones, where they were forced to spend their days eating Pringles and watching 'Psycho!' on repeat? I think so.)

But anyway, back to reality with one hell of a bump.

There are no handbooks, there is no singing Peter Andre frog and there is no rest for the wicked.

Here I am, having gathered as many marbles back in to my quality street tin as I possibly can over the last 3 weeks, suitcase in one hand, Addison, Doodle and The Irish One in the other, about to walk out of the mental hospital for the first and hopefully only time in my life.

Addy, The Irish One, Doodle Mcpoodleson and I, all holding hands (Doodle walking on two legs like a real life boy-bless him, he has such abandonment issues) getting ready to stroll off in to the sunset.

I am leaving behind my crazy friends, I am leaving behind my own room, I am leaving behind my 15 minute observations,

I am leaving behind the safety of being allowed to be mental, and I am heading off in to the big bad world, with a new set of coping mechanisms, a pot heart and a little leap of faith hoping to set me free.

I have tears running down my face as I say my goodbye's to the home I have hated, sobbed in, been broken within, liked and eventually loved.

I do not feel ready, but then I am not sure I ever will.

Will I live happily ever after?

I doubt it. (For all of the reasons above, plus add in a gastro-enteritis prone poodle, a bum shuffler with a penchant for licking plug sockets, a pelvic floor supported entirely by Tena Lady and an Irish one that eats more cow than can possibly be healthy and a permanently blocked bog... the list is endless...)

But more importantly will I ***live forever after?***

I plan to.

And really, that is what matters, I suppose.

The one that broke the camel's back...

I am currently inexplicably wedged in to an enormous brown leather armchair munching on a gigantic and sticky Starbucks caramel waffle, so although I feel for the main part, like a bit of a hog, (Starbucks sofa's must be made for people who weigh nothing! I am actually sinking!) As the gooey caramel lodges itself between my teeth, all over my lips and down my front and while the crumbly biscuit exterior makes best friends with my inner thighs (currently fighting to push each other away and failing miserably) the writing of this post feels strangely apt.

I am about to ask you a question,

She says cocking her head to the side, trying to take on the role of nurturing therapist while continuously munching away and slowly descending in to the back of the couch with every bite, so that my feet are now at a 90% angle above me,

But I would like you to have a *good think* about this question, and all the possible responses you can imagine before answering.

Ok?

Here goes.

I am about to offer you one of my Caramel waffles. Really, they are delicious, delectable, mouthwateringly gooey, appetizing, and scrumptious and completely calorie free.

Stay with me here.

They are the ultimate biscuit, a biscuit to rival all other biscuits in their category and you desperately want one. By the time I have finished showing you the full delights of the super tasty *taste sensation*, and by the time I have finished wafting it under your nose so you can smell the super sweet-scented *smell sensation*, you are *so* desperate for a bite you almost snatch my hand off.

And you can have it if you really really want it *(a zig a zig ah)* but as always in life, there is a catch.

Each and every time you take a bite of this waffle, the waffle you simply cannot imagine turning down at this point, for the disappointment would be too great, I am going to thump and thhhwack you over the head with a bloody big stick I have been surreptitiously hiding behind my back.

(You may have to help me up first though. I think I am actually stuck. I am typing this laying completely flat on my back but still sat on a sofa... only at Starbucks...)

This is the scenario you find yourself in ok?

The waffle is sat on the plate in front of you, calling your name, willing you to have a lick, just a single, tantalizing lick, but out of your peripheral vision you can now see me stick in hand poised and waiting to twat you across the head with every munch you try to enjoy.

(I am a full on bitch in this scenario, I know this. And really I am ok with it.)

So what would you do?

Stop reading now please, look away from your screen if you have to, and deliberate.

What would you do?

I REALLY REALLY want *(ah zig a zig ah)* for you to have a little think about it. (Get those cogs a-turning folks!)

Last week, while I was still *existing* on the ward and before I came up for parole, and therefore release, I was asked this very same question.

I mulled it over for a full 7 days.

Arriving back in my support group this morning, the air thick with dismay and rising damp, I was the epitome of smug

Sally Wanker. (There was a girl in my class called Sally Wanker. There really was... or maybe that was a nickname. I can't remember, but either way she was smug.)

'I know what I would do James.' I proclaimed to my therapist, plonking my bag down, taking a load off (quite literally, I had dressed for Antarctic adventures but somehow it was now 80% and snowing outside...what the hell is going on with our summer??? Anyway, I digress...) and whispering hello's to the rest of the mentalists with no identity at all. 'I totally, *full on,* know what I would do.'

'I am assuming this is about the waffle Lexy, but before you tell me, and as you have asserted yourself to speak first (damn,) could you please tell me about your week, we have missed you around here, what has been going on for you?'

'Not much' I say, keen to get this out of the way and finally be able to give him my answer to Waffle-gate.

'I notice you are wearing full make up today, including lipstick, that's a change from the norm, what has been going on for you?'

'Are you saying I look like a transvestite?'

'Did it sound like I was saying that?'

'No. But I think I look like a man.'

'Ok.' He smiles kindly 'I don't.'

'I am also wearing Skinny jeans James. Have you noticed my ultra-skinny Jeans? I thought I would look skinny in them, well at least that is the effect I was hoping for, but as it is, I can hardly breathe and you may think I am wearing deep purple lipstick James, but it is actually a lack of circulation to my upper repositories, to be honest.'

'You're upper *what now?*' He asks, concern pushing through the joviality in his voice.

'My upper repositories.' I retort confidently.

'Did you make that word up Lexy?'

'A little bit yes.' I smile.

"I am sensing that you are (completely mad) a little all over the place this morning, so let us start simple. Tell me one thing this week that made you smile secretly to yourself?'

'My son.'

'Stock response, something else.'

'He did though.'

'I am sure he did, what else?'

'Well I smiled when I saw a beautiful friend, and felt truly content for the first time in a long while.'

'Great but again, stock response, anything else? And really try to hear my question now. Please tell me one thing this week that made you smile TO YOURSELF SECRETLY.'

'As in, is there something I am secretly proud of myself for?'

'If you think that is what I meant, then yes.'

(FOR THE LOVE OF GOD!!!!!)

'I'm taking back control?' I state, as if asking him permission for this to be true.

'From who?'

'Everybody.'

'Who is everybody?'

The million-dollar question.

Who is everybody?

I know **my** answer to this, and I am sure in **our** own way, we all know **our own** answer to this.

Who shreds our confidence, who pushes our buttons and who do we have to fight to regain some of ourselves back? Each individual story is completely unique, but sometimes (and just to be completely enigmatic here) sometimes the person who commits all these heinous crimes against us, is **us**, Isn't it?

Sometimes we need to take control back from ourselves, before we can even consider attempting to win it back from others.

I know I do.

How many times do I beat myself up with a big bastard stick? How many times over a 24 hour period, do I call myself incapable, stupid, fat, ugly, thick, not as good as that person over there, unhealthy, miserable, idiotic. The list is endless. And ok, I may not say them out loud. I may not say;

'Hey Irish one, sorry I burnt your chips, it is because I am a thoughtless, worthless great big lump of wasted blood and organs ok?'

I may not say it out loud. But I think it.

I may not say;

'Hey Irish one, please don't look at me, or try it on with me or touch me because since having this baby my body is truly disgusting and the very thought of you touching it makes me want to curl up and die in shame. I hate myself and I would really prefer if you did too, thanks.'

I may not say it out loud. But I think it.

(I may *actually* try being honest next time, as I am quickly running out of excuses to not be intimate. Last night I literally told him I couldn't, as there was a strong possibility of me having scurvy. Luckily, he has no idea what scurvy is, and I assume he imagines it to be a long the same lines as having thrush. Either way I got an early night so all's well that ends well... Except it isn't. Because I miss him, and I hate feeling like this... Damn houseboat. Anyway.)

I beat myself up constantly.

And not only that, I allow others to do it too, usually because I am in complete agreement with them.

I deserve to be hit with a huge stick while eating a waffle.

Don't you?

'Would you eat the waffle Lexy?' James asks, eyes wide open.

'Yes James, I would eat the waffle, I wouldn't mind so much really,' I pause for dramatic affect 'the pain of being hit, because the waffle would be worth it.'

I state this sitting smugly in my bubble of insightful intuition I have learnt over the last three weeks.

He urges me to explain further.

'I know now,' I explain thoughtfully 'after being here for three weeks, just how much pain and torment I can handle, it is nothing new. So the waffle would be worth it you see. Sometimes a small amount of discomfort is worth the enjoyment...'

'Would you now,' his eyebrows knot in intrigue 'you would eat the waffle, are you sure?'

'Yes. I would eat the waffle.' (FOR THE LOVE OF GOD!!)

He is thoughtful in his silence, before looking at me once again and continuing.

'You would eat the waffle, even while being hit with a great big cricket bat?'

'Eh? I thought it was just a stick.'

'Ok. Now it is a cricket bat. Would you still eat the Waffle?'

'Yes.'

'What if the immense pain the cricket bat was now causing, began to completely outweigh the enjoyment of the tasty waffle, then what would you do?'

'I would run away with the waffle James.' I roll my eyes wondering to myself why I didn't think of this response sooner. Running with the waffle is the ideal solution. I would be burning off the calories immediately (mine isn't calorie free) and would avoid being battered.

'Both of your legs are broken. Would you still eat the waffle?'

'Do I have a wheelchair to escape on?'

'No! Would you eat the waffle?'

'If I had two broken legs?' (Is it me, or is this getting a little out of hand now? It's a bloody waffle. They aren't *that* nice!)

I sigh, 'I would have probably given up on the waffle by now to be honest.'

'So', his turn to pause for dramatic effect 'You would deny yourself the pleasure of the waffle when it became too painful?'

'Yes,' I reply with a deep sigh 'If you had broken both of my legs I would be most displeased as not only have I just bought new shoes, but I cannot eat when I am pissed off and although Starbucks waffles are delicious, I would not want my legs broken, so I would leave the waffle where it was.'

I am aware that I am waffling (no pun intended) but when I stop he urges me to go on.

I falter slightly before believing I finally grasp what he is getting at and ploughing on with what I deem to be **his revelation** full steam ahead 'because some pleasure isn't worth getting hurt for is it? I wanted the waffle, you offered me the waffle, but it isn't worth the pain, so leaving the waffle seems the perfect solution. Even though I miss out on what I wanted...'

He smiles slightly before leaning slowly back on his chair, not losing eye contact with me once.

I am completely confused.

Now I have said it out loud, that doesn't seem right at all.

The room is deathly quiet.

'Can I ask you something Lexy?'

'Go for it.' I say shitting myself now; sensing something important is about to happen.

'Did you never consider, even for a moment, that you could just take the stick off me?'

I hadn't.

'...And eat your waffle in peace, with no pain, just enjoyment?'

I hadn't.

Had you?

This idea was brought to you by Postnatal Depression. Finding the inner courage to take the stick away, personal insult by personal insult, believing in myself little by little and opening up and peeping from behind the wrought iron door, tiptoe by tiptoe.

'Hey Irish one, I burnt your chips because I was busy being a brilliant mummy playing with Addison, and I set the oven a little too high. Ill bang some more in.'

Shit happens.

Want a bite of my waffle?

The Art of memory making...

When the instant finally arrived, hurtling towards me like a ton of concrete bricks I had spent 8 months evading, my heart began thrashing and kicking, screaming for me to escape. My chest became so tightly knotted I found myself forgetting to breathe and against my will my eyes started releasing tears brimming with pure anguish that seemed to burn tracks of hatred down my face.

It was at this point, with James staring in to my soul, and an audience of six strangers, that I found myself unable to fight any longer.

All it had taken was the sheer terror, hiding behind some heavily carved distraction techniques, to be glimpsed at, for the briefest of moments and my carefully painted masquerade, filled with dancing clowns, cotton candy and merry go rounds, came thundering down, landing around my battered and tired feet, before shattering in to a hundred tiny, finger cutting, soul destroying shards of malevolence.

In this moment, the risk of not sharing my pain, by far outweighed the fear of not knowing what would happen to me if I did.

This became my element of freedom.

Which incidentally is also the name of Alicia Keyes' last album.

And fair play to her. It is a great name, and a great album.

However, as I have not been blessed with a figure that allows me to confidently carry off shoulder pads on a regular basis (I always end up looking like I am about to play American football) am unable to wear hot pants without Greenpeace showing up with a huge net and a shit load of placards (Blubber is not fashionable, leave it to the whales!!) and am so tone deaf, that even singing Happy Birthday sets off the neighborhood dogs howling to the moon and running around in manic circles frothing at the mouth, can we just pretend, just for a heartbeat that I came up with that last line all by myself, and that Alicia is ok with this?

Thank you.

I think at the very least, under the circumstances, she owes me that.

Interestingly though I have visited the concrete jungle, so in fairness we do have *that* in common. I climbed up the Empire State Building in 1996 (not in the same way King Kong did, just to be clear. Although I do own a gorilla suit. I am not sure why I feel this is relevant. I wasn't wearing it or anything... but anyway.)

Addison's godmother and I took the stairs, as petulantly at the time, I refused to get in the lift. I am claustrophobic see, or at least I thought I was, but according to my therapist James (the one with the eyes that can tear through your soul like heat seeking missiles) I am not.

I am, in fact, Agro phobic (aren't we bloody all!)

Which isn't a fear of wide-open spaces as I thought it was, but a fear of not being able to escape. So although we both have a love of New York, Alicia and me, I wouldn't have been able to wax lyrical about it as she did, while I was there, as after mounting 186 floors (in a gorilla suit) I was too busy coughing up a lung, to sing anything. (Much to the relief of New York pet lovers anonymous.)

So...

My favourite Disney film is Lilo and Stitch.

Yes I am aware that was a very tenuous link but *really,* if *you* can link Alicia Keys and a tiny blue, four handed alien that burps the Kauain national anthem better than that, then please let me know, and I will add it in here, and claim it as my own... I seem to be doing that a lot today.

Ohana Means Family and Family means nobody gets left behind.

Five years ago this small sentence said by a mongrel experimental alien life form (that isn't even available in HD) would have either reduced me to tears or sent me in to a fit of anger that would have resulted in me shouting at the television and branding the shit out of my arm with my hair straighteners.

Utter bollocks I would have thought. Family brings nothing but pain, rejection, loss and hurt.

So in that moment, taken unawares, with my circus tent falling to its knees, in a room filled with tortured souls, luke-warm tea and stale biscuits, I took a deep shaky breath, and I faced it.

And it hurt.

It hurt like hell.

And in many ways, it still does.

As I sit here munching on my waffle (seriously. If you poke me, I oink) I am still feeling an underlying sensation of vulnerability and acute sadness but, and there is always a butt (and mine is huge) the fear of feeling this way was actually a million times worse, and more anxiety inducing, than actually the way I am feeling right now.

Sometimes the dread of the feelings we **may** feel, is actually worse than the actual feelings that follow from tackling the unknown, and the fear of the unknown.

I was terrified I was going to break, but actually I was already broken, and sometimes the only way to fix things is to remove all the jagged edges, and piece them back together part by part.

Yesterday, following on from a moment of utter carnage, during which Doodle had secreted a horrifically wet runny poo on to my neighbours knee (Sorry Gary) in the garden (I honestly couldn't make this shit up, is it any wonder I ended up in a mental institute?) and following on from the ensuing screams of delight from Addison, who had found a worm and was presenting it to me at the same time as me trying to find wet wipes that could not only wipe the soggy doggy squit off my neighbours jogging bottoms but also from his memory, I caught sight of the Lilo and Stitch DVD peeping out from behind an old box of Ski gear sat in the hallway, and thought, after 5 years of avoiding it, maybe now (not at that *exact* moment per say, as my neighbor was still sat in his deck chair retching manically at this point) but soon would be a good time, to process the past while looking to the future in the hope of creating some new family memories.

Ohana means family and family means nobody gets left behind.

Two hours later with the neighbor back in his own house no doubt showering in bleach and scrubbing at his knee with a wire brush, Doodle wearing one of Addison's nappies, The Irish One wearing most of Addison's dinner and me, wearing galoshes and moon boots, we all sat down together (under duress) on our manky old sofa and prepared to create a loving family memory I would no doubt cherish for years to come, with no anger involved!

Great expectations and all that.

Turns out, making perfect memories is a certified nightmare.

The film was only on for 15 minutes before The Irish One fell asleep, Addison was repeatedly biting my leg and squealing for Toy Story and Doodle was shaking, panting and making some decidedly squelchy noises.

I could feel myself becoming upset.

I wanted a happy memory for god sake!!!! How hard could it be???

Why could things never go according to plan???

I shook The Irish One awake and bellowed in his face.

'CAN YOU JUST BLOODY TRY TO STAY AWAKE LONG ENOUGH FOR ME TO MAKE A NICE FAMILY MEMORY PLEASE? IT SHOULDN'T BE THIS HARD!!'

He jerked awake with a look of shock, wiped the dribble from his mouth, (he will love me for that – serves him right) and smiled openly.

'I think today's memory's will last a lifetime for all of us Lex, let alone next door. I love you. Now please let Addison get down before we all go deaf, open the door for Doodle before his bum explodes and lets go for a walk in the garden and enjoy the sunshine.'

'What?' I shouted back

'Lexy, take off your ear muffs if you can't hear me'

'Oh right yeah. What?'

'I said' he sighs getting ready to repeat himself before stopping, smiling a secret smile and adopting his know-it-all face 'I said, let's take the stick away.'

So we did.

(Smug sod. Ahem...)

And even though I had to let go of making the 'perfect memory' we actually had a lovely afternoon.

But don't think they got away with it. Even if I have to drug them, we will all sit down and watch Lilo and stich together at some point.

That's how I'll mark my progress!

Stop biting the lady...

There were five of us huddled outside of that shop, early on Friday morning, waiting impatiently, eager for the doors to open, and let us in out of the cold.

Most of us were sporting the very same bedraggled, *I slept in a bush*, hair-style, the same bin bag, *I'm trying to hide I'm still in my pajamas underneath this coat*, winter wear and all of us were staring at the warm and cozy woman on the other side of the glass with the exact same look of desperation etched on to our features.

Let us in you shop whore! We are bitter cold, we are dog shit tired and we are all teetering precariously on the edge!

All of us except one, that is.

Cyndi Lauper is chanting 'girls just wanna have fun' over the outdoor tannoy and I can't help but smile to myself as I picture her cavorting in leopard print leggings and a stomach revealing crop top, glass of bubbly in her hand singing this, while I furtively glance around at the clan of bag women surrounding me, a clan that I have inadvertently become a part of.

Fun was a thing we were all having when we got in to this mess, I mutter at Cyndi realising from my reflection in the sliding glass doors that I have come out of the house with no bra on; and by the looks of things, mascara only enhancing one eye, yesterday's eye-liner spread generously around the bags under it.

I look like a pirate, and Addison my yoghurt encrusted first mate.

There are four other beautiful bouncing babies joining us, my captain bonkers included.

One in a buggy sucking her thumb and playing with her hair, both nostrils flourished with a snotty garnish. One sleeping peacefully in a pearl coloured maxi-cosi, all new, her tiny fists scrunched up and angry. One stood patiently by her mother's side singing *'everything is Rosie'*, fruit shoot in one hand, lollipop in the other and mine, crouched down on the floor, face pressed up at the glass shouting 'Thomas' at top volume while pushing out a smelly one.

'When the working day is done, when the working day is done... girls just wanna have fun.' Cyndi Lauper finishes serenading us from above, as the rain starts to pitter patter on the flag stone car park and we all shuffle a little closer to the protective haven of a very much closed Mothercare.

'Addison' I murmur half-heartedly stifling a yawn and wondering what the hell I was thinking leaving the house at this un godly hour (oh yeah, a vain attempt to wear out the child and give Doodle a few moments respite from having all manner of plastic equipment shoved up his bum) 'you'll wake the baby up, try not to shout.'

My weak and futile effort to be a good parent in front of these other mums' falls on deaf ears.

But hey, I think to myself proudly, at least I tried.

Although bearing in mind the only word he understands at the moment seems to be 'jelly' I don't really expect him to respond.

'Yes, please god' I hear quietly from beside me, the woman rubbing her face 'yes Addison, stop shouting, please god don't wake the baby up.'

I turn and (unwittingly) stare at her (I am bog eyed, everything is a stare these days, while my brain catches up with my eyes) trying to decide whether or not to be angry that she has quietly admonished my little pooing angel, bellowing for his idol in between forceful grunts, or to smile warmly and ask how old her little girl is, and whether she has received her *'Well done you made it to a month'* certificate yet, when the moment passes and we are interrupted by *well put together* woman.

The well put together and very *smooth* woman, who is immaculately dressed in black leggings, riding boots, a white coat (YES WHITE!) with hair spray finished beehive hair, interestingly enough, has no child by her side.

'Aww' she coos at me while watching Addison's face turn beetroot from exertion 'He's adorable, so cute doing a poo, how old is he?'

'Do you want him?' I respond, my hand thrust in to the dark depths of my handbag, the wrong handbag, hoping that against all the odds that this handbag, the wrong handbag, also contains a nappy. 'Because if you want him, you can have him.'

Clearly I am joking, but she doesn't laugh.

'What?' she probes a look of confusion passing over her face, her hand automatically connecting with her uterus, leading me to believe that actually she is in fact brewing one of her own?

'Just joking,' I shrill.

She says nothing more, my early morning (half) humour (half seriousness) clearly not touching her before we all return to our incessant faffing about.

Searching for wipes, quietly asking our children not to burp or shout 'shit' (not mine! Clearly everything is not Rosie...) Bending down to check they aren't too cold. Removing a layer, adding a layer... it never ends.

Well put together woman is just silently watching us all, a slight look of disgust on her face, I can't help but notice.

At bang on 10 o'clock the doors open and Addison is off like a shot, the smell of poop following him in.

The tired woman with the small baby and the woman with the buggy smile at me as well put together woman marches in and over to the maternity wear.

'She won't get 'it' for at least another 10 to 12 months' the one who's child is now shouting 'bugger!' at top volume whispers to me as she hurries past and I laugh, thankful I am understood.

It is on my way to the Mothercare till, approximately 35 minutes later after running around after monster mash, locating a nappy , changing a bum, asking him to not touch everything he comes upon, please do not climb on the car seats, please leave the lady alone, just let mummy buy you some long sleeve vests, Addison please don't do another poo, buying some nappies, changing another bum, prizing a Thomas the tank engine out of his hands that he already has, surreptitiously reading him a book while I keep a look out for incoming sales assistants who would no doubt remind me it isn't a library, grabbing some long sleeve vests, getting to the till realising they are pink, chasing him out of the door and dragging him back in just before he runs in to oncoming traffic, locating the boy vests, asking him repeatedly not to throw all the sale items out of the basket by the window, removing his fingers from my eyes, and finally, finally, being in a position to pay and leave, when the same well put together woman appears behind me, her arms filled with tiny white baby –gro's.

'Do you ever watch Supernanny?' she asks pointedly, clearly displeased that Addison is now attempting to bite her leg.

I remain quiet as I pick Addison up and tenderly give him a kiss while reminding him that we don't bite strangers, type my debit card pin numbers in to the machine incorrectly twice, before finally guessing them correctly, much to my relief, all the while jiggling Addy about to keep him entertained, thank the woman on the till and turn to leave.

'Yes' I address the perfect goddess face to face 'she is brilliant. God knows what I would have done without her. He wouldn't eat for month on end, he wouldn't sleep either, and we didn't know *what* was going on. Turns out he is allergic to *everything*, so we are so pleased he is putting weight on, although we still only average about 6 hours sleep a night that is actually brilliant in comparison to the first few months. I actually met Jo Frost and thanked her to her face, for all the handy tips which really helped get us to this point, right before I was institutionalized for Post Natal depression which nearly killed me. Yes, thank god for Supernanny, she really has been a godsend, he is like a different child now. He is happy, and so am I, finally.'

She says nothing but her ashen and frozen face speaks volumes.

'When are you due?' I ask back mightily pissed off but trying to kill her with kindness.

'April.' She almost whispers swallowing hard

'Addison was an April baby too. Good luck.' I say with a head cock and sympathetic smile. 'I am sure you will be *perfect.'*

And with that my beautiful baby boy and I bounce from the shop followed by an aroma of coffee, farts and no frills wipes.

It is only when I get home I realise I paid, and left without my shopping.

Motherhood.

Flying the flag for black coats, red bull and going with the flow...

God I love it.

The perfect mother is one, who is yet to have kids.

The Heebie Geebies...

Someone, somehow, has downloaded the entire Bee gees album on to my iPhone without me noticing.

There I was trying to relax after a long day of looking after Addy, my heart beat slowly returning back to a normal rate after nearly blowing up the microwave with his Thomas the tank engine bowl (yes the one that says **Do Not Microwave** in massive letters on the underside) and slowly feeling my muscles loosen after having to apologize to my ever so tolerant neighbor for his massacred rose garden when out of nowhere Sheryl crow was rudely interrupted by an inappropriate amount of Jive talking.

So there I am in the bath and...What?

Oh the roses?

I was busy trying to respond to my best friend in Florida and researching glandular fever on my phone (bad mother)) when I looked up to see Addison in his walker, pulling the heads off Gary and Stuart's, precious flower garden arrangement. Well by the time I made it over to him, he was so proud of his efforts, picking up each individual petal and passing it to me, snot streaming down from both nostrils and shouting 'TA! Ta!' I just didn't have it in me to be cross.

It was my fault anyway; I should have been watching him. Interestingly though that isn't what I said to next door. This is the very same next door neighbor who had joined me for a cup of tea last week and was relaxing with Doodle sat on his knee, when unfortunately for him the dog decided to open his bowels, all over his favorite tracky bottoms. It was runny too. Makes me shudder just thinking about it. Funnily enough, I think they actually just put their flat on the market too, but I am sure that is just a coincidence.

No, I told him I was watching him like a hawk and I couldn't understand how he had got there and ruined each individual rose bud so catastrophically when I was honestly Gary, watching him like a BLOODY HAWK! NEVER TOOK MY EYES OFF HIM, honest.

He said it was fine (between gritted teeth now I come to think of it) and asked to borrow an onion, and it just so happens I had a spare one, so all's well that ends well I suppose.

The not having the heart to get cross, however, did not last long as one after the other, a catalog of errors the likes of Basil Faulty would have been proud of proceeded to occur one right after the other. (I liken it to being stuck in a huge game of domino's and being the one right at the end who gets twatted, really hard!)

Are you ready for this?

•I slaved over a hot stove for at least 12 minutes putting together a delicious and nutritious pan of pasta, which instead of ever making it to Addison's mouth, actually ended up being sent by *air mail* to each and every corner of the kitchen.

I somehow managed to punch the pan handle sending the contents flying in to my face and all over the floor.

•Not long after, just as I was prizing long strings of buttery and **strictly** forbidden (he has a dodgy tummy, in case you hadn't gathered) carbohydrate from Doodle's mouth, Addison came crawling inside with a worm hanging out of his.

There are really no words, but seriously? Can children get lung worm? Should I get him a vaccination? I feel like I should.

•And to top things off, about 20 minutes later the credit card company rang asking if I was possibly considering doing them the great honour of paying the minimum payment any time soon.

Nope.

•And finally, finally, just as I am getting over all this, settling down in to the bath with Sheryl crow and her Tuesday night music club (which is a total coincidence by the way) I find myself asking how can I mend a broken heart and then bloody *jive talking.*

Yes, I sat through 'how to mend a broken heart', trying to figure out who it was. (I thought maybe Radio one live lounge at first.)

'Irish one!!' I had screamed from behind the bathroom door (which now stays locked for reasons each and every female reading this will understand – not only do I NOT want you grabbing my boob, but unplanned shits just aren't on ok? THEY ARE NOT ON!)

'What?' he had shouted back 'I am watching the football.'

Shocker.

'Why the fuck am I listening to the Bee gees?' I had elegantly responded. 'I didn't put this on and now I can't change it because my hands are wet!' I shout back irritated 'Keep your shit music off my fancy laptop!'

Struggling to hear his response over the crooning trio, I beckon him (with words that would probably get me arrested if I were to publish them on Amazon) in to the bathroom. (I listen to a lot of Eminem and on occasion my white trash mode, gets the better of me. Bitch.)

'What? He says unlocking the door from the outside (damn.) 'What do you want? Wayne Rooney has just knocked one off at the side of the pitch, and I really want to see how Fergie reacts.'

(At least I *think* that's what he said; I'm not very *up* on my football terminology.)

'Turn this shit over for me *please*, and stop downloading weird folk music on to my iTunes account.'

'Only if I can grab your boob' he replies grabbing my boob just as the opening bars for 'tragedy' ring throughout my steamy bathroom, the aura now completely ruined.

'Tragedy!' he shouts as he walks out without changing it, the git, and unbeknownst to him, we both do the dance hand movement, at the exact same time.

Because, really, it really is, and if you can't beat them (with a great big stick) you may as well join them.

Did you ever see that program on tele where that woman walked down the aisle to 'tragedy' doing all the dance moves, like in the S club 7 video?

What a random.

Can I get a Rewiiindddd...

I re-visited the mental facility today, as I do every Wednesday at the moment.

I miss Jeff. (Which isn't why I go, but bear with me.)

Each time I approach the sign, welcoming me back with its green and white calming lettering, I automatically move down a gear. Almost as if by just turning a corner off the busy main road I am instantly shrouded in a cloak of peace and tranquility that the sanctuary provides, and my heartbeat automatically slows in adjustment to the surroundings.

I am astounded and overcome by the memories that this place holds for me now.

It seems a million years ago that I lived here, cried here and wanted to die here, and yet here it is a few weeks later, welcoming me in to its open arms, providing me with unconditional protection from the outside world, but more crucially from myself and the guilt, self-loathing and anxiety, I am tortured by. Less now that I was, but tortured all the same.

Each time I step out of the car and glance towards the grey and clinical hospital building overlooking the car park, peeping out from between two deep-rooted majestic oak trees, I am proud of what I have achieved.

Albeit for for a very short time.

I am alive, I am well and my son is alive, well and thriving.

I should be proud of myself.

Or so I am told.

But although, I know all of this, I do not really believe it.

(I am an evil horrible person with post-natal depression remember? I don't deserve to be proud of myself!)

I kept my eyes peeled for my favourite magpie today as I was walking towards my dreaded one on one session with James but unfortunately I did not spot him hiding around the dotted nutter's and crispy autumnal foliage.

(*Dotted nutters* would be a great name for a breakfast cereal, don't you think? I would TOTALLY buy them. I imagine them to be a little like lucky charm's but less Irish and more marshmallows. They could make them in to tiny nutter shapes! Me, Ozzy Osborne, Kerry Katona... the list is endless.)

So although I searched for him and did spot couple of impostors, and of course performed the obligatory salute to both, (does anyone else do *like*, an *actual* army salute, or is that just me? Recently I found out it is only supposed to be a *good morning* or whatever, as in that kind of salute? News to me. Superstitions are *hard work yo!!* I will be doing both from now on anyway as I ain't taking no chances!) But no Jeff.

Jeff and I spent some wonderful times together while I was an inpatient.

He would sit on my window ledge peering in at me from the outside and *peck peck peck* each and every time I needed him. Letting me know that although he understood I was on my own, incredibly depressed and hugely confused at how I had arrived here, when my pregnancy and subsequent birth was meant to be *perfect,* that he was there, listening and watching me, supporting me from afar while I sobbed and snotted my way through many a six pack. (Of square crisps.)

Today however, there was no Jeff and that made me gloomy.

He had clearly moved on, found himself a nice bird with long legs and the perfect figure (probably a tit) and was busy getting on with his life.

Whereas I, if I am honest, seem to take 2 steps forward and 12 gallops back.

How is your self-esteem? (I am asking you. So answer me.)

How is your self-esteem?

Because I thought mine was all right thanks, Jack. (I don't know who Jack is, but I hear people say this a lot and I like the way it sounds.)

I had a great night out on Friday at an award ceremony for MAD WRITERS and am honestly still in awe that I came away with an award, especially seen as you know, I am an idiot, and I haven't stopped grinning since. Not even in my sleep.

So when I was asked the question today,

'Lexy, how do you think your self-esteem is?' By James the man with the X-ray vision.

(As in, he can see in to my soul, not beneath my bra, thank god...as I am sure he would be most disappointed. Although I am pretty sure he is gay, so I am not sure why he would be looking in the first place.)

I told James, while crossing my arms across my boobs, that yes, my self-esteem was 'grand.'

But at the end of the session, after he had ignored me of course and continued to pester me like he usually does, clearly sensing something I wasn't, with those eyes that could skin a chicken in seconds, I was seriously starting to question whether this *was* the case, or like with everything else leading up to the grand event of being admitted in to that place, I was just kidding myself.

Was my self-esteem 'grand?'

'How is your self-esteem Lexy?' He asked peering so far through my windows to the soul I was pretty sure he could see what I had eaten for lunch.

'Aright, yeah, all right yeah thanks James, you know. Alright.' I stuttered trying to break eye contact and failing miserably.

'Shall we test that theory?' he asked smiling kindly.

'Why not?' I responded shifting in my seat, feeling the discomfort starting in my chest.

Usually when James tests a theory, he is right and I am proved wrong. So you can understand my awkwardness at that point.

I hate being wrong, and being wrong to a man is just damn insulting, no matter how insightful that man actually is. (You get that right?)

I mean yeah, when I get dressed I tend to focus on the things about myself that I dislike, like my arm fat, or my hairy thighs, my huge nose, my flabby drooping arse, my kangaroo pouch, my stretch marks, my sagging boobs and my yellow teeth, but who doesn't?

And sure, occasionally I will bring myself down a peg or two if I have done something to be proud of, and yeah intermittently I will forget to do something for Addison, for someone special or for an organisation (like paying a bill, *interestingly* this one is the most common) and give myself the living amount of grief over it, but that is normal isn't it? We all bloody do it. (Don't we?)

So other than hating myself, forgetting to buy myself dinner sometimes as I am so busy looking after others and never really accepting compliments without explaining my opinion;

('Oh Lexy I love your bag.'

'What this old thing? I have had it ages, it is actually really dirty and I don't look after stuff.'

Or

'Oh Lexy you should write a book, your blog is great.'

'Nah honest, it is just fluke that I won an award.')

My self-esteem is *pretty good.*

I don't hate myself *all* the time.

'Ok Lexy so let us start.'

'Actually James I am not sure you need to.'

I had already come to the conclusion that my self-esteem was pretty shit actually.

He looked at me and nodded.

'Thought as much' the slight nod of his head as the understanding passed across his features, told me.

Damn it I hate it when men are right.

'So ok,' I began to ask 'my self-esteem since giving birth has been rock bottom, what can I do about it?'

'Do you treat yourself?' he asked.

'Yes' I replied instantly, safe in the knowledge that treating myself was something I was great at.

'How?' he fired back unconvinced.

'I buy stuff.'

'Like what?'

'Shoes, clothes, nice food'

I paused and he urged me to go on, the way he always does, with a slight flip of the hand lying in his lap.

'But I probably shouldn't as we don't really have the money.' I finished as he sat up, barely able to contain his glee.

'Ah' he exclaimed, holding a finger in the air before continuing 'so you treat yourself, but then beat yourself up about it?'

I didn't respond but looked down at the scarf lying in my lap, smoothing it over my leg again and again, as if to methodically push away the pain slowly beginning to rise to the surface from years of self-abuse.

'So ok,' he continued sensing my unease 'do you relax?'

'Yes.' I replied, once again feeling in control of the situation.

'How?' He asked.

'I write, or read a book, or watch television or have a bath.'

'You watch television?'

'Yes.'

'Do you actually watch though, or do you think about other things, while you just aimlessly stare at the screen?'

I shifted in my seat at this point.

It was all getting a bit too much like that film SCREAM for my liking.

How does he know these things?

Will he ring me tonight when I am in my pajamas staring at something The Irish One is forcing me to watch on discovery channel and say 'I can see you Leeexxxxxyyyy, what are you thiiinnkkkiinggg abouuut?'

I shuddered and taking this as an affirmative, and not noticing I was now glancing about looking for a stashed freaky scream mask, he continued.

'Ok, and when you are in the bath what do you think about?'

I will be honest.

I burst out laughing.

'That is a bit personal James.' Fnar, smack of the leg.

'Is it?' he replied without flinching, 'because I think that probably the only thing you think about when you are relaxing is what you have to do in the morning, or what Addison needs for dinner, or how much washing up is left in the sink, or oooo I don't know' he pauses reaching in to an imaginary suitcase in his mind about to pull out the *piece de resistance* 'how many people dislike you, or how fat you think you are, or perhaps, just perhaps, you talk yourself out of every success you have achieved over the day, by telling yourself you could have done better and will do better tomorrow.'

He looked at me looking for signs of recognition, his eyes brimming over with kindness, but saw nothing, as by that point I had put my lovely new scarf over my head and face, and was doing a very bad impression of Darth Vader, against my will.

'Lexy?' he asked tentatively 'what are you doing?'

'I am hiding' my muffled voice came from beneath the scarf 'you know too much.'

'Ok' he laughed 'good to know where we stand. I will still be here when you feel you can look me in the eye again and if you can't I will leave, it is almost time anyway but I am giving you some homework ok?'

'This week' he announced 'I want you to do something nice for **you,** without beating yourself up and without feeling guilty about all the other things you SHOULD or COULD or NEED to be doing at that time.'

He continued 'Go to the cinema, watch a film, do some writing for you, not for anyone else, buy yourself something and ENJOY the pleasure of treating yourself without the guilt, the constant need to put yourself down or tell yourself you SHOULDN'T have spent the money on that.

Be kind to yourself, and try to enjoy the moment, guilt free.'

'What would be the point?' I had asked a little nonplussed and now sweating from beneath the thick wool scarf.

'You may start to believe you deserve it and that you are worth it.' He had replied as I pulled the scarf off my face and decided to rise to the challenge. 'You may just gain a little bit of pleasure and either way, what harm can it do?'

None.

So this week, I am taking a small step to help my self-esteem.

I am going to find the time to treat myself. Guilt free.

Will you join me?

I think I may give myself a facial.

What about you?

I may also say a little prayer for Jeff's happiness; he was a great bird.

It is a small step for mammy kind, right?

But an important one.

Go on, treat yourself.

The world won't end on a Thursday...

Never at any point in my entire lifetime, did I ever once imagine, that I would end up questioning the fragility of life and the prospect that the end of the world was most definitely upon me, while slapping too much mayonnaise on to a very unhealthy ham sandwich, while arguing with The Irish One, on a very mundane and monotonous Thursday night.

I don't know about you, but *I* always imagined, that if the end of the world was about to materialise, I would be prepared (well, as prepared as I could be, given that I am quite possibly the most unorganised person alive) you know? Because *clearly* we would have all been given some warning by sky news.

'Next Thursday at four o'clock, the world will end. Breaking news. Don't worry about your credit card debt.'

And there I would be, at 4 o'clock on said Thursday, on high ground, wearing fabulous new clothes and glitzy shoes courtesy of NatWest, rifling through the changing bag looking for a tissue or something, surrounded by my loved ones and worrying about whether I had left the oven on.

So most disappointingly it seemed the world was going to come to an end while I was making a crap tea.

As the clock struck 8 last night, while Addison was sleeping like a drunken angel, bum in the air, dribble on the pillow and trumping like a beast, and while both myself and The Irish One were in the middle of a deeply heated 'discussion', and doodle was most probably licking his bum, we, as a whole family, experienced a very dramatic incident.

A dramatic incident that without a doubt has changed the way I think, the person I am and how I will live my life from this day forward, forever more. It has shaken the very foundations at the core of who I am, leaving my deep rooted beliefs feeling incredibly vulnerable and exposed.

Nah not really, but please, do read on, it was proper dramatic honest.

Elbow deep in washing up and seriously unhappy about it, my Irish child rearing colleague and I were arguing about whether or not I should be allowed to take Addison to the zoo without him, the following day.

'I am asking you not to go without me' he had muttered from between very gritted teeth, so gritted in fact, that he had given himself a bit of a speech impediment, which I am *pretty* sure wasn't the effect he was going for. His jaw was set firmly and he was blowing air through his nose like a mental bull about to go on a seriously damaging rampage.

'But that's the thing,' I replied using my sing songy voice, turning to face him from the opposite counter, the conversation with the therapist the day previous still ringing in my ears and attempting to appear the epitome of cool, calm and collected 'you aren't though are you? You aren't actually *asking* me anything. The word *asking*' I pronounced slowly, limp armed and waving my knife around '*invariably* makes me think there are **two** possible answers to this *question,* when in all honesty' I continued slopping mayonnaise all over the counters he had just cleaned 'there isn't. You are **telling** me not to take him to the zoo and James said that when people tell me to do stuff I should question their motives as most people should ask, as I am my own person and...'

'I don't want you to go without me because I don't want to miss out' he interrupted me loudly 'I already miss out on **so** much, how can you not understand that I am **asking** you not to go because I miss out on **so** much already?'

'And that is fine' I replied, mopping up the spilt mayonnaise with my finger and giving it a good suck 'but let us not pretend you are *asking* me, because you aren't, you are actually *telling* me not to go and I won't anyway, as I respect the way you feel, but it wasn't a question, you were telling me not to go, so you can stop pretending it was a question.'

At the time, it seemed like an important argument.

At the time it seemed like I was making an important point, and that perhaps we were heading for a relational breakthrough.

Now of course, looking back, I can totally see I was being a complete anus.

Hindsight is a funny thing isn't it?

We were arguing about two completely different things though.

He didn't want me to go to the zoo, and obviously I wasn't going to go, that was obvious, *but I just wanted him to stop saying he was asking me when he wasn't, he was blatantly telling me, while he just wanted me to say I wouldn't go. Which I never would because I totally understood his point, but he didn't hear me and just kept repeating his reasons for not wanting me to go, which I understood and never would have gone, but I just wanted him to stop saying... You know what?*

Men just don't get it. (Ahem.) It doesn't matter.

Shall we move on?

'Are you ever going to wash up again?' he had mumbled from under his breath as the argument drizzled off because I had a mouth full of pig sandwich 'or has *James* told you that by washing up I am somehow controlling your underlying need to be a complete pain in the arse...'

I swallowed hard (on my sarnie, this isn't a porno) and was on the precipice of behaving just as sanctimoniously back, when from behind the window came the most god almighty bright flash of light, illuminating us both in our tedium from the outside in, immediately followed by the loudest crack and tumble I have ever heard in my life.

It literally sounded like the hospital across the road was blowing up.

It sounded like a bomb.

And the moment seemed to go on for ages, because within, what in reality could have only been a couple of seconds of sheer terror and panic, the following thoughts went through my head.

Oh my god what the hell is that noise.
Oh my god is the building coming down on us?
What the hell is that flashing light outside?
Has somebody let off a gun?
Are we blowing up?
Why can't I see anything?
Oh yeah open your eyes!
If The Irish One doesn't look scared then I don't need to either.
Shit Irish One looks scared.
I can't believe he got the last word!
Where the hell is Addison?
He is bed, is the world coming to an end?
I need to get him out of his bed.
Has somebody targeted Salford hospital?
Why would somebody target Salford hospital?
I know it isn't the best but blowing it up seems a bit much!
Oh my god where is my phone?
What underwear am I wearing?
I can't die in a g string.
I should have put a wash on.
Oh my god it is the end of the world.
I think I just weed a little bit in fright.
Is it 2012 yet? (Mayan calendar and all that...)
This shouldn't be happening yet
Where is Doodle?

Is this happening?

I should have eaten the rest of that Twirl this morning.

Never save chocolate.

What was I thinking?

We need to get outside.

I will grab Addison and my chocolate and he can grab Doodle.

Can Doodle swim?

I need to get to my boy and my poodle.

We need to make a makeshift arc.

I need a cuddle.

I am scared.

I want that chocolate.

I think a bit more wee just escaped.

Heart pounding and knees threatening to give way beneath me (and seriously trying not to poo) I looked at The Irish One, now turned towards the window, both hands dripping wet and looking decidedly worried (from behind anyway) and screeched.

'What was that?'

'I don't know' he replied quickly, as I was running out of the room to check on my beautiful son. 'But calm down, it isn't the end of the world!'

But how does he know that?

Why are my feet wet?

The floods are coming I just know it.

It's the miner's prophecy, or something.

Oh my god why did I buy a ground floor flat?

Where did I put Addy's swimwear?

Why are my feet wet?

Turns out it was lightening.

It had hit the chimney stack above our flats and caused quite a bit of chaos.

So not the end of the world, actually.

Turns out my feet were wet because Doodle had also been a little shocked by the horrifically loud noise and had immediately and unintentionally released his bladder in the hallway. (I am just thankful he wasn't lying on my bed. Like last time.)

The neighbor (the one that Doodle poo'd on that *one time at band camp*) called by shortly after moaning that he too, had released his bladder with the shock of it all and then went on to ask if I was I aware, that if the chemical factory down the road blew up there was no evacuation plan for our flats as we were too close and would die instantly.

Cheery bunch this lot.

Anyway, this morning following on from this *near death experience;*

I put a wash on.

Bought some more chocolate and ate the lot.

Didn't go to the zoo,

And mostly sat around feeling happy (ish) to be alive, but a little bored.

I have come to this conclusion though,

Life is too short to leave chocolate in the cupboard.

(And I really hope the chemical plant doesn't blow up.)

A whole lot of nakedness and the Odd truth...

'You do realise, that by ignoring the issues, by closing your eyes, sticking your fingers in your ears and singing La! They aren't *actually* going to go away right?'

'I am not three, Irish one.'

'I am aware of that, oh befuddled one,' he sighs 'and please stop referring to me as The Irish One. Doing it on your diary is one thing but in person? I feel like a piece of meat.'

'Ok,' I respond trying not to laugh, and attempting to craftily change the subject 'when are we going on the London Eye? I won it for us you know, with my hard work! So when do you fancy going?'

'Nice try.'

I sigh. 'Go on then, what do you want to discuss?'

'Well, so tell me then, what day are you returning once again, to work?'

'I er, I er, um, ar, Oh look!' I shout, pointing at the television my mouth falling open aghast 'Angeline Jolie has no clothes on!!'

And while his head swivels at the speed of light towards the odd children on Waybaloo that have clearly been dubbed but I will never understand why (Naked Angelina Jolie? Seriously Irish One? On Cbeebies?) I make a run for it in to the bathroom and switch on the shower.

It isn't that I am not aware it isn't going to happen I just don't want to talk about it you know?

I am like Julia Roberts in pretty woman, not a whore, I am not a whore just to clarify here, although on some days I do wish... never mind, but I like to 'fly by the seat of my pants.'

Some things I just don't like to face.

Like bills.

I hate facing bills.

Which is why they usually only get paid when a man knocks at the door holding a spanner and asking me where the electricity meter is.

'Why?' I ask aghast.

'I am here to cut you off' he speaks solemnly in a broad Boltonion accent.

'But why?' I inquire again aghast 'I deserve light.'

'Because you haven't paid missis, and if you don't pay, you get to live in the dark.'

At which point, just as everything is about to be emerged in to obscurity I will reach for my debit card, face up to the fact we can't cook Thomas the tank engine pasta shapes by candle light and make a payment.

It isn't laziness, or irresponsibility (although I suppose it is a bit) and it isn't because I don't have the money, or because I am stingy and would rather spend my money on shoes than electricity (although clearly I would. I saw some lovely heels today in Topshop...)

It is because, well, it is because... I don't know why but I blame Spain.

Yes the whole country.

I grew up over there and brilliant country that it is, the general rule for living seems to be 'why do today what you can clearly put off until tomorrow?' And seriously, I was brainwashed.

This excuse unfortunately didn't wash with my therapist when I visited him last week though, and when I pointed out of the window and screamed that Jennifer Aniston had just turned up butt naked and waving a cucumber about, he didn't even flinch. (Damn it, he is gay, I KNEW I should have gone for brad Pitt.)

But it seems most people currently, want to ask me things I am not ready to answer or to think about even, and in all honesty, it is driving me insane.

'Do you blame yourself for the last year?'

'What do you mean?'

'Do you regret the way things have gone since Addison was born?'

'Regret it?'

'Yes. Do you wish you could have behaved differently?'

'I have a feeling you are trying to trick me here.' I respond looking towards the door.

'I can assure you I am not, I am just trying to find out if you blame yourself?'

'Look!! Brad Pitt with no clothes on waving a jar of hummus about!'

'Nice try, answer the question.'

'Why do you want to know?' I sigh, looking everywhere but at him, anxiety creeping out as my legs becoming possessed by Michael Flatly.

'Humour me. I'm your therapist.' He smiles.

'Of course I regret it,' I say quietly looking down at my open palms staring back up at me 'and of course I wish things could have been different, who wouldn't in my position? I don't remember the way I felt when I first saw my son, I don't recall feeling love, I don't remember huge chunks of his life, people tell me I was happy, that I was a great mum, but I don't remember him as a tiny baby or me even, I can't even look at photos from that time, I missed out on so much, of course I regret it. I mean, no I don't regret it,' I stumble as I see him latching on and about to go in for the kill 'I just wish things could be different.'

'Lexy?'

'What?'

'Why are you crying?'

'Oh,' I exclaim surprised, wiping my eye 'I didn't realise I was.'

'You are. Do you blame yourself?'

'I guess I do yeah.' I shrug 'but who else is responsible if not me?'

'Why does anybody need to be held responsible? Postnatal Depression is an illness, you need to grieve what could have been, that is true, but it needs to be let go of, maybe it is time to stop punishing yourself, as it is getting you nowhere.'

'Right,' I smile slightly 'except it is.'

'It is.' He confirms nodding slightly. 'You are right it is. How could I have missed this? It is allowing you to remain static in a nonsensical circle of self-harming and avoidance. Blaming yourself for things that are out of your control feels comfortable to you doesn't it?'

'That's right.' I laugh. (Although he is mistaken, everything is within my control. EVERYTHING!!)

'Why are you laughing?'

'Because if I don't I will break.'

'It isn't funny Lexy. It is heartbreaking.'

I laugh almost sarcastically, annoyed. I am angry with him. Indignant. What does he know? This isn't heartbreaking, this is life, he isn't a mother, he doesn't know, he has no idea of the pressure, heartbroken? I am not heartbroken I am nothing! I am a big fat sodding failure.

'I am not heartbroken' I spit out at him. 'I am nothing.'

He looks deep in to my eyes, a look of shock on his face.

'You are nothing?'

'Nothing.' I confirm. 'So let's just change the subject.'

He is silent again.

'Who is allowed to call you worthless?' He continues, ignoring my pleas to move on.

'No one' I say annoyed that he should even suggest it. I am not worthless, much.

'Who is allowed to shout at you?'

'No one.'

'Really?' he says an amused look playing on his features 'I don't believe that.'

I just look at him blankly. I am not in the mood.

'Ok,' he tries again 'who is allowed to call you worthless?'

'No one!' I almost shout 'of course, no one!'

'Just you then?'

'What?'

'You wouldn't stand to be treated like this off anyone else, and I am damn sure you wouldn't dream of inflicting this behaviour on anyone else, so why is it ok to do it to yourself? Why is it ok to call yourself a failure, a nothing, a piece of shit?'

I don't answer for a long time, defiant.

'How can you regret something that isn't your fault?' he asks chin jutting out towards me breaking the atmosphere.

I look up at him solemnly from my chair in the opposite corner of the room 'it *is* my fault though' I disagree with him, 'that is what you don't know' and I lean in to him, trying to make him hear. 'I could have been different if I had tried a bit harder. Look at all those other mothers, they did it.'

'Ah.' He nods 'So you chose to be this way?'

'No.'

'So then?' he sits back in his chair, and slaps his knees lightly in exasperation.

'But I allowed it to happen' I shout louder than I intended to. 'If I had been stronger, not so selfish, not an evil selfish bitch then maybe...'

'Did you try and stop it?'

'Yes.' I whisper quietly, alarmed 'of course I did.'

'And what happened?'

'You know what happened, can we move on?'

'So, again, did you choose this?' he repeats himself.

'No. I didn't chose it but...'

'Would you change it if you could?' He interrupts me.

'In a heartbeat.' I nod, wiping another trespassing tear. 'Just for Addison. I would live through it a hundred times to keep him here, but it is just not fair on him, to have half a mum, he didn't chose this did he?' I am faintly aware of my face being wet again.

'No and neither did you. Did you?'

'No.'

'Can you regret something that isn't your fault?'

'I don't suppose you can, but you can regret not trying harder...'

He sighs, not the answer he is looking for.

I cannot let him win this point, I am not ready to.

'Do you love your son?'

'Yes, but not as much as I should. Not as much as all those other mum's love their children. I see them and they look brilliant, while I am on the outskirts, failing to be...' I trail off.

'Can you measure it?' He asks kindly

'No' I sob again 'I can't. I am a failure.'

After a few minutes of silence, only broken by my sniffing and trying to hold back the tears he draws the session to an end.

'That is enough for today.'

'Ok.' I nod mutely, glancing at the clock, wiping my nose.

'Before you go, I want you to think about something and next session we can talk about it. Ok?'

'Ok.' I say glumly about to stand up.

'I want you to write it down.' He directs and I immediately reach in to my bag and pull out my notebook and pen.

'Ok' I say pen poised.

If your child became poorly with an illness out of his control, how long would you punish him for?

And if you wouldn't punish him for being ill, write down all the things you would do.

Write down five reasons why it is time to stop punishing yourself.

I put my book away, stand up and smile. Bastard.

There is no way I will be able to answer those questions without admitting it isn't my fault and he knows it.

'Bye James, see you Wednesday.'

'Bye Lexy, and oh, one thing...'

'What?' I ask, turning to face him from the door.

'You do love your son enough.' He smiles up at me 'you have nothing to worry about there. You aren't a failure, not at all. And contrary to what you believe, you love him more than you will ever realise.'

My heart skips a beat.

'How do you know?' I ask hopefully.

'Because every time you talk about him you cry.'

....aaaannnnnndddd this is why avoidance is probably a bit poo. (That and the fact I potentially won't have running water in a couple of days...)

Because ever since he said that, anytime I look at Addison, I cry.

Of course I love him enough, I always have.

Maybe it is time to stop punishing myself?

But I am still not paying the bills, or ringing the council tax people, or even discussing my return to work...

One step at a time yeah?

'Look! Mr. Bloom with no clothes on!!'

(I wish.)

And look at the state of Roger...

'Jessica Rabbit was curvy wasn't she? And she was a full on knock out.'

I turn to look at him.

'Seriously? You are trying to make me feel better about my body, by comparing me to a cartoon rabbit with bigger boobs than me? How unrealistic is that?'

'Ok, bad example.' He grumbles walking out. 'I couldn't have won anyway.'

Conversation over.

And he is right.

He wouldn't have done.

He thinks I am gorgeous.

He tells me all the time.

So why can't I just believe him?

Because the truth is, the expectations I have of myself are *way* higher than any expectations I would ever have of anybody else.

It is not *ok* for my body to look like this.

He may think it is.

But I don't.

I have to be *perfect*. I am *supposed* to be perfect. I need to try harder.

And yet, as I sit here taking a *ridiculous* amount of time to type this due to the fact that one hand is currently fumbling around in the dark depths of a bag of Walkers Taste Sensations and the other is about to reach out for a pot of hummus, I should be saving for tonight's tea, I am finding it hard to care.

(I am actually typing this with my chin, as I chew. Honest.)

The thing is, it is all very well having therapy to 'sort your head out' but unfortunately the down side of this *mood reboot* seems to be that as my mood increases, and I start to see sense, due to therapists whacking me on the side of the head and switching me off and on (the tried and tested technique for anything that requires technical assistance...hey! Have Blackberry tried this? I should call them...) unfortunately so does my waistline, which is playing havoc with my internal scoring system.

Hang on, just to backtrack a bit here... when I mentioned that the therapists turn me off and on, I meant purely within the realms of that metaphor. I can assure you I have not once been *turned on* by any of my therapists.

Honest.

Seriously. I haven't.

Ok, I suppose there is *one* who is quite fit but it's not like I am available, or would ever dream of approaching him and he doesn't have to know that he has done things to me, I mean *for* me, that ... you know what? Let's move on.

He is good for my self-esteem. End of.

Back to the point.

With every day that passes, the stronger I feel emotionally, the more I shove down my throat, and the less I get done.

(Including the washing up. - I was told to put that in here, he feels very hard done to, poor love.)

Which literally is sending my fragile brain and sense of what is normal, in to a tail spin, because for as long as I can remember my self-esteem has been entirely based on how thin I am, and how much I can achieve as the 'perfect mother' on a day to day basis.

If I was thin I could be happy.

If I could just complete the last 8 things on my list, including re carpeting the living room floor, while changing Addison's bum, in the next hour, I would be worth it.

If you could see my ribs I would be winning, we would be a happier couple and the world would make sense again.

Seriously, I don't know why I ever worried in the early days about other mothers judging me or my lack of parenting skills, because if truth be told, I was judging *myself* enough for bloody everyone.

However as I begin to crawl out from this dark hole of self-hatred, self-punishment and unrealistic expectations I set for myself, I am trying to see things a little clearer.

I don't have the perfect body, but the fact I now have a kangaroo pouch that covers my hairy thighs, nipples that I could clean my belly button with (if I wanted to, which I don't, cos that would be gross) and bits that resemble something literally, that the cat dragged in, they shouldn't really serve to make me feel worthless should they?

Sure, it isn't ideal. And I would prefer the body of (not Jessica rabbit) Jennifer Anniston but hey, she doesn't have kids, a poodle with the runs or a hectic schedule that involves more poop than scoop does she?

(Scoop being cocktails and Botox.)

So why do I compare myself to these people who mostly, are airbrushed?

These things about myself that aren't *actually* perfect are just tantamount to the life we have created for ourselves. (I say we because I refuse to believe I am the only woman with serious perfectionism issues here, and misery loves company.)

Because as WE start to look in the mirror and see OUR true worth, worth that should be based on a million different things, good things, friendly things, caring things, hugs, words of support, words we give out, friendship, love, our children, the reaction I get off that Irish bloke that lives with me, the fact we are loved, the fact we can love, the ways we manage to succeed on a daily basis, be it just getting out of bed, or be it telling somebody they are worth it, I really am struggling to put importance on the parts of my body that can no longer be considered *thin.*

I am struggling to put importance on the things I haven't achieved today, when there are a good few things that I have. (Like eating two massive bags of crisps and having a rant.)

I know I could be healthier, thinner and a million different other things on my list if I really wanted to be, I could run around like a blue arsed fly all day trying to achieve everything right this second, rather than in a week, rather than in a month, but why should I?

Think of all the moments I would miss out on, if I carried on this way?

Why do we need to be perfect???

I wouldn't punish others the way I punish myself, I wouldn't expect others to complete as much as I expect myself to complete, Jaysus, if I gave The Irish One a list of 12 things to do in an hour, I would be happy (and amazed) if he completed 3 things. So why when I give myself a list, do I have to complete them all in *half an hour* and then add stuff?

I do not have to be perfect all of the time.

I am not Jennifer Anniston.

Whoa.

Hang on, I need a new bag of crisps, this is all getting a bit deep.

I have to be honest, I am pretty damn sure that if the 20 year old me, the one who was obsessed with work and a career and drinking and being thin, and having to have achieved EVERYTHING by the time she was 30, was to see the 32 year old me now, living the way I am, having achieved not much of what she wanted me to, she would probably be a bit appalled.

But you know what?

She can sod off.

She doesn't have my son, and I do.

And there is time yet for all that other stuff anyway.

(My Aunty Et always used to say 'The washing up will still be there when the children are in bed dear...' And I see what she means now.)

So, I will sit here and I will eat these crisps, and rather than starving myself, like I used to, or standing and texting work stuff while at the playground, watching a film with Addison while beating myself up and punishing myself for missing out on all these moments that could be enjoyed if i wasn't so busy trying to get EVERYTHING DONE NOW, I may actually just try and be kind to myself for a change and enjoy the moments for what they are and *then* list all the things I *have* achieved by the end of the day.

I know it will be easier said than done, but I owe it to myself to try right?

And if I don't succeed at first that is ok too right?

Because I am starting to see what really matters to me.

And that is me.

And the moments that can never be bought back.

So if eating a Big Mac makes me smile?

I'm going to eat it.

Enough punishment for now.

Yeah?

And maybe, just maybe, next time The Irish One calls me gorgeous, I may let him win. (Briefly.)

Alpine goats, winter coats and...

'Yooodeley Yooodeley Yodelayyyyy HuuHuuuuuuuuuuu!!'

'Again, again!!' Addison roars, pronouncing it 'Gin gin!' (which is actually pretty embarrassing/handy particularly when I am in the wine aisle at the supermarket) at top volume from his car seat where he is now strapped in looking very much like a trussed up turkey, unable to move like a little cardboard man, due to the sheer chunkiness and bulk of his new winter bomber jacket.

I am not the only one who buys clothes too big so he 'can grow' in to them right?

I may, however, have gone a bit far this time; I think to myself looking back at him from the driver's seat, it reaches his feet. He looks like a mattress with a little blonde head.

'Yooodeley Yooodeley Yodelayyyyy HuuHuuuuuuuuuuu!!'

I yodel back at him channeling Dolly Parton and sticking my chest out. (Does Dolly Yodel? She totally should.) While he once again hoots (albeit completely motionless) like this simple and strange noise emanating from my lips, is the funniest thing he has ever heard.

I put the car in to gear and promptly stall (I do this a lot, but try and make it seem like I meant to) and whisper my thanks to the universe as I check the clock and notice with glee that for once, woohooo for once!!!! We have actually managed to get out of the house on time and without any of the usual D.I's

(Dramatic incidents, which can include but are not limited to, losing spot the dog, losing Doodle the dog, banging our heads, taking off our shoes and throwing them in the toilet bowl, trying to shove our toothbrushes up Doodle's bum hole, banging our heads again for attention and not being able to leave without our favourite Dummy, which has been missing since the dawn of time.)

I smile to myself at his continued merriment circling its way around my healing heart, like a great big hug, from the back of the car.

It is honestly just so lovely to hear the fruit of my loins giggle, it is a sound that makes me feel like I have arrived home, the best sound in the entire world. I love it.

It is also such a lovely change from what currently seems to be the sound track of my life, which isn't the Benny Hill theme tune anymore, but instead Addison telling me his teeth are hurting.

Pronounced, just so you are fully aware,

'Waaaaaaaaaaaaaaa waaaaaaaaaaaaaaaaa errrrrrrrrrrrrrrrrrrrrrrrrr waaaaaaaaaaaaaaaaaaaaaaaaaaaaaaaaa waaaaaaaaaaaaaaaaaaaaaa

'Waaaaaaaaaaaaaaa waaaaaaaaaaaaaaaaa errrrrrrrrrrrrrrrrrrrrrrrrr waaaaaaaaaaaaaaaaaaaaaaaaaaaaaaaaa waaaaaaaaaaaaaaaaaaaaaa

'Waaaaaaaaaaaaaaa waaaaaaaaaaaaaaaaa errrrrrrrrrrrrrrrrrrrrrrrrr waaaaaaaaaaaaaaaaaaaaaaaaaaaaaaaaa waaaaaaaaaaaaaaaaaaaaaa

'Waaaaaaaaaaaaaaa waaaaaaaaaaaaaaaaa errrrrrrrrrrrrrrrrrrrrrrrrr waaaaaaaaaaaaaaaaaaaaaaaaaaaaaaaaa waaaaaaaaaaaaaaaaaaaaaa

'Waaaaaaaaaaaaaaa waaaaaaaaaaaaaaaaa errrrrrrrrrrrrrrrrrrrrrrrrr waaaaaaaaaaaaaaaaaaaaaaaaaaaaaaaaa waaaaaaaaaaaaaaaaaaaaaa'

While he is making this god awful racket he is also *always* attempting to shove everything and anything in to his mouth, including but not limited to, my new Ugg boot, Doodle's bed, Doodle himself, the Dyson, the bath plug, my handbag, my leg, Doodle's leg, a full toilet roll, The take away menu and sometimes, if I am not quick enough, the 50 inch flat screen TV. (Which now has flickery teeth marks right in the corner... No Irish one! Of course I was watching him! I have NO IDEA what those marks are!)

During these times we also, and by *we* I mean me and Doodle, have to don ice skates due to the overwhelming amount of dribble, spit and snot that leaves the entire house saturated and soggy.

I could do with one of those yellow flip signs. Or a boat.

'Right Addy, let's go and buy you some new shoes before nursery!' I holler over-excitedly before finally getting the car to move, 'YEAYYYYYYYYYYYY NEW SHOOOESSSSS ADDISONNN, NEW SHOES YEAYYYYYYY!' I look back at him inviting him to join in with the excitement, hopeful that he will take me up on the offer.

You'd think the kid *would* be excited *anyway* at the thought of new shoes, him being *my* kid and all, but unfortunately and true to form, I am met with the customary response.

"Waaaaaaaaaaaaaaa waaaaaaaaaaaaaaaaa errrrrrrrrrrrrrrrrrrrrrrrr waaaaaaaaaaaaaaaaaaaaaaaaaaaaaa waaaaaaaaaaaaaaaaaaaaaa

'Waaaaaaaaaaaaaaa waaaaaaaaaaaaaaaaa errrrrrrrrrrrrrrrrrrrrrrrr waaaaaaaaaaaaaaaaaaaaaaaaaaaaaa waaaaaaaaaaaaaaaaaaaaaa

'Waaaaaaaaaaaaaaa waaaaaaaaaaaaaaaaa errrrrrrrrrrrrrrrrrrrrrrrr waaaaaaaaaaaaaaaaaaaaaaaaaaaaaa waaaaaaaaaaaaaaaaaaaaaa

'Waaaaaaaaaaaaaaa waaaaaaaaaaaaaaaaaa errrrrrrrrrrrrrrrrrrrrrrrrrr waaaaaaaaaaaaaaaaaaaaaaaaaaaaaaaaa waaaaaaaaaaaaaaaaaaaaaaaa

'Waaaaaaaaaaaaaaa waaaaaaaaaaaaaaaaaa errrrrrrrrrrrrrrrrrrrrrrrrrr waaaaaaaaaaaaaaaaaaaaaaaaaaaaaaaaa waaaaaaaaaaaaaaaaaaaaaaaa'

"Yooodeley Yooodeley Yodelayyyyy HuuHuuuuuuuuuuuu!!'

I try, and once again am thrilled to hear it working like a goddamn dream, so much so, that I end up yodeling like a mental Inga from Sweden (even Dolly has disowned me) all the way to Clarks Shoe Shop.

Which is a 40 minute drive.

I am aware I sound like a bad copy of a mad milk maid and that my voice is going hoarse but if it keeps him laughing and distracted while I navigate my way around rush hour traffic, taxi drivers and white van men sent directly from hell to taunt my insufficient high way code knowledge (amber means slam your foot down and go, right?) Then so be it.

Unfortunately by the time we reach the Clarks Sale and find ourselves waiting to be served behind a million other well behaved and surprisingly quiet school aged children accompanied by their calm and in control mothers and lurking Nannies, (Hale Barns- they have help, these women in Hale Barns and even though I know I shouldn't be, I am eternally Jealous) yodeling is the last thing I am prepared to do and Addison is far too annoyed at now being wedged in to the pram, for it to even be considered as an option.

'Waaaaaaaaaaaaaaa waaaaaaaaaaaaaaaaaa errrrrrrrrrrrrrrrrrrrrrrrrrr waaaaaaaaaaaaaaaaaaaaaaaaaaaaaaaaa waaaaaaaaaaaaaaaaaaaaaaaa

'Waaaaaaaaaaaaaaa waaaaaaaaaaaaaaaaaa errrrrrrrrrrrrrrrrrrrrrrrrrr waaaaaaaaaaaaaaaaaaaaaaaaaaaaaaaaa waaaaaaaaaaaaaaaaaaaaaaaa

'Waaaaaaaaaaaaaaa waaaaaaaaaaaaaaaaaa errrrrrrrrrrrrrrrrrrrrrrrrr waaaaaaaaaaaaaaaaaaaaaaaaaaaaaaaa waaaaaaaaaaaaaaaaaaaaaaa

'Waaaaaaaaaaaaaaa waaaaaaaaaaaaaaaaaa errrrrrrrrrrrrrrrrrrrrrrrrr waaaaaaaaaaaaaaaaaaaaaaaaaaaaaaaa waaaaaaaaaaaaaaaaaaaaaaa

'Waaaaaaaaaaaaaaa waaaaaaaaaaaaaaaaaa errrrrrrrrrrrrrrrrrrrrrrrrr waaaaaaaaaaaaaaaaaaaaaaaaaaaaaaaa waaaaaaaaaaaaaaaaaaaaaaa'

He signals that he is about to pass out from heat exhaustion and I whip his coat off hoping against all odds this will quieten him down somewhat.

The shop is packed.

Other mothers are glancing over at my designer *Primarni* gear, disgusted, touching their Gucci wears as if to check they are still there and that making eye contact with my screaming son hasn't transformed them in to someone like me. (Nanny less! Oh the atrocity of it all!)

The shop assistant seems to be in a hurry to get us, due to the ear piercing disruption coming from my pram and I silently thank my son for his persistent reminder of the fact we are waiting.

Fast forward 3 very long years.

'Addison just sit still for one moment while we try this shoe on, OOOO ISNT THIS SHOE NICE? YEAYYYY!'

'Waaaaaaaaaaaaaaa waaaaaaaaaaaaaaaaaa errrrrrrrrrrrrrrrrrrrrrrrrr waaaaaaaaaaaaaaaaaaaaaaaaaaaaaaaa waaaaaaaaaaaaaaaaaaaaaaa

'Waaaaaaaaaaaaaaa waaaaaaaaaaaaaaaaaa errrrrrrrrrrrrrrrrrrrrrrrrr waaaaaaaaaaaaaaaaaaaaaaaaaaaaaaaa waaaaaaaaaaaaaaaaaaaaaaa

'Waaaaaaaaaaaaaaa waaaaaaaaaaaaaaaaaa errrrrrrrrrrrrrrrrrrrrrrrrr waaaaaaaaaaaaaaaaaaaaaaaaaaaaaaaa waaaaaaaaaaaaaaaaaaaaaaa

'Waaaaaaaaaaaaaaa waaaaaaaaaaaaaaaaa errrrrrrrrrrrrrrrrrrrrrrrrrr waaaaaaaaaaaaaaaaaaaaaaaaaaaaaaa waaaaaaaaaaaaaaaaaaaaaa

'Waaaaaaaaaaaaaaa waaaaaaaaaaaaaaaaa errrrrrrrrrrrrrrrrrrrrrrrrrr waaaaaaaaaaaaaaaaaaaaaaaaaaaaaaa waaaaaaaaaaaaaaaaaaaaaa'

As the shop assistant becomes huffy and it feels like all eyes are now on my little beast who has now doubled over the manky puff seat and is trying to fit the whole thing in his mouth, I finally give up on a magical nanny appearing out of a lamp to save me and go for the tried and tested calm and happy maker instead.

Throwing caution to the wind, believing will all my heart, that this will work, I yodel.

"Yooodeley Yooodeley Yodelayyyyy HuuHuuuuuuuuuuuu!!'

All eyes are now **definitely** on me, and during the year and a half's silence that follows my outburst, I am sure I hear someone snigger.

Addison eyes me warily as the shop assistant takes the opportunity to wedge the shoe on to his paddle foot. (Seriously, they are ridiculously big for such a small boy.)

'Yooodeley Yooodeley Yodelayyyyy HuuHuuuuuuuuuuuu!!'

I try again, and even at this moment right now, as I sit here re-living the horror, I am not sure why I decided in my infinite wisdom to do it again.

As if it wasn't excruciating enough.

I think, by this point, I was trying to *make* a point. Do you know what I mean?

'Laugh Addison, laugh.' I whisper in to his ear through gritted teeth, my face colouring up as I notice the shop assistant hiding her ill contained smirk behind a colourful shoebox.

'Addison please laugh for mummy, don't leave me hanging here!'

The child doesn't laugh.

Instead choosing this exact moment to remain completely silent, glowering at me from above the two dummies now sitting snugly in his mouth, neither of them recognisable as his own.

'Let this be a lesson,' his eyes seem to say 'I do not like carrot mummy, remember this the next time you are trying to intravenously force feed me carrot. I do not like carrots mummy, and **I** am the master. Let this be a lesson to you... you now look like a fool, and this could have been avoided, just like the carrot. This is what they call, in simple terms, so that you understand mummy, Payback.'

'Are these ok to be left on?' the shop assistant asks me, standing up and walking away, before I can respond, the entire shop I notice, still giving me their focused attention, most of the children smiling, the mum's horrified on my behalf and still completely confused by my lack of nanny.

'Yes.' I mumble quickly before tripping up over the pram in my rush to get to the till, this of course, raising a raucous bubble of laughter from my son.

Normal noise levels in the shop resume as we pay, but as we head out of the door, new shoes on feet, my face beetroot, a man that can only be described as a male daddy *model,* holding a tiny little baby motions to me.

'Yes?' I ask flustered, secretly hoping he was going to flatter me with compliments about my parenting skills and how he has always admired women without hired help.

'Great yodeling' he replies mouth full of plums and hilarity.

'Thanks' I mutter, before shooting him daggers and skulking out, cursing the child and his evil plot, and driving at warp speed to nursery internally reliving the hell over and over again, while Addison cackles evilly in the background 3 dummies now wedged in his mouth, none of which seem recognisable as his own.

He is an evil genius by day. Teething menace by night.

But hey at least he has a new pair of Clarks, and there are *loads* of branches of those, meaning I never have to return to *that* particular place again.

Well, that *would* have been the case anyway, if I hadn't left his old shoes the ones that never saw the floor once, which I desperately want to keep forever as a memento, (they are Adidas high tops - the chav in me loves them) behind.

This time though I intend to walk in with my head held high, wearing my old Oktoberfest outfit, carrying Doodle dressed up as a goat under one arm and my hair dyed blonde and plaited down both sides of my head.

Once a yodeler, always a yodeler, and it isn't like I have any shame left in me, so why not?

*** He *is* having sprouts for tea. He may think he is the master, but I am the Mammy.

Evil cackle

I don't know *where* he gets it from. I really don't.

Life in slow motion...

Shopping I must shop today, I need sponges and cloths, the one on the sink has been there since New Kids on the Block were at number 1. It is manky. Which reminds me I need to buy some drain un-blocker too. The plug is filled with hair. Gross. I wonder if I will ever stop malting, which reminds me I need to hoover the dog hair off the sofa before The Irish One gets home tomorrow night or he will go mad. Oh we need fish too. I must make Addison's lunch from fresh tomorrow, he will eat fish, he always does, yes that is a good idea, it will need to be put on at eleven while he naps, or should that be half eleven, what if it goes cold while he is still asleep? You know people don't like you right? They think you are a terrible mother.

Maybe I should just cook it when he wakes up? But what if he climbs on the TV stand while I am in the kitchen and knocks it over on himself? No I will cook it while he sleeps then wake him up and he can eat. If he is tired he could sleep again this afternoon while I do some writing. If they liked you, you would feel it. I am sure they call you things behind your back; it is because you are worthless.

Shit, when will we go to the shops? I need sponges and cloths, oh and washing up liquid and nappies. Damn I will need to go to the bank first. Right so if I wake Addison up and give him is lunch then we can go to the bank and then I can go to the supermarket. Nobody will ever love you enough Lexy you are hard work.

Right but before all of that I need to make him breakfast and I need to wash up and let the dog out. What time is it? Oh. 3 Am. I really should get some sleep. Ok I will try and sleep. Don't forget the sponges tomorrow. Maybe you should get out of bed and write it down in case you forget...you are pathetic.

Oh and drain un-blocker! Do not forget that, and make sure you hoover...shit the shopping! I went to Asda before! How did I forget that? Because you are an idiot...

It is happening again.

I am starting to run too hard, too fast and for too long.

When I say *I am staring to run,* I don't mean in the literal sense because I do not run and never will. Occasionally I will jog, but only if I am jogging towards someone holding a chocolate bar, or maybe after the pizza deliveryman if he forgot the sweet chili sauce, but running has never been my thing and I am not ashamed to admit it.

What I *actually* mean is, I can appreciate when I am making myself ill again by never stopping for breath, by driving through the Starbucks 'Drive thru', paying and leaving without the coffee, and forgetting to smile at the realisation.

I suffer with depression, this much is true but sometimes I forget I can do things to help myself.

I start to fall in to old behavioral patterns, and one by one I start leaving my marbles behind, losing them, leaving them and most disturbingly, abusing myself instead of coming to my own rescue.

A while back, when my sheets were starched white, a magpie was my best friend and a doctor would pop his head in on me to check I wasn't dead every fifteen minutes, I learnt a lot about recognising the signs of illness, and how to live in the moment.

'Take one day at a time,' is a phrase I have heard countless times over the last few months, from health professionals, friends and family. In fact I have heard it so often, I sometimes wonder if Addison will whisper it to me as his first full sentence.

And although I nod and murmur my agreement while shooting a Wallace and Grommit type grin back, I don't really listen, when perhaps I should be doing.

Before being admitted in to hospital I would say I didn't understand or know how to 'live in the moment', I thought it was just an annoying cliché.

Since being hospitalised I would probably say I do know how to, but usually forget the importance and the need for doing so.

How can I only think about today when next Tuesday I am going to the dentist? (And we all know what happened last time!)

How can I only think of today when I have to find the money to pay nursery on Wednesday?

How can I only live in this moment **right now**, when I have to put Addison's lunch on in the next hour?

I need to plan.

Life is too fast and too important; there are too many things to think about, to worry about, to fixate on, to only think of today, to only think of this moment right now.

There is no time to slow down.

Getting everything done matters more.

Doesn't it?

On Monday evening I left my lifeline, my laptop, in its newly bought leather case, sat on the top of my car for two hours in the middle of Salford, while I took all my other belongings (my son and his paraphernalia) in to the house to commence the regimented bedtime routine. I didn't realise that this is where my life line, my laptop, had been sitting like a time bomb, waiting to be stolen until 8pm when I sat down to write and remembered with a minor heart attack the last time I had had it.

It was still there.

On Tuesday I left the gas on the hob, crackling and bursting away, turned on full for an hour after warming up ready brek. I only realised after I had started to feel drowsy and had wandered in to the kitchen to get a glass of water. After feeling my legs go weak with relief that I had caught it just in time, I ran with a pounding heart, and opened every window in the house.

Thank god Addison was in nursery.

On Wednesday I was so anxious about getting everything done I needed to get done, I was in Asda with my belongings (my son and all his paraphernalia) by 6.30 am. I woke him up to take him.

After no sleep.

On **Thursday and Friday** I forgot to eat. I wasn't hungry. At least, I don't remember feeling hungry.

I probably wasn't.

On Saturday I dropped my belongings (my son and all his paraphernalia) off with my mum while I went to a wedding. My mum called not long after and said she wanted to take Addison to the on-call Dr again as his temperature was high *again,* but not to worry, it was just for her peace of mind. I raced there, in my dress, insisting they wait for me and I went with them.

Returning a couple of hours later, prescription in hand and wanting to get my exhausted belongings (my son and his paraphernalia) in to my own car, and go home, I couldn't find my car keys. The car keys that also had my house keys attached to them. After an hour of searching and panicking, my mum reminded me 'I saw you put them on top of the car when you strapped Addy in before we left for the Dr's, did you pick them up again?'

No I hadn't.

Miraculously though, they were still there, sat on top of her car, inexplicably wedged under the roof rack. We had driven on the motorway, we had been to Wythenshaw hospital, got lost, taken at least four U turns, and we had driven home on the motorway and yet, there they still were. Heart pounding, knowing The Irish One was away with *his* keys and Doodle could have been imprisoned at home, I got in the car and thanked whoever it was, who was watching over me.

I also acknowledged that maybe; just maybe, it was time to slow down.

But didn't...

On **Sunday,** struggling to function, the depression having seen it's opening and thrust itself in, an uninvited guest at the party, I lost my cash card. And 2 credit cards. I shouted at Addison over nothing. I made him cry. Over nothing. I self-harmed because I shouted at Addison over nothing and more so than ever before, I wanted to give up. I am a terrible mother, a failure. I researched brain tumors in my spare time while Addison slept, and convinced myself I had one. As if I wasn't anxious enough. I thought a lot about dying. I hated everybody. We went to Asda and did a shop. A shop I only remembered was in the boot of my car at 3 o'clock this morning.

After eating nothing for dinner.

Again.

When I was first in hospital, I thought I wasn't depressed because I got out of bed every day and got on with my day. I kept telling the doctors I was just a drama queen. I can laugh. I can *organise*. I am not depressed.

'You are depressed.'

'No I am not!'

'What makes you think you aren't?'

'I get out of bed every day!'

'Do you sometimes think about dying?'

'Doesn't everybody?'

'No.'

'Oh'

'Do you ever stop?'

'Not really.'

'What do you enjoy doing?'

'Not much.'

'Do you ever stop?'

'No. There is no time to.'

'It is critical that you stop.'

Like plunging head first in to very cold water, I am reminded once again of those words.

My illness is one I have fought long and hard with.

So why am I giving up now? Why am I ignoring all the advice now?

I am not. I will not.

It is time to slow down again.

Before something catastrophic happens.

When I am playing with my son, I have to put my phone down, remind myself that in an hour, I will deal with that hour, but right now, we are playing. The fish will cook. The day will go on.

When I am making dinner I have to be making dinner.

When I am meant to be sleeping I need to be sleeping.

The days will take care of themselves.

No more multitasking for now.

It is too dangerous, for my belongings (my son and all his paraphernalia) and for my mental health.

And that includes you, voice in my head.

(Voice, *not voices!*)

No more multi-tasking for now.

One thing at a time.

But what about picking The Irish One up from the airport, you need petrol, you'll need to put your foot down, you'll be ok doing 80, make sure you pick Addison up, you need to feed the dog, and have a shower, you need to wash, The Irish One will think you are stinky, nobody likes you stinky...

Shut up.

*And whoever you are, that has been looking after and out for me up there, as if I didn't know; I am listening, and I owe you one. I am listening. I love you and miss you every day. A hundred times, thank you. X

Passion is the genesis of genius...

I am a genius.

A genius wearing more colours today than is strictly necessary on account of having to get dressed in the dark, due to an electricity failure in the bedroom coupled with the fact that yesterday, in a moment of sheer madness I bought myself some new clothes and wanted to wear them all at the same time, in preparation for today's therapy session, but a genius nevertheless.

There is something about a new top, or a new cardigan, or new trousers that really make me feel special. Yes I can't afford them, and yes I told the lady to forget the bag so The Irish One wouldn't see me coming home weighed down by more credit card debt, but oh it is so worth it.

Wearing new clothes I feel, I don't know, special, attractive, young and well...unburdened by the everyday humdrum of depression and the unrelenting routine of motherhood.

Do you know what I mean?

My new top meant I didn't mind when I woke up to find the light switch had given up, the very thought of it sat there, waiting to be worn, motivated me to get dressed even though I couldn't see what I was doing and once again, experienced the seemingly monthly inconvenience of bounding out of bed to the dulcet tones of my baby screeching, directly on to an upturned plug.

My new top closed its ears to me swearing at The Irish One and threatening, like one may do a teenager, to throw out his items if he didn't pick them up!

(This year alone, I have stood on three upturned plugs. THREE. I will need surgery if it happens again. SURGERY!!!)

My new cardigan meant I didn't mind when I let Doodle out and he wandered back in, while I was in the kitchen trying to find the coffee I finally remembered to buy, muddy footed and jumped straight on the sofa to eat Addison's toast.

The thought of my new trousers, waiting patiently in the cupboard for the day when I eventually shed the last few muffins worth of top, did not however, keep me focused on happiness, when I stepped in to the shower and found myself shin deep in used grubby and bitty Irish water.

My home is slowly falling to pieces, much like my mind, but unlike when I try and fix my faulty mind, I am able to think logically, unlike the man in my life, and rectify the wrong doing in a matter of moments.

The drain has been blocked in the bathtub for weeks. (Ok, so maybe not moments, but I got there in the end.)

Threatening to buy a plunger, call a plumber and buy some drain un-blocker for weeks, I finally gave up on The Irish One and took matters in to my own capable and shaking hands. (I think my meds need tweaking. I am currently walking around shaking like an old Volvo going up a hill, and can literally do nothing about it.)

'Are you ok?' The woman at Starbucks asked me yesterday when she handed me my coffee and I proceeded to scatter it, like one would someone's ashes, all over myself.

'Yes' I replied smiling and thinking on my feet 'I've just had a shock that's all' which I thought was probably a better response than 'Yeah it's just the concoction of anti-psychotic med's I am taking to stop me going completely mad that make me shake.'

Turns out I should have been honest.

'Oh no what happened?' she asked nosily.

And of course I had to make something up on the spot.

'I thought someone had stolen my son, but then realised they hadn't.'

First thing I could think of. (Which does actually happen on occasion though in fairness. Again it is the meds.)

'OH my god!' she gushed 'Where is he?'

'At home with his dad' and I shrugged.

I left her looking confused and fled. She may think I am an idiot, but she is completely unaware of my genius status, so I will let her off.

Sometimes though, I do wonder why my brain doesn't step in and gag my mouth in times like this, but genius that I am, I can only cope with so much.

Wearing my new top, my new cardi and promising my new trousers I would see them soon, I took drastic action on the plughole.

There are only so many times I can listen to 'I promise to fix it tomorrow' off himself, especially when I am knee deep in his *Gak* so I seized the hoover nozzle off the Dyson, and yes I know the correct term is vacuum but it's *a hoover* ok? Just like a tampon will always be a Tampax to me, even if it isn't. Life is too short to split hairs, which actually brings me to my point nicely, and stuck it over the plughole.

With a whoosh and a *phaaa*lunk 7 years' worth of hair (sorry if you are eating right now) was sucked up by the magic flute and hey presto!! The drain was unblocked.

Now I know this isn't an inspiring tale of recovery or a poignant tale of woe but still, it felt important enough to share. (I am in therapy in an hour, so I promise the next one will be better.)

As I looked down at the 'hoover' now grumbling and whining, sodden and severely pissed off at being used as a make shift plumber, horns and trumpets started celebrating my ingenious plan.

The water ran down that plug hole like horses galloping towards a finish line at the Grand National!

I was victorious.

Too too too toooot!!!

And yes ok, now the hoover smells like something died in it, and yes maybe with it being an electrical item it probably wasn't the best idea to plunge it in to a bath of water but hey! My hairy shins are now free from second hand water, and that feels marvelous!

I do sometimes wonder about the need for The Irish One.

If Doodle could get a job, I would probably marry him, to be honest.

Because my man, **can** do a job...*eventually*, if he has all the right equipment, and the right *light*, the universe is pulling in the right direction and it is a Tuesday in May, but sometimes, just sometimes, it isn't worth the wait.

Especially when one owns a Dyson.

If you want a job doing?

Get me round.

I am a genius.

Anyway, I am off to therapy... and then I need to call an electrician about the bedroom lights... or do I?

Hmm

It's ok not to be ok...

'I stare at my reflection in the mirror, why am I doing this to myself? Losing my mind on a tiny era, I nearly left the real me on the shelf. Don't lose who you are, dreaming is believing, it is ok not to be ok. Sometimes it is hard to follow your heart, tears don't mean you are losing, everybody is bruising, and just be true to who you are.'

I am drunk as I write this.

It is 1.20 am on Friday night. (1:20 and I am already home with my laptop on my knee! *What* a *party* animal!)

Tonight I left the house and *faced* Jessie J in concert, courtesy of a very good friend who I met during my stay at the priory.

We have a shared journey.

I didn't want to leave the house, which is why I say I *faced* Jessie J.

I wanted to disappear but reaching an understanding with myself while drying my hair, I realised with iron certainty it would not matter where I was (in or out, shake it all about) I would undoubtedly feel the same way, so with a heavy sigh, I put on a skirt and left the house.

I was wearing a top too, just in case you wondered and boots. I am not lady Godiva, as I do not have a horse and my boobs are too saggy. But fair play to her and thanks mum, as we are on the subject, for sending me to a primary school fancy dress party as the *blessed mad woman,* wearing only tights and a hobbyhorse, at the age of 3. It really didn't scar me for life. Not much anyway.

The skirt however, is significant.

I talked myself in to making an effort; the aim being to re discover the part of me that used to be confident enough to wear a skirt and unearth the tiny morsel of me that used to be able to *strut.*

I don't like going to concerts usually, especially concerts of artists whom I love.

The reasons being that normally, as I stand crushed in the crowd, too hot, claustrophobic and bursting for a wee, I often find myself looking up at them, the artiste I admire, living their dreams, fulfilling ambitions and inadvertently and irritatingly sink in to a pit of self-hatred.

And then I drink too much.

I could have been somebody, gulp, I am nobody, gulp, what is the point? Gulp.

This time though, was a little different.

For a start I avoided the mosh pit and found myself with a seat. (God I am SO old. I did have a pint though just so you know, it wasn't like I ordered a pot of tea or anything.)

As she exploded on to the stage, her eyes bright from excitement, wearing, well, not much, welcomed by a million screaming teenagers and greeting us all with the token 'Hello Manchester!' I caught myself just in time and cautioned the approaching negative behaviour and my inclination for what I can now see to be jealousy at my unfulfilled ambition with strong words, learnt over the summer.

You are somebody, focus on that, remember who you are, what you have achieved and listen to the words, they *may* touch you.

If you feel worthless at the end of this evening, I will allow you to sink.

Deal?

Deal.

(Apparently when you talk to yourself you are mad, but I have to be honest, I find it madder not to. Who wants to live in silence?)

At 1 am, after leaving my friend behind in a busy and overcrowded bar, after admittedly, having a bit of sing to Kylie, I did something I promised The Irish One I would never do.

(It is ok, I doubt he will ever read this far in, and if you do Irish One? I am sorry. I don't know what I was thinking.)

I strolled, completely alone, around the busy night time streets of Manchester, purposely placing one foot in front of the other, as my boots clicked on the stone pavements, my arms wrapped around myself tightly, to warn oncoming revelers I wasn't up for a chat, with a half-smile on my face, heading nowhere and with no direction.

I needed some time.

I could have stayed in the bar, but I didn't want to.

I could have jumped in a taxi home, but I didn't want to.

I needed some time. To just... be.

Deliberately I slowed as I reached a heavily packed pub and looked through the window. A group of four women around a table, warm with drinks in front of them, throwing their lined faces full of experience, back in laughter.

I watched briefly from the outside looking in as they touched, and giggled, sharing secrets and enjoying the arrival of the weekend together.

One of them noticed me stagnant, peering in from the cold outside and as her eyes briefly made contact with mine I hurriedly started back on my journey.

The air was biting cold; it brought me pleasure, soothed by the alcohol buzz as it numbed my pain and wrapped its arms around me, a blanket of protection making me feel free.

I walked around the city that used to feel like home, that I used to know so well, knowing that I would be safe and that I could leave this trip behind at any time, as the taxi lights flowed past me in fluid motion.

I could have been anybody, a student with no responsibility, just a girl.

Anonymous.

I couldn't help but grin.

Two policemen gazed over at me as I crossed a deserted road picking up my pace.

I didn't care.

I was doing nothing wrong; it felt that way, for the first time in a long time.

I was just walking.

Will I get run over?

I glanced down a dark alleyway filled with dustbins and discarded rubbish however I did not feel fear.

Can I disappear in to that darkness and be forgotten?

Can I forget?

I queued for cigarettes behind two bouncing young girls buying pick and mix, wearing ballet pumps and talking about boys.

Freedom.

Youth.

A slap in the face.

A reminder I still had life in me.

A middle-aged man behind me talking to his friend 'What I love about tonight is, it could go anywhere...'

I smiled to myself and carried on.

His feeling of promise washing over me as for a split second as I remembered.

Two young women in shoes too high, both too wrecked for them to navigate properly at this hour, being supported by two younger men 'I don't usually get this drunk' was howled in to the night as she fell, he friend collapsing in to giggles beside her.

I continued on.

I'm past that.

I watched myself as I approached the library in the full-length glass.

I was a teenager again for a moment, laughing, surrounded by friends, full of promise, full of hope, enjoying the moment.

And then I saw me.

A woman in a skirt, half drunk, alone, unable to hold her pelvic muscles when she sneezes.

When did I lose that ability to enjoy the moment? I questioned myself, not realising I was enjoying this moment.

Will I ever sneeze again without wetting myself?

The library so majestic back then, full of promise.

Back to work for me very very soon.

A future where each day is longer than the last.

Maybe.

Back to my silence, back to my prison.

Maybe.

Will those moments where I could have been anybody, always haunt me?

Or can I let go?

Too old to dance too tired to try.

Maybe.

Life.

How did I get here?

When did I lose me?

Will I ever find me again?

Yes.

Maybe without realising.

Do I actually want to die?

No, I just want to be saved. (Not *shaved.* Saved.)

But how?

Creeping back in to the house, fitting my key silently in to the lock and turning, I am greeted by my over excited poodle, full of kisses and warm welcomes.

My little boy, face down and snoring.

The Irish One asking me 'Good night?' as I trip over his bloody electric razor discarded (ONCE AGAIN!) on the floor, before sleepily turning over with an 'I love you' and falling back in to a deep sleep.

Smells like home.

In this moment, the answer is clear.

This is how.

I just hope I remember that in the morning, when I have sobered up.

Jessie spoke to me tonight by the way, and I *was* touched.

'You'll never leave me, you'll never leave me, I just want one more minute to finish this fairytale, how did you disappear? I won't say this is over, you are still here, in my shadow, everywhere I go. I don't see the need to cry, you'll never leave me...you're in my shadow.'

I enjoyed the concert.

The deal paid off.

Pop...

It is a dangerous and overpowering illness, and one I can see now I am helpless to control.

I once spoke of radio silence.

A detailed account of how I used to wake up, in the early days of diagnosis, after an elongated period of feeling content, thinking I had beaten the monster, that the doctors were wrong, that I was better, before realising with a sinking heart that they were right, I hadn't beaten anything.

I wasn't winning after all.

My head would muddle up, my thoughts would screech to a halt, my entire being would gradually become stagnant as I lay there, powerless to fight the early morning and extremely menacing ambush of the blanket of doom as it settled over my head, my heart and my ability to speak, to reach out and to ask for help.

In those days I had more control.

Pop.

I knew it was coming and I would prepare.

Stock up.

The monster has changed, the monster is clever, and the monster is out for revenge.

Pop.

Recognising in me that this slow muddy and creeping onslaught no longer takes effect as it used to, that I have learnt to fight, have learned through therapy and hospitalisation that I am strong, that I don't want it to overpower me, that it is not my fault, it has found a new hole-in-the-wall, a new chink in the chain, a loop hole.

If she is not prepared, if she isn't expecting me, she will not be robust and she will be blindsided.

The element of surprise, no wonder I didn't see it coming.

Saturday I had a lovely day.

We played, we enjoyed each other, I laughed, I witnessed a fairytale, and I was in the light.

With my son.

Enjoying our moments.

Pop.

A train steaming through the fog, a force of nature preparing to beat me down.

Unsuspected.

Sunday morning I awoke, put on my glasses to the sound of my baby calling me, left the bedroom heading for him, a smile on my face and was unexpectedly punched, hard and long and repeatedly in the face.

Good morning my beautiful boy.

I ducked and I dived.

I can beat you.

Breakfast my beautiful boy.

I was pushed against a wall and held by my throat while it breathed in to my face.

Pop.

Let's go and feed the ducks.

I was kicked in the stomach with a crushing blow and winded with anxiety.

What if he falls in the water?

What if my car gets broken in to?

What if I lose him?

I couldn't bear the pain.

What if he doesn't love me?

Black and blue.

Naptime and I lie down.

Pop.

The unexpected ambush self-congratulatory in its victory.

I walked around as the hours sped past, no longer resisting, and feeble.

I played; I sat and stared at the wall and I self-harmed.

Everywhere we went, everything we achieved, I was pulling a heavy suitcase with a dodgy wheel behind me, pulling and tugging willing it to hurry, so we could get on with our day.

So we could be happy.

So I could enjoy him.

Walking up the never-ending staircase towards freedom wearing a heavy backpack filled with individually lead wrapped stones of domination, lugging a hefty suitcase, mentally exhausted, pleading for it to stop, while my beautiful baby boy, his eyes so blue and so wide, stared up at me a questioning smile on his face.

Smile back.

Pop

Smile back.

I cannot control this illness and I know it is not my fault. I can stop punishing myself, I can tell everyone I am feeling better I can push and struggle and fight back but then the day comes to an end.

Pop

I sit with the pills in my hand.

I sit and I cry, with the pills inviting me in, while my little boy sleeps peacefully dreaming of an orange fish called Nemo and red cars called Lightening McQueen, his mammy is in the next room, her luggage multiplying, boxing her in.

Pop.

I am exhausted with being better.

I am exhausted with life.

Pop.

I look down at them in my hand.

Nothing is enough to live for.

Nothing.

I am tired.

I am lonely.

I am isolated and exhausted in this illness.

It has beaten me.

Pop.

Doodle walks in and cocks his head to the side, Addison stirs in the next room, the phone rings and the doorbell goes.

I put the pills down and attend to what is needed, there is no time now.

Faith found me.

Someone is watching over me.

Later, much later, after my neighbor has left, I have put the phone down and Doodle has been fed and long after I have kissed Addison's head, I go and look at the pills.

They glare at me.

I stare back.

And flush them down the toilet.

Faith has found me.

Someone is looking out for me.

I am broken.

But I can be repaired.

I cannot put my son through what I have experienced.

I know this is what he is trying to tell me.

I know he is watching out for me.

I hate this fucking illness.

I hate it.

I thought I would come out of hospital cured but that isn't how depression works.

But there is a smidgen of fight left in me, and maybe that is all it takes.

I am not giving up!

Faith has found me.

If you never try you will never know your worth.

I'm worth it.
I just wish I believed this more consistently.

Catching the egg...

When a priest in a Volkswagen blocked me in to an unmovable position in the car park last night, with nothing more than a raised eyebrow and a slight smirk, I knew it was time to drop the charade.

I took it as a sign from God himself. (Kind of.)

LEXY 1; VERSE 12.

'It is time to pack up your fake smile in an old tin case (or something to that effect) and get the feck home so you can go to bed'

That's the message that *I* heard anyway.

I ripped off my smile with a distressing amount of frustrated energy as I sat in my cold and dusty car, littered with empty fruit shoots and Starbucks cups waiting for that (grrr, *must* not swear in relation to holy man) *holy man* to buy his bag of chips, and allowed the real me to seep back in through my bones, like a hot drink working its way around my bloodstream.

My shoulders drooped; I rolled back my neck and breathed in to the silence a long and slow breath, a breath that in that silence belonged all to me, with no audience.

Here it comes, I thought to myself, feeling the floodgates open.

I am coming back.

For the past few days I have been conducting a social and personal experiment on myself.

'The power of positive attitude.' is a poster I am faced with each and every time I visit my GP.

Usually I walk past it and shoot it the middle finger, usually I *march* past it summoning all my remaining strength not to rip it off the wall, screw it up it to a tiny ball and jump up and down on it, usually when I *trudge* past it, my bags weighing me down, it makes me sad.

It reminds me of all the times I have been told to *get a grip*, to *just* smile more and to *just* be happy and then '*you will be.*'

Of all the times I have told myself, I am not *normal,* not *worth it,* useless.

A lack of understanding from those who you love, including myself, has been for me and probably always will be, like the most hurtful of shots fired from a weapon, which I could never recover from.

One of the biggest lessons I have learned from all of this therapy?

Realising it is ok for me not to be numb, that to have those mixed emotions, to feel angry **and** sad, with others, with myself, with the world, both at the same time is actually perfectly acceptable.

Just because I own the diagnosis 'depression' doesn't mean I am not entitled to feel.

And hey, get this!

You are actually allowed to feel more than one feeling at a time! Who knew?

It is ok, to feel angry and sad, as an example, instead of feeling angry BUT sad.

(The 'but' negates the feeling prior to the latter. It takes away the importance of the first feeling, and in doing so, makes us feel like we shouldn't be feeling it. Does that make sense? But hey!! We can feel many things all at the same time; no one says we can't, except perhaps ourselves, when we so effortlessly put ourselves down, with a great big 'BUT.')

'Think positive and watch your life change.' The poster screams at me.

This last time though, on my way to pick up my never ending subscription of medicine (or 'meds' as they say in the mentalist business) I paused directly in front of it and stared it down, like one of my demons.

I remember struggling to shrug my shoulders from the weight of the guilt, self-hatred and confusion resting upon them but definitely attempting to, thinking 'ok, as my 2nd return to work in a two month period is looming in front of me, why not, I may as well *try* to be positive, it isn't like I have anything left to lose, and as I am now struggling to control this depression again as it seems to once again be mauling me on a daily basis, I may as well give it a go.'

I thought that possibly if I hit *it* with the element of surprise for a change, instead of IT slamming me up against the wall, I could rid myself of the fear that had been growing up my mood like wild ivy since the week previous.

It worked for a while too.

Monday was a success in work, smile plastered on my over made up face and acting like a show puppet filled with coo's and ooo's and yeay's! And slaps on the back and beams.

Tuesday was ok too as the show carried over. 'Woohoo I ran out of petrol!'

The only truth in the act, being the overwhelming sense of love that every now and again, tugged at my heart strings as I watched my son tap dance to Thomas the tank engine in his bouncer. (It is the Irish gene I am sure.)

I feel it some days now you know, that sense of the future being exciting, that all these women kept going on about, right at the beginning.

Every now and again.

And that gives me hope.

By Wednesday, I thought I had beaten my diagnosis.

I really did.

I was all ready to ring the manufacturer of the poster and thank him (had to be a man) personally for his contribution to mental health.

Somewhere during the performance I had lost my heavy, down trodden and sodden suitcase containing all my self-hatred, depressive thoughts and dark inner turmoil and yeah ok, the underlying murky water was ever present lapping at my feet, but it had become more like a puddle Addy tries to stick his tongue in, rather than a lake I have to rescue doodle from, and yeah I was exhausted from all the fakeness but hey! That isn't important is it?

As long as I seem to be winning, that's all that matters!!

Could a positive attitude be working?

Then I met James for therapy.

I love Wednesdays because of James.

For the first time in my entire life I have an emotional safe zone.

As I type the words 'emotional safe zone' my stomach clenches up with the discomfort of it all, and I have to fight the urge not to stick my fingers down my throat and call myself pathetic.

To need somebody?

To trust somebody and for them to have told me they trust me?

Erghhhhhh makes me want to peel my skin off and set myself on fire.

I am actually physically shuddering.

'Wow' he exclaimed at seeing me bound in to the room, bounce in to the chair and shoot him with a grin I thought was sure to make him believe I was all better, and there for re-confirm to me, that I was cured 'That's scary!'

I laughed at his insightfulness, but it was as hollow as my misguided recital.

Two weeks ago I glanced over at a piece of paper I shouldn't have peeped at during an appointment with a consultant, and saw the words 'Postnatal / Clinical depression' scrawled in blue ink below my name.

I will be completely honest with you, the tears streaming down my face as I type this; it has knocked me for six.

I am little girl again, scared, looking for a leg to cling on to for protection from those evil words, words that make me feel like a failure, hoping to find nothing but the familiarity of an empty hardened gate post.

'Feelings aren't facts. You are not a failure. You will be ok. You *are* ok. Things are changing for you, you are learning, educating yourself about yourself, opening up and accepting new rules for living. Being kinder to yourself, recognising the need for living in the moment, being proud of your achievements. Every little step is a new beginning Lexy.'

I am once again curled up in a ball at the sound of all this horrifying and unwanted, desperately needed but horrendous support.

But, this is the thing I notice, I am hearing it and allowing myself to be comforted by it.

The egg is no longer sliding off the glass.

Depression may still control me, and currently there may be nothing much I can do about it, except continue to fight, but control is always overpowered with knowledge.

Understanding is key.

Right?

The curtain came down on my performance as the rain hammered on the roof of my dustbin of a car and my beliefs of needing to win went up in flames.

It isn't about winning against the illness; it is about treating myself thoughtfully, considerately and with care while I am experiencing dark times.

Treating myself the way I treat others, one moment at a time.

These dark times will not always be present, and it isn't you *will* be ok, it is you *are* ok. In this moment.

And fear is good, fear is healthy, it keeps me fighting.

It isn't a competition, it is my life, and I am about to start living it for me.

Maybe the vicar blocked me in on purpose to make me stop and take stock.

A positive attitude is all very well, if it serves a purpose, if it supports you and it feels honest, but not everybody can coast through life like the Duracell bunny, not all of the time.

LEXY 2; VERSE 13.

'Do not swear at a holy man, he wanted chips AND you needed your wheels turning to bricks' (or something to that effect.)

Does God rhyme? I should probably check that out.

Can I borrow a bible please?

I think I am finding some faith.

I am hopeful AND scared.

Reve Rouge...

There is a certain type of music, of pain, I know better than to inflict upon myself.

I haven't dared even approach this particular kind, for over 7 years.

The memories of it too ruthless, for me to have even had any hope of survival.

And yet, tonight, my low mood receding further in to the wing mirror on this long journey I am on, for now, I thought it was time.

I stared at my glowering reflection, at the wariness and caution emanating from my eyes and found it quite easy to ignore, to contradict.

I am not a masochist...anymore.

I just need closure from these memories.

I am desperate to heal and disoriented, adrift, but all the while trapped within a maze too perplexing and foggy to navigate myself out of, without facing the inevitable.

This for me is one of the last notches on the ladder, heading upwards, always upwards, towards my freedom.

I am conscious that throwing myself underneath a moving bus would flatten me and bring no healing, and yet with this type of pain, this kind of bus, this music, these memories, I know that by ignoring the caution, discounting the increasing beat of my heart advising me to stop, and ploughing on full steam ahead, I may be opening myself up too soon, in fact I am sure James would not advise it, but it now feels the only option.

I have to endure this to see how far I have come.

It has been whispering to me from its home on the highest shelf, gnawing away at me, as the dust collected and my heart slowly unfurled.

My method although terrifying, is clear.

De-sensitization by torture.

Something I seem to have always been very adept at.

The difference now being the power of knowing what I can handle.

The memories will hurt, but it is time.

I am strong enough.

I will move through this, the way I have been taught to.

With a bottle of beer and a bar of chocolate, understanding that for me to successfully complete this process, I will need to be kind to myself somehow.

I switch the DVD to play, and instantly I am there again.

Sat anonymous in a packed theatre in Downtown Disney, filled with thousands of other people, all shuffling, all breathing, all laughing, having travelled in packs from all over the world, hugging their family, surrounded by love, by those who have always been near them and always will be, enjoying the holiday of a lifetime, and about to witness an enthralling performance by Cirque Soliel.

La Nouba. (To 'live it up.')

I am sat on the outskirts of their security looking in, abandoned by those who I thought were mine. Left behind with the tattered furnishings, a screwed up piece of paper tossed to the side, about to treat myself with incredible cruelty, inflict abusive and almost brutal pain on myself by witnessing the same show, completely alone.

I see now, after weeks of torment and learning, by choice.

A show I had been to see with my family years before, when... well...before...

Before everything was irreplaceably broken.

Too shocked and too withdrawn to even consider unwinding myself from the tightly wound knot I had become and yet too frightened not to, I sat in that auditorium, and had to physically hold my heart, to keep the pain contained.

I am back there.

Overcome by the memories.

The music swelled intoxicatingly, an ancient Russian lady singing of a broken heart, her rich and heady voice becoming one with a ballerina dressed beautifully in white, fresh and new, just beginning her life, moving on tiptoes in quick succession with the beat, together they become one, her courageous, long languid and lingering movements, telling the story of a time long ago, that didn't belong to her.

But now did.

The effect is so clean cut and pure I found myself then, struggling to keep my barriers up, struggling to protect my beaten heart as the images mingled with the music soared with ease through the prison I had so carefully erected, each carefully constructed note toying with my fractured heart like a kitten with a ball of yarn.

The ballerina turned quickly and I caught my breath as I watched her hair flying around her, as if in slow motion.

She ran with unbridled speed in to the future, the freedom of security lifting her, propelling her through the air caught and held by sinuous and magnificent enormous red ribbons.

They lifted her up and kept her safe, sure to catch her should she have ever fallen.

A freedom I have never felt, allowed her to grasp her loved one, the one she had chosen and who had chosen her, mid-flight they clung to one another, kissing, embracing, and independent in their mutual dependency.

A performance maybe, but a deep mutual trust, an understanding of one another's body, souls and the rhythm of each other heart beats is on show for all of us to see.

Somewhere 50 feet below them, surrounded by hearts beating in unison and excited gasps, the 25 year old me sits in the audience, lost amongst the love, overcome by a loneliness so overpowering I am frozen in to my seat, sitting upright, observing this couple dance me to the top of my own dreams, as if parading in front of me what will never be, and my heart literally shattered right down the middle.

And I had thought it was already broken.

If I could have, I would have run.

I would run and I would run and I would run.

I would have liked to have heard my feet pounding the sodden earth, would have liked to feel the tears like acid, scorching down my cheeks, I would have liked to scream, to throw my body out wide and howl in to the night with the unfairness of it all. To torture myself further, to pound my fists in to the ground and bite down hard on the wet earth, but when my last breath had been taken and my heart was exhausted, my tears running dry in the cold, where would I have found myself?

I had nowhere to go and no one to run to.

Least of all myself.

I did not and could not have ever understood that this wasn't fated, but self-inflicted.

I was 50000 miles from home and completely alone.

Two strangers were sat beside me as the performance from above reached fever pitch and I trembled. An older couple, wrapped up in one another, enjoying the holiday of a lifetime, no doubt excited by the rest of their lives. Building another memory to add to their scrapbook of friendship.

I sat there and shook from deep within, needing to break but unable to find the chink, to release the torment, because even sat there, none of it seemed real and yet I knew it was.

'Are you ok?' The older woman clutching her husband, eyes shining brightly, tears brimming by the emotion of it all, whispered at me over the music.

She had noticed I was unaccompanied and she smiled kindly, a lack of understanding passing over her features before turning back to the show, the question forgotten.

Probably the only person in the history of the world to visit Walt Disney world completely alone.

I used to be a masochist.

I can see that now.

I didn't answer then, and now, as I sit here watching the same show on my laptop, on my sofa, in my lounge, surrounded by the smells and photos of my little boy, of the life I have created and the debris I have accumulated over the 7 years since then, I finally feel I am ready to.

'Yes.' I reply, turning my head to face no one, my beer empty and the room completely silent, the baby asleep, but the old lady still so clear in my mind's eye. 'Yes, I will be.'

I am no longer broken in half, no longer fragmented, and yes, I still feel the need to scream and shout and pound the earth, but through understanding I am slowly on the mend.

Learning how now not to.

How could I have failed to notice, 7 years ago, that by doing what I was doing, I was inflicting upon myself unnecessary and relentless agony?

Why would I have chosen to torture myself like that?

What made me think I deserved it?

One day soon I fully intend to start living my life for me.

To make the changes that I want to make to ensure my days can receive some light.

A caged bird for so long, with the door now wide open, I am slowly having to reach for the courage to fly out.

But right now, in this instant, I need to cry.

To let go.

I am learning to heal, and have ultimately realised the importance of being kind to myself by watching and re-living my own personal cruelty.

I think I may have another beer, maybe even reach out and ask for a hug. (Shock Horror! I may be able to actually *ask* for comfort! To *trust* in it.)

I will try to remember the choices I am able to make for me, to be kinder to myself, I really will.

I will re-visit this show for real one day, no longer alone on the inside, or the out.

By choice.

No longer afraid to live.

That will be my freedom.

Reached.

One Day.

Side Effects may include honesty...

I stopped taking my medication 6 weeks ago.

Nobody but James knows this.

Not The Irish One, not my best friend, Not my Psychiatrist.

'Enough!' my brain screamed when she, my Psychiatrist, routinely suggested another alteration to my chemical imbalance, to supposedly help with the anxiety, 'Four sets of medication is ridiculous!!! Are you even yourself anymore?'

I took the new prescription, signed with a flourish of her navy blue Cartier biro (no doubt one of those insanely heavy ones that only rich people have - a status pen if you will, I swear she was grunting with the weight of it as she wrote) and promptly threw it in the bin.

What a rebel.

For the first few days, sans meds, the time during which The Irish One incorrectly believed (as in, I lied to him) I was 'just' in the middle of a little medication change, he became completely unapproachable.

He honestly behaved around me in the same way I imagine I would behave, if I was sharing my home with a rabid Pit-bull.

Edgy, wary, alert. (Fucking scared.)

'Just chill!' he barked at me on day 3 from the safety of the door, as I sat crumpled on the bed, a Red Hot mess. 'How can I help you when you don't even know why you are crying??! You are low because you need to let your new meds kick in! Chill woman!'

There is no denying it.

He was being a prick.

But really, I guess, Can I really blame him?

Maybe he was trying out tough love, as a way of telling me to be strong.

Or maybe he was just being a prick.

Anyway.

It left me feeling completely alone and completely stuck, and more determined than ever to get through the withdrawal stage and be medication free.

I have feelings. I am a person. I am not the sum part of an anti-depressant.

People like me need medication to live a normal life, that's what they say.

And I do agree with them, mostly.

I haven't always though, it took me ages to 'give in.'

I just had too many doubts about it.

I would sit in group therapy and suffer just as much as everyone who was taking medication, so what was the point?

They seemed no better for it?

Medication, I guess, at that time, on some level, I saw as a failure.

Confirmation that I had an actual illness.

A label.

'I don't want that kind of help, I don't need that kind of help. I don't want something chemical that is going to stop me being me. I can do this on my own, I am not ill, I am just pathetic, I need to get a grip.'

And besides, what if I take it and have some sort of awful reaction?

These are all the thoughts I am now re-experiencing, now I am without them, and having to consider re -starting.

What if I get **all** of the millions of side effects written in Italics, covering one whole sheet of A4 paper?

Difficulty sleeping. - What if I get even More night terrors? The Irish One is already sick of finding me pulling up the laminate flooring looking for hidden gems.

Dry mouth - I cannot bear those little white crusty bits people get, what if I get them and don't notice? I'll look like I have rabies. How can I sell face to face, do my job, looking like that?

Increased sweating - Brilliant. Just brilliant.

Abnormal orgasm in women. - What? As in, at random times of the day, without provocation? (Well ok, maybe I could get on board with this one.)

Constipation, Diarrhoea - What? Both at the same time? Is that even possible? So, wait, does this mean each time I fart I will follow through? Amazing.

Ejaculation failure- Um.... Not a party trick I have ever managed, so I am guessing this is aimed at men. Hoping. Hoping it is.

Feeling agitated

Feeling anxious

Feeling dizzy

Feeling nervous - Well I feel all of these without medication so....

Increased salivation- So wait, which one is it? Will I be cotton mouthed or drooling?

Itchy- Ok, itchy where? On my head? Like nits? Or Itchy elsewhere? Like Thrush? I need to know!

Vomiting- So basically what they are saying is, I could potentially turn in to an itchy, vomiting woman, who occasionally orgasms mid conversation, who has a drooling dry mouth and never stops sweating? Yeah, no wonder ill experience agitation.

Hair loss- Oh, and I'll be bald too. Brilliant.

Weight gain- And fatter. Awesome.

Convulsions- Yeay!

Anaphylactic reactions- Hurrah!

Anger - Ok.

Angioedema - Now they are just making words up!

Feelings of hostility - So I will become even more hostile than I am normally?

Impaired judgement - Ha. No change there then.

The list is endless.

And then this.

Psychiatric problems such as uncovering symptoms of depression or suicidal tendencies and self-harming behaviour.

So it could all be for no reason?

So what is the point?

First time around, I resisted and resisted, because the side effects frightened me.

This time around, yeah, also feeling pretty frightened, except, this time, I know they do offer some relief.

But back then, there was no way I was giving in.

Until one day, during my hospital stay, for some reason, I did give in.

I hit a big wall.

And I guess I realised it was my last shot.

If Addison was going to have any hope of keeping his mother, I needed to give it a try.

So, I reluctantly joined the army of people swallowing 40mg of Fluoxitine, and 750mg (or whatever) of Quetipene to keep Amelie away, on a daily basis.

I spent 2 days feeling sick, but only with anxiety and worry.

(I did not want to be a convulsing, itchy mess, even with the promise of random orgasms.)

But over time the anxiety of side effects all but diminished and I began to notice I could get out of bed in the morning without thoughts of killing myself, without the overwhelming hopelessness, the heart gripping feelings that the future was too long a prospect.

2 months have passed in a blur.

A blur - yes, but a stable one.

I have been Apathetic to everything.

I came off my medication because I was sick of the numbness.

I couldn't remember how it felt to feel.

And now I can.

Six weeks without anything, it is definitely safe to say, I can connect with all of it.

The anxiety, the paranoia, the misery, the overwhelming love, the excitement that creeps up on me and sends me reeling in to an almost manic state, and also, of course, the overwhelming grief and disappointment that I am without doubt, a complete failure, in every sense.

The taking of everything personally.

The fear of being seen, full stop.

Seen.

Cared for.

Noticed.

I can connect with all of it.

I don't want to be looked after, seen, hated, disliked, spoken about, loved, enjoyed, seen.

'Are you considering going back on medication Lexy?' James asked me last week in our, once again now, weekly sessions.

It's a tough choice.

I feel now, like I can actually feel.

And sometimes I enjoy that.

But the negative, it does far outweigh the positive.

Medication numbs the bad, but also the good, it takes no prisoners, makes no choices, cannot decipher between the two.

It's a catch 22.

'I am doing well though James. I feel like I am winning most of the time.'

I can tell he doesn't believe me.

Hell, I don't believe me.

But I would like to believe I don't need medication.

I wish I could just be balanced.

It is my greatest wish.

The reason I argue with people who state-

'Happiness is a choice. My husband was depressed and one day he just decided not to be.'

I wish it was that easy. I don't want to be 'happy' just balanced!

And Yes, I have tried.

Each and every day for what feels like my entire life.

"It surprises me you say that.' James goes on, interrupting my thoughts.

He is going to say it like it is, I can tell.

I can also tell I am not going to like it.

'In the last 6 weeks without medication I have heard you speak nothing of joy. The joys. Only of the pain, the irritation, the misery, the hopelessness. You have once again pushed away all of the people who care for you. You are suffering, and badly convincing yourself that you aren't't. A little fogginess allowed you to smile and to feel without fear...' he trails off as I glare at him belligerently.

'Now, without that medication, you need to check in with me every week again, there is no relief from any of it, and last night..... Last night you considered an overdose again. There is no shame in being medicated.'

So

It seems I have hit that wall again.

For the sake of Addy, I must, without further ado, swallow another white pill - daily.

And most probably for the rest of my life.

Tomorrow marks starting over again.

No more sudo-making it.

I need medication for the illness I suffer with.

And if it gives me thrush, so be it.

A little Numbness is underrated.

At least I will be able to cope again.

Find balance.

Bring on the Random Orgasms.

And don't ever again tell me about your husband, who 'just decided' to get better.

Because each illness is different.

Each story unique.

Each person a fighter.

Square One...

Today's date is a date which has been looming in front of me, taunting me with its ever so slow creeping arrival, ever since Tuesday the 13 of March, over a year ago.

I had clambered slowly up the 12 flights of bitter cold, rock hard and dirty, concrete stairs heading towards my car for the final time, my breath freezing in front of me in heavy bursts.

Heavily pregnant and facing the very real possibility I would need a lung transplant by the time I reached the top, and wondering if there would ever be a time I would feel confident enough to tackle the lift on my own, I remained ecstatic.

My enormous, 80% KFC/20% baby belly bulging out in front of me, swinging from left to right, my arse protruding out from behind me, the sheer volume of my weight increase ensuring it was now so heavy it bumped each and every step on the way up, I stopped for a breather upon reaching my floor.

Leaning heavily against the grimy, dirt stained car park window looking down upon the work place, which had been the absolute center of my universe for the last 8 years, I felt nothing but pleasure.

I was free.

I had a whole year off to play, I was the center of everybody who cared about me's attention, I had a full month before he arrived to eat as much as I wanted without guilt and then the most exciting moment of my life was going to occur.

I was going to have a baby.

Me, Lexy Ellis, was going to have a baby.

The world would never be the same again.

Labour would be a cinch.

Everybody said so.

It would be a drop in the ocean; nothing in comparison to the years of magical moments and everyday tenderness that would herald his arrival.

Yes I have put weight on, I thought to myself, heaving myself back in to the standing position, my centre of equilibrium massively squew-wif, nearly toppling over as I picked up the numerous bags crammed with presents from my work friends, but that too will drop off in a jiffy, everyone said so, so let my 12 months of freedom begin.

I will miss work, but it will still be here in a year's time, maybe six months if I can get things organised quickly enough.

I am free and am about to have the happiest 6/12 months of my life.

I cannot to wait to see his little face, I cannot wait to cherish his every breath, and I cannot wait to hold this little angel in my arms and feel like the world finally makes sense.

He will be my all, and in my all I will find my true happiness.

This will be the best year of my whole damn life.

This will be the best year, although he may not remember it, I will, of my precious baby's life.

Great expectations and all that.

This morning as I scrambled from my car and headed in to work for the first time in 12 months, a slender size 16, with my nervous system ensuring I was encased within a permanent aroma of bum, I remembered back to that day.

How full of hope I was at what was about to happen.

How excited I was over the coming months.

How happily overweight I was.

How content I felt that everybody seemed to like me, love me during that time.

How bloody deluded I was about the weight falling off.

And how optimistic I was about my shared future.

I leant against that same window this morning, feeling melancholy, and looked out at the work place which had once been the be all and end all of my life, and which now, most unexpectedly seemed like an intimidating and daunting structure, and I thought back to the day I had left, arms filled with dreams and my heart filled with hope.

And I cried.

I did not cry the tears of *a victim* who does not want to return to work.

I did not cry the tears of a *hard done to child* who wants her own way.

I cried because I wanted to rewind the clock.

I cried, because I felt I had every right to feel that way, and yet still, there was nothing I could do about it.

I wanted to snatch back the moments I was supposed to have felt, the moments I was meant to have enjoyed. The moment when he first grabbed my finger and I had felt nothing, the moment when he first said 'Mammy' and I had shouted that I didn't care, the moment when he handed me my first mother's day card and I had run to the kitchen in search of a knife to cut away the pain, the moment when he would come for a hug and I would run away as fast I could, and the many moments of hidden tenderness between a mother and her new born that I heard so much about but could not find or feel.

I sobbed because looking out of that filthy window on the world I was now heading back in to, I wanted to snatch back the moments, which post-natal depression stole so brutally from out under me, that I could never re-claim.

I sobbed because the journey I have actually been on, is not the journey I so desperately craved, felt I deserved and had longed for since I was a little girl walking around with my dolly dressed in dungarees.

I grieved for the person I once was, who still lay dormant inside of me, but of whom I had to let go.

12 months ago I was a girl on a mission to enjoy becoming the perfect mother.

Today I am a woman who has been broken, fixed, broken some more and glued back together, for the interim, while she still tries to find a few missing pieces.

I have to let go of the loss of my dreams, I have to let go of the person I was, and I need to release the guilt I have harboured for the little boy, who arrived in this world bursting with love, but who received nothing, from the one person who was desperate to give it to him.

I have to build new dreams, be the person I am now, and replace the guilt with contentment.

At some point I am sure I will be able to do all of these things.

After spending a few moments cleaning up the gunk now splattered across my face, the mascara from below my mouth and the snot from all over my hands, I turned my back on the window and began to totter unsteadily down the same unforgiving stairs I had fought so hard to climb up 18 months ago.

Still not brave enough to take the lift.

'Hey Lexy.' My boss had greeted me kindly. 'You look great, how are you feeling? Within a few hours, it will be like you have never been away.'

I couldn't help but think, as I waited for my new gate pass, that it will never in one hundred years, feel like I have never been away, this I can guarantee.

How am I feeling?

Frightened, scared, anxious.... But ready for the next chapter of my life.

The one where my only expectation is to take every day as it comes, and to forgive myself for 'my year off.'

It was not my fault.

They say, don't they?

The first chapter of a book draws you in, but the second is where you find the real depth.

I am back in my office, and although my son is in full time nursery now, he is actually right here with me, engraved in my heart, so being back in work seems small fry.

I hate it yes, but in 3 hours I will see my son.

And once again, I am filled with hope.

And who knows?

Maybe tomorrow, I will be brave enough to tackle the lift.

I'd say no anyway...

I sometimes wonder, usually late at night when I am unable to sleep, due to too much caffeine and too little romantic pillow talk (last night we discussed the origins of the humble sprout, apparently they originated in Ireland, like most things) if it is likely I will be married before my face starts to resemble a walnut.

At the rate The Irish One gets around to things (faulty light switches, smoke alarms and fixing the washer) probably not, which unfortunately can only mean one thing.

Botox. (And no clean clothes for months.)

These are the thoughts that tumble across my skull as I toss and turn in bed trying to ignore the (Irish) snoring and disregard the tugging from my darker self, willing me to lie there and regret everything I have ever done in my life.

Insomnia isn't nice especially when your insomnia taunts you, so while lying there the other night regretting a cake I made, which gave everyone the most god almighty shits, **when I was 17**, I decided to try and coerce my brain in to thinking about something a little more pleasant.

Inadvertently, because of this, as the nights have turned in to days, and then back in to nights, my wedding plans have taken flight.

The one small snag being, he hasn't asked. Yet.

But it is ok, as I have decided, that if and when he finally gets around to dropping to one knee, (Yes, my proposal is planned too) if my face looks like a gnarled tree, I will allow myself some Botox.

I do believe in growing old **gradually** and of course, I do believe in growing old gracefully. (Although I also love Donatella Versace for her complete denial of the passing of time. If I had her money, my belly button would already be a chin dimple. Believe me.)

I completely believe though, that lines can make women look beautiful, they tell a story, they show laughter, they show pain, they show immense strength but most of all, to me, they show courage.

A life being lived.

But, soppiness aside, here is the issue I currently have.

I seem to have caught some sort of *era ignoring condition,* which is making me grow old before my time.

I am only 31 but on some days I am sure people in the street assume I am Addison's grandma.

Hell, on some days I feel old enough to be his grandma. (And the stoop doesn't help I suppose. It's that bloody pram though. It's too low! And seriously? Car seat in the back? With the weight of this child? My back in in bits!! Never mind looking like a walnut as I walk down the aisle! I will need a Zimmer soon!)

It may be conjunctivitis, this condition, as according to my not very proficient GP, it does *seem to be,* as my eyes *are* all swollen and puffy.

(What is it with Gp's these days? Are they so scared of being sued they now refuse to diagnose? Excuse me Dr. Quack; 'I seem to have a baby coming out of my bum, could I be in labour?' 'Well you certainly *seem to be!'* Ergh!)

It may be called Lazy-itis too, according to The Irish One, as some days I *do* wear the same clothes from the day previous due to (THE BLOODY WASHER STILL BEING BROKEN!) Tiredness.

But if I were to be completely honest, and I usually am, I actually think the condition I have definitely caught causing me to look less yummy mummy and more scummy *granmummy* has been with me a lot longer than the last few weeks.

It started around the same time the postnatal *condition* I have suffered with, did. (I.e.; Post NATALLY.)

68 hours in to labour, The Irish One ready to take a blunt fork and perform an impromptu caesarean section at my sweaty, teary, insistence, noticed a shock of my hair, right at the back, had turned completely white.

Since then, my natural highlights, as I like to call them, have been coming thick and fast, even hair dye doesn't cover them. (Spray paint does.)

Since being hospitalised, Eczema has ravaged, chomped and chewed my poor fingers away to that of a 90 year old, dashing my dreams of being a hand model, and the only way I can hide the bags under my eyes is by touching them up with black makeup, so it looks like they are part of *my look.*

As if I still have a look. (Dodgy old rocker is what I seem to be pulling off these days... is it me? Or does that sound rude? Moving on...)

I really don't know what the condition is, but every time I look at my face in the mirror, I seem to have grown another crevice.

The last one to materialise runs right across my forehead from left to right, (or right to left, if you are Japanese) and after a few minutes of screaming, for the first time in my life, I flirted with the idea of a fringe, before I Google searched face lifts and affordable on a shoe string surgical enhancement.

Botox of course, being a much safer option than a fringe in The Irish One's opinion.

His reasoning being that my chin is too big for a fringe, (nice huh?) and the effects of Botox, should it all go "*awfully*" wrong and I end up with shelf at the top of my face, wouldn't last long enough for it to make too much of a negative impact and hey! At least he would have somewhere to rest his brew while I was...

Who was it that said romance was dead? (Oh and FYI? That NEVER happens.)

Yes ladies and gents, this is the man I want to marry.

And yes, questioning his motives for our relationship, green snot pouring from my eyes, face all bright red and wrinkly from an hour in the bath and my knickers holding my hair back, I am probably doing myself no favours.

But I want to know you know?

It's not that I don't already think I will be ~~stuck with him~~, enjoying his company until death do us part anyway, and it isn't that I plan on leaving him if he doesn't propose soon, it's just...

It's just...

I need something to think about (Read; stare at in the form of diamond) at night instead of the long days ahead.

And er, yeah, I suppose I love him.

I didn't dream of a wedding as a little girl, in fact I never believed in marriage until recently, I just never thought it could work, that a legal piece of paper with your names on it could ever or would ever make a difference to the inevitable. (That you break up, hate each other and unsuccessfully plot each other's deaths at least twice a year, from a far, for the rest of your lives.... In case you were wondering, my parents don't get on.)

But now, after 18 weeks of therapy, 132 stiches in my *vaganzza,* a year of absolute hell and the love still going strong... (ish)... despite all infrequent ups and soul destroying lows, I want the bloody fairytale all the Disney films promised me.

I actually believe we could have it, check me out, I believe in love.

(You can stick your fingers down your throat now, it is ok, I am.)

We've had our bit with the villains, as far as I am concerned, and now I want a great big flipping dress, a teary declaration of our love, and a baileys fountain that you dip chocolate in.

I want to thank him, for everything he has supported me through, as he really has, by giving him a promise I will be around to enjoy our future.

And I want a hen night/hen world tour. (I will be honest, most nights this is what I can be found planning. Rio De Janiero, Australia for 6 weeks and Route 66 have all been on the 'When I finally win the lottery and *finally* get married/ Hen night' list.)

I want a party and I want to be able to say I have been committed in to something other than a mental house.

I want **him.** (Even if he doesn't fix the washer.)

So married ladies, help me out here please.

Do I need to stop wearing my trackies to bed and bitching about his razor being on the floor? (AGAIN!!!!!!) Do I need to start cooking steak and giving him a foot massage? Do I need to plaster my face with make up every day and hold my trumps in again? Do I need to avoid onion breath and change Addison's every bum, while chasing his every whim and making his dreams come true? Do I need to start allowing him to have a poo while I am in the bath? (In the *toilet,* just to clarify, turns out there is a limit, and that would be mine!!!)

Whatever it takes, I will do it, (within reason!) as I have spent the last few weeks planning this between the hours of 10pm and 5am.

The longer it takes the more outlandish it is becoming, so really, more fool him.

Brazil at sunrise, is where I currently am, him wearing a toga, me looking like a Brazilian goddess (courtesy of Tantastic in Bolton!) and believe me I am completely focused on getting the party of my dreams!!!

I mean man.

Of course, hahaha, I mean man.

But just in case, it takes longer than planned...

How much is Botox and does anyone have Donatella's number, or a winning lottery fund they want to share?

(Route 66 would be a hoot girls, marriage or no marriage!!)

*The condition seems to be known by most as; Mother *(posh mum, still harassed as child will only use this when child wants something.)* Mom *(American mum.)* Mommy *(Still American mum- and yeah I'm still jealous.)* Mum, *(Stop drinking cold tea immediately and get me what I need!!)* Mummy (*Dogs body but loved.)* Motherhood (film.) Motherhood *(makes you look gnarly, and not in a cool surfer way.)*

The fear...

You know what it is right?

(The 'right' at the end of that question doesn't actually need to be there, I know that, but it is the Mancunia in me. You know what it is *RIGHT?* Is just how I speak... can we move on?)

I have been stamped with a tag, (not an electronic one just to be clear. I am from Manchester yes, but I am not someone who behaves so atrociously that she would end up being electronically tagged, although The Irish One would probably disagree with this statement for five days of every month. The very same five days of the month when he has every right to fear for his safety) and now that I have worn that tag for a while, looked at it *full on* in the mirror, glanced at it a couple of times out of the corner of my eye in the reflection of the huge shop windows I pass on the way to the supermarket and back, and see it clean as day glaring back at me, sometimes hidden behind or underneath something, like a sleepless night, or a cheerful weekend, but still there somehow, it just seems impossible to disconnect from.

Like even when I am feeling happy, the underlying tag reminds me not to get my hopes up, not to give myself any credit and certainly not to take any of this, this *happiness, hope, wishful thinking, belief in a greater good and joy* for granted.

It almost feels like now it is written in stone, its sinister grin will always be watching from behind a corner mocking the very person I am trying so desperately to become.

Suits in the living room, drinking coffee, making plans to change my world.

Dark mornings, the smell of toast and an overwhelming fear leaking from my heart in to the very pit of my stomach that at some point soon, this happiness, this love, this dream I seem to be living in, where everything is ticking along tickety boo, that these moments almost pleasurably seeping now in to sepia never forgotten memories, will come to an irreversible end.

I am actually waiting for something to happen to kill me off. (It is like living in a Scream movie.)

I am anticipating it, knowing that it will prove the way I was living, isolated by choice, frozen in time and very much alone, was actually very sensible.

Was safe.

I can feel it watching me, a shadow lurking at the edge of my life, like an unwelcome sinister guest at a party for angels.

I will be kidding about, catching myself laughing, catching myself living and getting to know the new me and the life I am still learning to live, and somehow seem to be enjoying, and my stomach will flip over with the realisation of how mellow things have become.

Sometime soon, a dirty great big rock is going to land with great force in to the middle of this serene little man-made lake I have been working so hard on and I am dreading the sound, the feel, and the shock of the splash of cold water that will no doubt douse me in misery from head to toe.

This is the pattern of my life, this is why I haven't allowed love to break down my door. (Not my back doors. Just like, the front door. Look I am trying to be poetic ok? So can we just be serious for a moment please?) This is why I have spent my life pushing people away, anyone who came too close, anyone who wanted me, needed me to need them in any way at all.

I am scared that something horrific is going to happen now that the door has been opened.

Now, that I am in love.

Now that I am allowing myself to be loved.

Something is going to happen.

Something is coming and this feels like a warning.

My fingers flying over the keys of the paper sat in front of me, a warning to batten down the hatches, to prepare, to stock up for the winter where everything will once again change irreplaceably.

I can feel it coming.

Is this happiness, or is it the quiet before another storm?

Is this real, or is this the old me, struggling to bring *me, the real me* back within my comfort zone, whispering at me to push everyone away again.

Reminding me over and over again that nobody cares, that none of this will last and that ultimately, I am worthless.

Is this me?

Or is that me?

I know people care. I care.

Who the hell am I now?

Can I live with the old tag all the while creating a new tag?

Can someone with clinical *forward slash* postnatal depression recover?

Travel back down that road...

A year ago today, and I am certain of this because I remember the upcoming Father's day being a giant pain in the arse inconvenience to my plan, I found myself, sitting isolated in my little cloud of doom, in a room filled with happiness and laughter, family and loved ones.

In the background, behind the obvious and flamboyant sounds of Thomas the tank engine coming from the telly, Addison trying to squeeze out a hard poo and the voice of The Irish One singing loudly while he cooked sausages for our breakfast, from behind the sound of my own deceitful laughter and forced enjoyment at what really should have felt like a genuinely happy scene playing out around me, however, was a malicious and spiteful undertone.

Only I knew this of course, but I wasn't't aware of it.

An undertone in the form of a significantly 'heard' voice, that came from deep down inside of me, extensively and intricately trained to remind me at my most fragile of points, that I was irresponsible, disgusting and a pitiful excuse for a woman.

An accomplished and incredibly proficient opinion of myself that reminded me relentlessly with every task I attempted, I was thoughtless, and weak and could never succeed.

I was over sensitive and rash, dumb, and I hurt people without even realising. I was spoilt and a nightmare to be around, and everybody knew it so I may as well accept it. I should be ashamed of needing comfort for I didn't't deserve it, I should feel embarrassed of not being happy when I had so much to be happy about and I should feel incredibly guilty too, because so many people had problems worse than my own.

So many people had *real* illnesses, and *real* problems and mine were no more than vain and self-indulgent dramatics.

It barked at me that I was lazy and ungrateful and hated.

I was a failure as a mother and I was ugly and fat and a letdown. I was ugly inside. Everything about me was ugly.

It was so loud, and proud, and so convincing and had gone on for so long, that the truth is, I didn't't even hear it anymore, or realise it was even talking. It had just become part of me, hence not being aware of it.

I hadn't even started therapy and I *needed* to get better. I owed it to everybody. The pressure to succeed at 'getting better' was immense before I even got help. How did I think I could do it without?

If I couldn't 'get better' I deserved to be dead. 'Better' from what though, I would ask myself with ferocious disdain? THERE IS NOTHING WRONG WITH YOU.

The voice constantly reminded me of the need to be absolutely perfect all of the time, so failing? Even if it was only the voice in my head advising me I was failing? That meant I was. It was a fact.

Trying to come to terms with being a terrible mother?

Even when The Irish One would assure me I was in fact the opposite, and that I was loved and beautiful, I knew he would never understand the truth. Nothing I did would ever match up to the expectations, I set for myself, and my inner voice was only too happy to remind of that. I was a failure. It was a fact.

Trying to hide my disappointment at who I should be but was unable to be, behind laughter? Was exhausting. Especially when my inner voice was laughing too. *At* me, all the while calling me pathetic and evil, and obnoxious and worthless. All facts.

I was too selfish. Also a fact.

The three of us laughing, normal and happy, well, it was a family photograph of a memory, like so many others that have been taken since, but the difference on that day, was the ever present and intensely secretive threat of murder which had been lurking just behind my watery grin for a while, was now about to come to fruition.

It was making plans.

As we got dressed and the happy family park day played out, as I pushed Addison in the pram grinning from ear to ear, as I skipped off to buy ice cream, as The Irish One hugged me and told me he loved me and I kissed him back, as I shrieked and clapped and loafed about putting on the best show I could, the last show of my life, the finale, I was silently plotting, I was wordlessly preparing and I was busy considering, what the best time to take an overdose, so as to not be saved, and so as to cause as little commotion to those left behind as possible, would be.

I was going to commit murder.

It wasn't a cry for help. I wanted me dead.

I wanted to die as I put my baby to bed. What kind of mother thinks that?

My inner voice screamed. You should be filled with love, you selfish useless cunt. I wanted to die as I broke open the packet and hesitated, my inner voice whispering sinisterly, that I was a cowardly insect. Grime.

It was relentless.

I was stuck in a cube of cement with an inner voice that was certainly not guiding me with love. And I didn't even realise or believe that I was broken.

Not really. I had refused medication, for I didn't trust it. Medication for what? This isn't an illness, I would cry, I am just selfish. I ignored help, because how could anybody help me, there was nothing wrong with me, other than being pathetic. Even when I was taken in to hospital, I still didn't see it. I am just a drama queen. I am not ill. I am too pathetic to even kill myself properly and look how many people I have hurt now.

"You won't be able to silence it immediately,' My therapist carefully and quietly whispered to me this afternoon from his side of the room, after I had I spoken of how disappointed in myself I was, as that voice, that overpowering voice was once again, becoming louder.

'You can't expect yourself to be able to just turn it off, that voice is old and wise and strong. It has been around a lot longer than the knowledge that you can inject a new voice. But you **can** learn to turn it down.' He went on. 'This new voice telling you that you are ok, and a good mum, and deserve care, well it is young. It isn't strong yet, it is new, the important thing to remember is that it is there, and that you are trying.'

'Whatever.' I mumbled petulantly back in response, like a teenager refusing to take on that I wasn't't pathetic and a failure. It felt oddly comfortable to be insulting myself again.

'Falling back in to old patterns is what we do when we find ourselves vulnerable and fragile. This doesn't mean we have 'relapsed.' Only that we are learning to recognise the difference between *then* and now.'

'Alright.' I carried on. 'What time is it? Can I go yet?'

'No.'

'Why not?' I asked trying not to stamp my foot.

'You have ten minutes left. Have you moved on in the last year do you think?' He asks silencing me with a question he knew I would have to think about.

Have I moved on?

As I pick up the building blocks and listen to my son trying to get to sleep singing a song this evening and find myself genuinely laughing, I know that I have, but I also know, I still have a long way to go.

There are two voices now, that's true, but it is still one hell of a battle. When things get difficult and I feel like I can't cope and am to blame (like getting suspended from work for making a terrible mistake) she shouts loud and clear about how pathetic and evil I am for long periods of time, and sometimes I hear her, and I listen and I struggle for a while, I get paranoid that everyone hates me again and I spiral.

And at other times when I drop a bollock, (like letting Addison eat Play Doh... it is ok to let them eat it, isn't it? I don't mean as a *main meal*, I just mean, if he swallowed some when I had my back turned that doesn't make me a bad mum does it?) I find the strength from god knows where, with the help of medication, because I deserve to be helped, to tell her that not everybody hates me and actually I'm not as bad she thinks I am. (So take that bitch! - I'll work on my fighting talk as time goes on I suppose. Baby steps and all that.)

Right now I am fighting. (Cos I'm awesome. – cringe!!!)

I have learnt a lot off James this year. (Why am I so god damn mean to him??)

Including that it is ok to be a victim sometimes, and that those thoughts your inner voice tells you – well they aren't't fact.

They are just thoughts, and thoughts can be changed.

Thoughts aren't't facts.

Feelings aren't facts.

'What would you say to your best friend Lexy, if she felt weak and pathetic and was constantly beating herself up? What would you say to her? Think about how you would react to her, then do the same for yourself.'

'It isn't as easy as that James' I bite back at him (for no reason whatsoever?!?! He is lovely to me and all I do is stomp around acting like he just told me my skirt was too short!)

'But to quote pink, I'd probably say;

'Change the voices in your head, make them like you instead! Cos your perfect, your fuckin perfect!' and with him rolling his eyes and laughing, I stormed out.

(I really don't know why.)

I wonder, how I will be, a year from now?

One of the voices in my head just answered very quietly.

It said;

I hope I win.

Twinkle Twinkle...

'Is it going to hurt?'

'I *honestly* thought I was going to die last time.' She says searching in her Vivienne Westwood handbag for a cigarette and then looking directly in to my eyes.

'I thought an angel was going to appear from the ceiling and take me to heaven...'

I feel the blood drain from my face as she goes on.

'I felt this *warmth* on my back, and thought *oh god this it*. This is me. I'm off. Off in to the clouds I go...'

Stood on the corner of a quiet street with a gorgeous and hilarious gal pal *(she wanted me to call her that)* the cool morning air biting at my face, making my lips tingle, the sun just setting up shop, not yet on full throttle but inching it's way across the road and on to the pavement behind me, as if trying to chase me with a warning of the deep heat I could be in, I take a deep breath.

I am what some may refer to as, *shaking like a shitting dog.*

I am hopping about like *a long tailed skunk in a room full of rocking chairs.*

I am feeling *no doubt*, what every cow *must* feel right before it gets branded with a red hot poker.

Like releasing a huge cow pat.

'Then what happened?' I ask breathless and giddy, my stomach turning over reminding me to clench my buttocks in case I let one rip *and embarrass myself.*

'Well. Basically the minute the needle went in' she takes a long drag on her cigarette as she lights it and grins at me 'I passed out, and the warmth I felt on my back was the big bloke *who caught me* waking me up.'

I explode in to nervous and slightly horrified giggles.

'So not an angel?' I ask, slightly disappointed. An angel would have been cool.

But fainting? Oh god. What if I faint? I tend to dribble when I faint, and everyone knows that dribbling in a tattoo parlour is social suicide!

'No.' she laughs back 'Aw but he was honestly so lovely. It does hurt, but it's nothing like childbirth so you should be fine, and at least if you faint you know he will catch you.'

I am about to respond that the catchy 'it's nothing like childbirth' line has actually done nothing to calm the bowel movements I am currently experiencing when a heavily painted arm, with a neck and head attached appears around the door.

'Lexy?' he asked, surprisingly softly spoken, considering how mental and grizzly he looks with his long beard, his beanie hat and the heavy metal rock music providing the soundtrack to his entrance in to my life story.

There is no turning back now.

As I walk through the door I can hear the voices in my head.

'Do not go ahead with this, or you will regret it! You are an embarrassment! What if it looks stupid? You do realise you are 32?'

'I forbid you from doing this! You'll never be cool enough to pull off a tattoo you stupid moose like knob jockey!'

'You are 32 years old. It is your life, your body and you own your own mind.'

The tattoo man asks me to sit down on the stool opposite him and extend my right wrist.

I am shakily finding somewhere to prop Arthur *(my new handbag – so beautiful he deserved a name)* when another man appears to the left of me (presumably this is the *body catcher*) and asks me if I know who Black Sabbath are.

'Is that the bloke who bit the head off a rabbit?' I respond nervously, my eyes darting between their faces to the big feck off needle resting on the bench beside the *'yob'* opposite me. (*Yob*, was my mother's voice muscling its way in to my psychic.)

'Bat.' He laughs. 'But yes.'

Right.

Bat.

Not rabbit.

Damn it. There goes my street cred.

(Oh Jesus, am I actually turning in to my mother? Mental note to self, stop thinking in my mother's voice.)

'Are you ready?' Yob one asks, turning on the *stabbing needle gun of death* and aiming it towards my clear white beautiful and innocent arm.

I would like to tell you at this point, I calmly and coolly told him I was *born ready,* and everything went fine, but alas, I didn't and it didn't.

'Hang on!' I end up shouting directly in to the weapon yielding grizzly's face before re-adjusting the volume setting on my anxiety and trying to appear calm and collected.

'Can I ask you some questions?'

'Shoot!' he said smiling kindly (which would have been lovely if it wasn't't for the *jerking metallic buzzing needle gun of disaster* he was holding in his hand approximately 20 cm away from my face.)

'Will it hurt?' I asked honestly, the question seemingly pissing off the body catcher as he sighed and stropped off with a roll of his eyes. (Big grizzly men can strop – *you learn something every day,* as my mother always... god damn it!)

Oh god. I have no body catcher.

I look down at the tile floor and wonder if Arthur would break my fall.

'What do *you* think?' Grizzly responds interrupting my thoughts and turning off the *animated injector of pain and ink.*

I breathe a shaky sigh of relief.

2 extra minutes to prepare.

'I think it will.' I respond with thought, moving Arthur on to the floor about a foot away from the stool.

If I feel myself going, I will *aim my faint* towards him.

'You are right it will,' he solemnly replies before nodding in the general direction of my left arm and making full eye contact.

'But I notice you are *covered* in scars, which tells me one of two things, either you are absolutely *crap* at fishing *(?!?)* or you are a self-harmer.'

I laugh in shock.

'If you are the latter, which I am guessing you probably are because you have that sexy but damaged and slightly unhinged look about you, then I will tell you now it won't hurt nearly as much as that.' He points at a deep bubbly scar above my left thumb. Burn?'

I smile at him gratefully.

'Yeah.'

He has totally put me at ease, bless his – evil clown tattooed, graveyard *scened,* burning Jesus dying on the cross-etched inky black- cotton socks.

'Degree?'

'Third.'

'Respect.' He nods.

(There are no words. In my opinion unless you are Eminem, you cannot get away with saying 'Respect.' but whatever...)

Before I get chance to jump up and run outside to tell my gal pal (*again* she *wanted* me to call her that) that the tattoo man thought I was sexy and unhinged which in my mind passes roughly for *cool,* he ran his plastic gloved thumb over the trace on my wrist and turned *the blade of doom* back on.

'Woo?'

'Yes.' I respond enthusiastically.

'Woo?' he asks again incredulously, a little louder.

'Yes.' I repeat nodding for extra effect. 'Woo.'

He sighs 'Go on tell me all about it.'

I close my eyes, as he lowers the tattoo gun towards me and take deep breaths as I do as I am told.

'Woo saved my life. I used to be cool but then I had Woo. He is my son, he is two next week, he says *bugger* a lot... I wee when I sneeze'

A pause, and he continues.

Wow this *hurts. But I kind of like it...*

'... but Woo also represents the thousands of people who have supported me and cared for me, through my blog Mammywoo, total strangers, I may add, since I had him. It also represents my dog Doodle...'

The buzzing stops so abruptly, I am forced to open one eye and peep at him.

He is hunched over my hand, pulling the skin on my wrist back tightly, but looking directly up at me, his eyebrows knotted.

'Doodle?'

'The poodle.'

The buzzing starts up again as he shakes his head and goes back to concentrating on scaring me for the rest of my *god-damn* life.

'So yeah, and basically' I continue, trying to remember my flow and closing my eyes again with a wince.

Breathe Lexy, breathe.

'I tried to kill myself, then I went in to a mental hospital, then my therapist asked me when I was going to take control of my own life, and I realised at that exact moment that it was about time I at *least tried* to free myself from the chains I have, I suppose kept *myself* under. I want to live my own life, but I never have. I have always asked others 'Am I ok?' without actually asking them? You know? Like if they are in a mood then I automatically assume I have done something wrong, and if people feel bad then I have to make them feel better or it could be *me that has upset them* and then they may not like me anymore. Like they may confirm to me, by not liking me that I actually don't like myself. I have always been so afraid, but I couldn't't tell you exactly what of. You know?'

'No.'

I carry on regardless as he bumps the needle over my crease. *(That sounds way ruder on paper than it does in my head.)*

'Well basically, I have always thought I have been living my own life when really I have always been controlled by these voices in my head.'

The buzzing stops again.

It's ok though. I kind of expected it to.

I open my eyes.

He is looking at me with an expression I am unable to read.

'Voices in your head?'

'Yeah.' I say, looking back at him, focusing on his mono-brow for courage. 'Like, sometimes it's my mother's voice and sometimes it's my father's voice and sometimes it's my own harsh voice, and they are always telling me what I can and can't do. And I am sick of it.'

The buzzing starts up again and once again I close my eyes.

'Argh!' I exclaim before continuing between gritted teeth 'so Woo represents everything I have been, everything I can be, my son, my dog and a new beginning where if I want a freaking tattoo I will get one and I don't have to answer to anyone.'

He turns off the stabbing needle gun and rubs the blood off my wrist.

'It represents control, and me, and my son, and my dog, and that poor mental health is ok and I am never alone.'

He ignores me as he turns away from me and grabs up for some cellophane.

'Finished. Do you like it?'

I look down at it, and tilt my head.

That's my wrist.

But.

It looks weird.

'No.' I reply honestly, feeling a bit queasy. *Oh shit what have I done?*

'Why?' he replies.

'It's too straight, do some curly bits.' *Oh my god make it better, make it better, holy hell make it better! That looks like a crab poo'd on me!*

The buzzing starts again and I add something.

'Woo *also* means, from now on, I am gonna be me, and only me, and the only person who will tell me if I am ok, is me. Or at least, that's the aim.'

The buzzing stops again. He sighs.

'Do you like it?'

I breathe a huge excited breath.

'Yes. I exclaim! I bloody love it! WOO!' I lift my wrist as I say this.

'Woo also means Woooooo!' I add excitedly, lifting my wrist in to his face.

He gets up from his chair and shakes his head.

'Women' he mutters as he wraps me up. 'You're all as mad as a bag of frogs.'

Whatever! I have a tattoo!!

Woo means 'Journey.'

Well today it does anyway... tomorrow it may mean destination.

Is it meant to be this itchy though? Don't scratch. Don't scratch. Don't scratch! It's so itchy!!! Like thrush but on my wrist!!

Oh hell.

I have Woo on my wrist.

How to expect what you aren't expecting...

There should be alerts.

There should be bells and whistles. Sirens and men banging on big drums.

At the very least there should be warning signs.

There is already?

No, I don't mean, the *'oh congratulations on your pregnancy now read this...'* type slogans.

'Here is what you can and cannot do for the next nine (ten) months' type pamphlets.

I'm talking about the full on, honest, *'trespass at your own risk, drink this bleach and your insides won't be clean and sparkly, you'll be dead'* type, easy to read picture and cautionary tale- warnings. Skull and crossbones that type of thing.

'Don't eat MacDonald's, accept pain relief and avoid un-pasturerised cheese' aren't useful at all!

They are completely redundant!

Like locking the gate *after* the bulldog has bitten the priest in the ball sack. (True story. And yes. He did take the lords name in vain. But I can't say I blame him to be honest.) They are like taking your tarmac stained boots off *after* you've trodden it all the way across the new carpet. (How my cousin's husband isn't dead right now, I really don't know. The Irish One would be digging his own shallow hole. Brand new cream carpets! Tarmac – everywhere!)

I'M TALKING PROPER, HONEST, AND EASY TO UNDERSTAND WARNING SIGNS.

I'm talking the kind of warnings you see on sign posts while waiting to board a great big scary roller-coaster. The ones you look at while you are waiting in line, and meticulously read, looking for some sort of get out clause. Or if you are a lover of roller coasters, the signs you read over and over again, while working yourself up in to a *'woohooo I could have a heart attack, this ride is gonna be amazing' frenzy.* (I used to be the latter, now I mumble about how I have weakened pelvic floor and toddle off to the bathroom. Well, have you been on a bouncy, spinny, upside down ride since giving birth? I have. It was NOT pretty. Let's just say I *told* people I had been on the log flume...)

Pregnancy, birth and motherhood is often described as 'the biggest rollercoaster a woman can ride' right? So why not? Why not give appropriate forewarning?

Your doctor should provide adequate signals and information! They could have them on the walls in the family planning clinic. They could swing over your head as you walk in to the Gynae's office. They could be stuck in pamphlet holders on your consultant's reception.

Some Bint in a smock could hand them out on the pregnancy test and condom aisle in Morrison's. 'Here you go love, just so you know. What to expect if you do, or if you are in the situation where you are *with child,* for the next 1-35 years. Thanks very much love. Have a nice day.'

I'm not talking any *mamby pamby, watery, slowly break it to you* type warning signs, here. I'm talking *honest, straight forward, hard hitting, no beating around the bush*, type signs informing you of the ride you are about to take; B*y taking off the condom/ stopping the pill/ getting drunk/ allowing him to take his wellies off in the bath.* – Delete as appropriate

Here are some examples of what I *feel,* the Side effects and cautions could be.

Do not ride – **If you have a bad back.**

As after labour you will affectively be crippled from the neck down. Walking around carrying a 23 pound boy with a snotty nose as well as having to push a trolley full of The Irish One's sausages and potatoes will ensure no sofa will ever be comfy again, and you will forever more inadvertently shout *'oof'* every time you bend down to pick up a discarded dummy. And yes, those jeans are a bit tight but yes again, you did just show the 68 year old man behind you the rather long crack of your arse. Perhaps tomorrow you should go back to the leggings....

Do not ride – **If you have a tendency to be ditzy.**

As after birth you will no longer be dizzy, you will automatically find yourself, against your will or say so, upgraded to *dozy bloody mare* status. You can blame the IPhone all you want for sending messages such as;

•'I can't wait to taste your cock' to an old family friend. (Cooking, I can't wait to taste your cooking!) Or,

•'You are one hot mammal' to a heavily pregnant and slightly paranoid about her weight gain, friend. (Mama, you are one hot mama!) Or even,

•'My hot cock tastes yummy' to over 1000 people on twitter, (Chocolate, my hot CHOCOLATE tasted yummy!)

But ultimately you will only have yourself to blame.

You were dizzy and you ignored the signs. You were already a bit *dazed* and you *still* embarked on the motherhood rollercoaster. Now you are just a dozy cow. And yes, maybe the IPhone is a bit pervy, but seriously, at least something is. When was the last time you *even* had sex?

Do not ride – **If you have high blood pressure.**

A mild nuisance can no longer be categorised as a slight irritant. A cat meowing outside your bedroom window at 11pm before birth, may have been considered cute. You may even have worried it was hungry and fetched a bowl of milk. *Post birth,* you will not care about being 'an animal lover' or even contemplate helping the neighbours call the 'RSPCA.' You will be looking for a shotgun. You will be fashioning a sling shot using a pair of old knickers and a heavy dirty nappy screaming 'Wake my baby up and die!!!!!" out of the bathroom wild eyes and busy haired. (You can make anything when you are a mother.)

Do not ride - **If you are a control freak.**

Nothing will be routine ever again. EVER. Even your lists will change minute by minute. You may follow Gina ford (Swearword in our house) but on occasion you will not meet her standards. The house will be a mess. No, you can laugh all you want. You can tell me you have OCD all you want. The HOUSE WILL BE A MESS. Even when it is tidy. Your trained nose will smell poo. And the cleaning starts again. IT NEVER ENDS.

Were you in control of your emotions before? You thought you were. But you got on the ride. Now you are out of control. Whether you like it or not. Now you are a sniveling, howling, hysterically laughing, sobbing, balling, shouting, walking round in circles heap of un-ironed baby grows.

Oh and there is a milk ring from the bottle on the TV stand. (Just letting you know!)

Do not ride- If **you suffer with memory problems.**

What was I just saying? No seriously! What was I talking to you about? Damn it, it was really juicy! I haven't seen you for ages. I wanted to catch up but I can't finish a sentence. I just walked in to the kitchen for something. Er, hang on. What did I need? I'll just pop back in to the living room that will remind me. Oh yeah, feed the dog and put the kettle on for a bottle.

No problem. So what was I saying? Oh yeah. If you have memory issues you are screwed. As after birth, when you are tired and... Was that the door? No? Ok, so yeah when you are... what was I saying? Hang on. I'll remember. Just let me give the dog a bottle and feed the baby some Pedigree chum.

- Have you seen my book? It's in the fridge? Well what the hell is it doing in there?

- Do you know where my boots are? They are on the bed? Why the hell are they *on* the bed?

- Have you seen my eye liner? It's in my hand? Oh yes, so it is.

I am not joking here. Auto-pilot is a fucker.

Do not ride -**If you are not ready.**

Hahahahahahahahahaha. When are you ever ready? I thought I was ready. I planned, I nested, I prepared. I was SO READY!! I was wrong. I was NOT ready! But then, are you ever ready to never sleep again? To hold a tiny anus open to help find trumps? To pick your Childs stomach lining from between your toes? Are you ever ready to constantly smell like an old sleeping bag? You know the smell. Musty, with a mixture of puke.

Do not ride – **If you enjoy sex.**

Anal stitching is somewhat of a deterrent.

Do not ride – **As some effects may be too intense for some adults.** Anal stitching. Even the midwife cringed.

Do not ride – **As may be frightening for some people.** Tearing afore mentioned anal stitching. My Screams made the neighbours call the police. They thought I was being 'maimed with a blunt hatchet' (True story.)

Do not ride – **If you suffer from claustrophobia, agoraphobia, oooegraphobia (fear of eggs) or irritatingmanaphobia (phobia of irritating men.)** I may have made that last one up, and the one before. But seriously, if you are scared of eggs, don't do it. Kids love them scrambled! Awful, just awful!

Do not ride if you expect to be perfect.

You ignored ALL my warnings? You got on the ride anyway???

Well, in that case.

Try not to judge those mothers whose children have already arrived.

'I will never give my child a dummy.' said to a mother in the process of giving her child a dummy will not help your cause for support once your baby arrives. And also Egg on your face is horrific. (See previous comment on eggs.)

Please keep arms, hands, shoulders (knees and toes, knees and toes) in the vehicle at all times. Do not try and disembark said vehicle while carriage is still moving. You will only cause unnecessary rocking of the proverbial boat.

Should you feel a little depressed, a little sad, a little guilty, and a little confused please seek help.

Should you feel like doubting yourself at every turn please try not to. You are amazing.

If you feel like crying every second day. Please seek help. You are not alone.

If you feel like knocking your other half out, please remove all sporting equipment from the home.

If you did not bond with your baby immediately, you are just like me. He is my world, now. Has been since day one, I was just too tired and overwhelmed to recognise it. You will get there. I promise.

If you still wear maternity pants on occasion because you enjoy having a warm tummy, ahem... what? I have no idea what you mean? These are just my stretchy pants!! Go you. You rock.

If you sometimes feel you aren't good enough. YOU ARE.

Is your child happy? Then you are more than good enough.

Are you struggling to be happy? Confide in somebody.

WARNING: ALL RIDERS DO SO AT THIER OWN RISK. THE ESTABLISHMENT TAKES NO RESPONSIBILITY FOR ALL CONSUMING LOVE, COURAGE ONLY A MOTHER KNOWS, PATIENCE ONLY A MOTHER UNDERSTANDS AND A FEELING OF CALM AND BELONGING, WHEN YOUR CHILD SMILES AND GRABS YOUR FINGER, ONLY A MOTHER CAN'T HELP FEELING PROUD OF.

You made a baby. You are a superhero. (Would batman endure hours of labour, nipple torture and a forced episiotomy or anal tearing, and still smile at the end of is all? No he bloody wouldn't. Batman is a frigging wimp. Bang! Pow! Wallop! My arse...(Literally.)

If you wish to ride again? (You are a mentalist.)

I am SO going to ride again***!

*Park attractions are currently closed for routine maintenance.

*No they will not open tonight.

*In other words; I have a bad back, I am a control freak, I get motion sickness, I am not ready and Ohmygod I suffer from Irritatingmanaphobia, so you've no chance. (Not for another 2 years anyway....)

Alternate CV...

Address:

The institute of mental illness and chaos, 1 child -1 man who never washes the knives and forks, Shattered Ville, edgy town.

Telephone:

Can I one bell you? I honestly can't remember it.

Date of Birth:

Sometime before now.

Personal statement.

An occasionally positive, occasionally suicidal, dynamic and passionate multi-tasker and head case, with 1 years' experience of wetting herself in public for no apparent reason, repeatedly scorching her ears with hair straighteners, running around in circles clearing up poop, accidentally interrupting funerals by running over squirrels and then screaming very loudly at the atrocity of it all, and managing to stand on a plug each and every time I am found running barefoot. Who is also proudly bringing up, nipple-less, I may add, a child with fully functioning bite reflexes.

Highly personable and honest with a great impending sense of doom I am consistently task focused on accomplishing an incredible number of missions during an unrealistic time frame – such as but not limited to – feeding the world, and making it a better place for you and for me and the whole damn human race, liking 75 of my friends Facebook status' and acting as camp counsellor for the dog who seems more depressed than I am, all before the bedtime routine starts at a time when I would rather stick my head down the toilet and repeatedly brain myself with the lid.

I achieve all of this of course, while also smiling for the public.

Work History;

Mum – present.

To lead and develop a child in to a well-rounded individual who doesn't need therapy in his teens and who suffers no lasting damage caused by repeatedly having to watch with his mother stick her head is down the toilet and slam the lid on her face in frustration.

To ensure a consistent quality of service by not appearing harassed when the dog vomits in the car just after being de-bollocked, by always talking in calming voices even when one feels close to a mental breakdown as the child has once again proudly announced he too has now shit his kecks all over the shag pile. And by always ensuring 5 back up dinners are cooking for a grumpy Irish man even though by this point in the day the idea of cooking seems less appealing that drinking a pint glass of one's own urine.

To be positively, passionately and completely awake at all times. Sleeping with one eye open will only ensure you get poked in it, by a finger that smells suspiciously of bum.

To instigate all areas of play as if one could not think of anything better one would like to do with one's time other than make **another** digger teddy dance the Macarena for 4 hours, bring the sandpit in the house, act out the role of trampoline, cultivate an ant farm and be force fed a worm, just to prove that people don't eat worms.

To pretend to like the sound of brain numbing screaming. To ignore the sound of perfect mothers giving unwanted advice. To wish you have gone deaf to the sound of brain numbing screaming. To eventually start screaming yourself, because if you can't beat them... to take this all out on your other half when he gets home and doesn't understand why you have your head in the oven repeatedly smashing the door in to your face in frustration.

To pretend to want sex as much as your other half even when you haven't slept in 6 months and you can smell something suspiciously like Bum. All. Of. The. Time.

To moan and groan and make all the right noises while surreptitiously planning tomorrow's activities (washing, ironing, world peace acquisition, cleaning up poop.)

To mentor and coach and support your other half by consistently nipping to the local off license and purchasing copious bottles of wine that undoubtedly increase productivity standards on his part. Using the time commonly known as 'mummy time' to set individual targets and feedback to your other half on why you are so much better than him at everything. Apologising like you really mean it when you sober up.

Thinking outside of the box to develop possible solutions for situations such as having no childcare and having to at some point return to work, only having enough money to buy beans and hiding mental illness by repeatedly singing 'old MacDonald had a farm' instead of a song you recently made up, titled 'Shoot me in the head. Shoot me in the head now.'

As a mother I have to consider and demonstrate sound and logical reasons for decisions such as 'No please don't eat your own poo.' 'No please don't roll off the changing table' and 'Stop putting your toys up the dogs bum.'

I also have to provide detailed and thoughtful responses to complex questions such as 'What have you been doing all day?' and 'Do you not realise how tired I am having to work?'

Normal Person – Up to Not long Ago.

Never weeing when one sneezed and enjoying control over all bodily functions.

Judging all parents who didn't seem to have a well behaved child. *'God have they never watched Supernanny? My child will never behave like that!!'*

Avoiding children at all costs but marginally feeling broody when I did see one, for like, a second before returning to my life.

Partying and showing my toned midriff. (Slight exaggeration possible.)

Having an idealistic view of how happy and relaxed family life would be for me in the future and how well behaved and beautiful my child would be and how my figure would simply 'snap' back in to shape after pregnancy. No Impending sense of doom, basically.

Lie in's, without the sound of 'Daddy' screaming and losing control in the back ground, while I fight to stay in bed to the sound of all manner of chaos just outside the bedroom door.

Television that didn't involve three Channel Five presenters dressed like cucumbers doing Heads shoulders knees and toes at 6 in the morning. (How have they not been victims of a bloody good beating yet?)

Being able to call The Irish One by his name, instead of the now commonly used 'Daddy' or 'Dickhead.'

Reading a book in bed without the use of a torch.

Sleeping.

Qualifications;

Stretch marks.

Broken Perineum.

Nipples that graze along the floor.

Ability to smile in the face of a hell of a lot of poop.

Snapped back.

Sore Legs.

Bags under eyes that resemble extra cheeks.

INTERESTS;
Gin.

Depression for Dummies....

It's not that I don't like my life. I do.

'Good morning Starbucks, yes I am fine, are you?'

I know I am very *lucky*.

I know from the outside looking in it would seem that I have *nothing* to be unhappy about, nothing at all.

I know I'm very *lucky* to have a beautiful healthy baby boy... who, has developed a fondness for throwing trains at my face when I won't give him pizza and ice pops for breakfast, but that's normal right? That's kids! I *should* laugh about it. And I do.

I know I have a lovely flat... and ok it is too small and we have no room and of course I would love it to sell so we could move, but that's understandable and nothing to stress about is it? That's life. I should be grateful I am not homeless. And I am.

And yes I know *both* my parents are still alive and healthy and supportive in ways I would never have thought possible... and ok, they are a bit crackers, but whose parents aren't right? You *should* be thanking your lucky stars you still have them. And I do.

And to top all this *luckiness* off I have the support of a sexy bearded man with a nice accent... and ok, sometimes I want to garrote him with my dressing gown belt because he seems incapable of finishing off the washing up, or for that matter, throwing away the used loo roll (!!!! The bin is right there!!!!), but that's just *a man thing* isn't it? I *should* be *grateful* he has stuck by me. I should thank my lucky stars. And sometimes, during moments of clarity, I do.

'Grande, extra shot, skinny dry cappuccino please... Yes he is nursery. No, no flavor today thanks.'

I know that I *should* be happy and living life to the full, not wishing my days away.

I know I *should* try harder to concentrate on enjoying the here and now.

I know life is passing me by and I *should* be relishing every moment.

I know I *need* to realize I am lucky.

I know this.

I know you think I *JUST need* to do all these things and I would be 'better'.

I know you think I am selfish.

I feel selfish.

'Yes it was lovely thanks. We went to Ireland. Lots of family and he loved his presents yes. Did you have a good one?'

And I also know you have *tried and tried and tried,* but you *just* can't seem to grasp why I can't *just* pull myself together, or why can't I *just* smile more? Or why am I unable to *just* give my head a wobble and see how *lucky* I am.

I can see in your eyes that you *think* you have the answers, that you think I am *choosing* to ignore you. I know when you hug me you think I am weak and I am pathetic, that I have issues, that I am dramatic and need constant attention.

I know you think living like this is a *choice I am making.*

The illness I am suffering from is not a choice though.

And it is that illusion, that perfectionist, *simple* view, which is damaging.

All of us.

Who would *choose* to wake up every morning and want it to be bedtime?

Just so they didn't have to pretend to be happy. *Just* so they didn't have to smile and play and swallow down the tears repeatedly every time they could see how many moments they were *choosing* to miss out on, unable to grasp hold of, unable to get back.

Who would *choose* to lie in bed all night crying silent tears of frustration?

Just because they have lost control of their own minds, *just* because they are being tortured over and over by demons so cunning and sly, so ferocious and cruel, that they can't reach out, they are isolated, no matter how many battles they *choose* to courageously fight in the hope it will stop.

Who would *choose* to feel nothing? Who would *choose* to become so numb that human touch evaporates before it even breaks the surface?

Who would *choose* isolation in a room bursting with family and caring faces?

Who would *choose* to experience only tiny moments of clarity? Who would *choose* to find natural laughter over something insignificant, so momentous that they remember back to it days later and wish they could experience it again? Be normal.

Who would *choose* to walk a lonely path in the darkness when there is light surrounding them?

Who would *choose* to die, over living?

'Oh how lovely. That must have been wonderful. I am glad your sister enjoyed it. Ok, well I am just going over by the window. Thanks again, have a good day.'

Who would *choose* to live with a hidden affliction, a disease, an overpowering sickness that nobody could see, that was incredibly misunderstood and was often treated with flamboyant disregard?

Nobody would *choose* this.

Depression **is an illness.** Not a choice.

Treat the illness itself, and those fighting it with the respect they deserve.

End the stigma.

Acknowledgments...

Thank you to the following folk;

My long suffering Irish Man, who supports me and lets me write whatever the hell I like about him and never has a problem with it because he just gets it. 'People can say what they fucking like, who gives a fuck about the people that say things. I don't.'

Dad. I don't need to say it. You know it. But just in case you forgot - Thank you and I love you to the moon and back x infinity. (I win.)

Thank you Doodle. My best bud.

Alison, Sarah, Helen, Natalie, Vanessa, Jonathan, Louise, Jon, Naomi, Paul, Simon, Pippa, Angela, Tom and Jess, Christine and T. Here's to tea in the garden, behavioural activation and not stealing other people's chips. Thank you for being part of my story, I feel honoured to have you in it.

Jamie. Thank you for protecting me from death. I am sorry I said I didn't find you sexy. It was a complete lie. You are definitely sexy in a 'you fucking terrify me when you dig through my soul' kind of way. You are a sexy beast.

Wonky Nana, The Boy and Me, Merry, Eliza do lots, Katie Bailey, Jen P, Susan KMann, Marylin, @the_moiderer, AdamPlum Transatlantic Blonde, Tara Cain, Nickie (always you Nickie) and Sally Whittle. You know why. You kept me going like the special little people that live in the cupboard, during the darkest of times.

The Mad Blog Awards, for teaching me not to shout 'minge' at the breakfast table. Oh and also - reminding me to live instead of merely exist.

Annette, Julie, Kate, Louise (yes, you in Canada) and Saz. You are so fucking money, my family. I would be nowhere without my sisters from another mister. Thank you the most of all. The crazy is good! Keep the crazy!

Gary And Stuart. We miss you and thank you Sarah Louise F, S.M Phillips, Gemma P and the Graphic shed, thank you for being my agent, my editor and my support. Without you this wouldn't be for sale. Thank you for your endless advice and support and an amazing cover!

Jake. It's been one hell of a long day without you. I will tell you all about it when I see you again.

Please don’t steal my shit, basically. – Author note.

Printed in Great Britain
by Amazon.co.uk, Ltd.,
Marston Gate.